Day by Day
COOKING

Day by Day
COOKING
Mary Berry

Hamlyn
London . New York . Sydney . Toronto

Acknowledgements

The author and publisher would like to thank the following for their co-operation in supplying colour photographs for this book:

American Long-Grain Rice *23 below, 28 below, 29, 30, 46 below, 55, 65, 79, 82, 91 below, 101*
Carnation Milk Bureau *137*
Cerebos Foods Ltd *113*
Cheese Bureau *33 below*
Cherry Valley Farms Ltd *95*
Christian Délu *41, 84, 92, 128*
Fleetway Studios *83*
Fruit Producers' Council *73, 135*
Gale's Honey *69*
Grand Marnier *46 above*
Grants of St. James's *89*
Guernsey Tomato Information Bureau *42, 44*
John West Foods Ltd *98*
Knorr *60 below, 63, 67, 86 below, 91 above*
Marmite *14, 85*

M.E.A.T. *61 below, 64 above*
Mushroom Growers' Association *10 above*
New Zealand Lamb Information Bureau *66 above and below, 99, 100, 162*
Olives from Spain *21 below, 23 above, 39, 60 above, 86 above, 159, endpapers*
Potato Marketing Board *33 above*
Quaker Oats Ltd *50*
R.H.M. Foods Ltd *9, 16, 26, 40, 48, 118, 120, 121, 145, 152, 155*
Syndication International *10 below, 13, 58–9, 81, 106, 115, 125 above, 134, 149, 165*
Thames Television *6*
Tower Housewares Ltd *24, 36 below, 54 above, 94, 96, 114, 158*
White Fish Authority *45, 49, 53, 54 below*

Cover photography by John Lee
Cover shows Cider pork chops (see page 70)

Some of the material in this book has appeared in the Hamlyn All Colour Cook Book.

Published by
The Hamlyn Publishing Group Limited
London · New York · Sydney · Toronto
Astronaut House, Feltham, Middlesex, England
© Copyright The Hamlyn Publishing Group Limited 1977
ISBN 0 600 31978 4
Phototypeset by Tradespools Limited, Frome, Somerset
Printed in Great Britain by C. J. Mason & Sons Limited, Bristol

Contents

Introduction

In this book I hope busy cooks will find answers to some of their most frequent questions, whether a bright new idea for a weekday supper or a splendid concoction to round off an elegant dinner party. Day by day cooking need not be a tiresome repetition of old standbys but can lend itself to new ingredients, variations on well loved themes, or even adventurous new ideas, without requiring hours of precious time in preparation.

Many of the recipes are illustrated with a full colour picture alongside the recipe itself. This can prove of inestimable help in preparing, garnishing and presenting a dish, as well as making it easy to leaf through the book for general inspiration. Readers have often written in to me asking that recipes be illustrated when-

ever possible, and I am glad that in this book we have been able to do this with such a large number.

In preparing the chapters I have tried to offer as varied a selection of recipes as possible. To cater for special occasions, some of the more expensive ingredients have been used in some starters, main meals and sweets. But for everyday cooking, I have included dishes using cheaper cuts of meat like offal and stewing meat, and have employed methods such as casseroling to make these more economical ingredients tender and tasty.

Special features are the chapter on roasts, including an invaluable table of roasting times, temperatures and suggestions for serving a great variety of meats, and the chapter on preserves, which begins with general tips on preparing bottles and kilner jars and how to test jams for readiness. I have also made suggestions for unusual party meals such as beef or cheese fondue, Spanish tapas and paella in the chapter on entertaining.

Some of the dishes are plain, some traditional and some are exotic examples of the cooking of other lands. Whatever the occasion or mood, there should be something to tempt you in this collection of recipes, and I hope that you, your family and friends will come to appreciate the challenge and fun of day by day cooking.

Mary Berry

Useful facts and figures

Notes on metrication

Exact conversion from imperial to metric measures does not give very convenient working quantities and so for greater convenience we have rounded off the metric measures into units of 25. The following tables show the recommended equivalents.

Dry measures

Ounces	Approx. g to nearest whole figure	Recommended equivalent to nearest unit of 25
1	28	25
2	57	50
3	85	75
4 ($\frac{1}{4}$ lb)	113	100
5	142	150
6	170	175
7	198	200
8 ($\frac{1}{2}$ lb)	227	225
9	255	250
10	283	275
11	312	300
12 ($\frac{3}{4}$ lb)	340	350
13	368	375
14	397	400
15	425	425
16 (1 lb)	456	450

Liquid measures

Fluid ounces	Approx. ml to nearest whole figure	Recommended equivalent to nearest unit of 25
2	57	50
4	113	100
5 ($\frac{1}{4}$ pint)	142	150
6	170	175
8	227	225
10 ($\frac{1}{2}$ pint)	283	300
15 ($\frac{3}{4}$ pint)	425	450
20 (1 pint)	569	600
$1\frac{1}{4}$ pints		750 ml
$1\frac{1}{2}$ pints		900 ml
$1\frac{3}{4}$ pints		1 litre
2 pints		generous litre
$2\frac{1}{4}$ pints		1·25 litres
$2\frac{3}{4}$ pints		1·5 litres
3 pints		1·75 litres
$3\frac{1}{2}$ pints		2 litres

Note When converting quantities larger than 16 oz or 20 fl oz, add the literal conversions in the centre columns and then adjust to the nearest unit of 25. As a general guide, 1 kg (1000 g) equals 2·2 lb or about 2 lb 3 oz; 1 litre (1000 ml) equals 1·76 pints or almost exactly $1\frac{3}{4}$ pints. This method of conversion gives good results in nearly all recipes; however, in certain recipes a more accurate conversion may be necessary to produce a balanced proportion of ingredients.

Oven temperature chart

Description	°F	°C	Gas Mark
Very cool	225	110	$\frac{1}{4}$
	250	120	$\frac{1}{2}$
Cool	275	140	1
	300	150	2
Moderate	325	160	3
	350	180	4
Moderately hot	375	190	5
	400	200	6
Hot	425	220	7
	450	230	8
Very hot	475	240	9

Notes for American users

The imperial pint is 20 fl oz whereas the American pint is 16 fl oz. The British standard tablespoon holds 17·7 ml whereas the American tablespoon holds 14·2 ml. Below are a few common liquid equivalents.

British	American
1 tablespoon	1 tablespoon or 3 teaspoons
$1\frac{1}{2}$ tablespoons (1 fl oz)	2 tablespoons
2 tablespoons	3 tablespoons
3 tablespoons (2 fl oz)	$\frac{1}{4}$ cup
4 tablespoons	$\frac{1}{3}$ cup
5 tablespoons	6 tablespoons
6 tablespoons (4 fl oz)	$\frac{1}{2}$ cup
$\frac{1}{4}$ pint	$\frac{2}{3}$ cup
6 fl oz	$\frac{3}{4}$ cup
scant $\frac{1}{2}$ pint	1 cup (8 fl oz)
$\frac{1}{2}$ pint	$1\frac{1}{4}$ cups
$\frac{3}{4}$ pint	2 cups (1 us pint)
1 pint	$2\frac{1}{2}$ cups

A large (1-kg/2-lb) loaf tin is similar to a 9 × 5 × 3-inch loaf pan, while a small (0·5-kg/1-lb) loaf tin is similar to a $4\frac{1}{2}$ × $2\frac{1}{2}$ × $1\frac{1}{2}$-inch loaf pan.

All cup and spoon measures are level unless otherwise indicated.

The following list gives American equivalents for some of the terms and equipment used in this book.

British	American
Baking tin	Baking pan
Baking tray	Baking sheet
Base	Bottom
Biscuits	Crackers or cookies
Biscuit mixture	Cookie dough
Cocktail stick	Toothpick
Deep cake tin	Spring form pan
Dough or mixture	Batter
Frying pan	Skillet
Greaseproof paper	Wax paper
Grill	Broil
Kitchen paper	Paper towels
Knock back dough	Punch down dough
Liquidiser	Blender
Loaf tin	Loaf pan
Minced	Ground
Muslin	Cheesecloth
Pastry cutter	Cookie cutter
Patty tins	Muffin pans or cups
Piping bag	Pastry bag
Polythene	Plastic
Prove dough	Rise dough
Pudding basin	Ovenproof bowl
Salt beef	Corned beef
Sandwich tin	Layer cake pan
Scones	Biscuits
Shortcrust pastry	Basic pie dough
Stoned	Pitted
Swiss roll	Jelly roll
Top and tail fruit	Stem fruit
Whip	Beat
Whisk	Whip
Wholemeal	Wholewheat

Notes for Australian users

In Australia the American 8-oz measuring cup is used in conjunction with the imperial pint of 20 fl oz. It is most important to remember that the Australian tablespoon differs from both the British and American tablespoons in that it holds 20 ml. The table below gives a comparison between the standard British and Australian tablespoons.

British	Australian
1 teaspoon	1 teaspoon
1 tablespoon	1 tablespoon
2 tablespoons	2 tablespoons
$3\frac{1}{2}$ tablespoons	3 tablespoons
4 tablespoons	$3\frac{1}{2}$ tablespoons

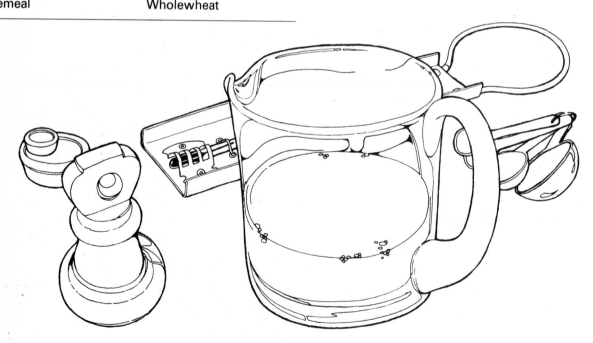

Good beginnings

What could be more warming on a cold evening than a bowl of steaming hot, home-made vegetable soup – or more enticing than a chilled luncheon soup on a hot summer's day? Pâté is another favourite many cooks mistakenly believe is difficult to make, but in this chapter a variety of recipes for hot and cold soups, chicken liver and fish pâtés, and a host of other easy but attractive starters prove them wrong.

Try a delicate egg mousse or oeufs aurore, or exotic moules marinières. Whether as a start to a family meal or a special luncheon or dinner party, this selection will prove a great source of ideas.

To give you the confidence to experiment with the many dishes based on classic sauces and dressings, easy recipes for Hollandaise sauce (both a classic and a liquidiser method), French dressing and mayonnaise are included.

Tomato and Orange Soup

Metric/Imperial	American
25 g/1 oz butter	2 tablespoons butter
1 onion, sliced	1 onion, sliced
25 g/1 oz flour	$\frac{1}{4}$ cup all-purpose flour
425-g/15-oz can tomatoes	15-oz can tomatoes
750 ml/1$\frac{1}{4}$ pints water	3 cups water
1 chicken stock cube	1 chicken bouillon cube
1 bay leaf	1 bay leaf
1 teaspoon salt	1 teaspoon salt
1 teaspoon sugar	1 teaspoon sugar
black pepper	black pepper
1 small orange	1 small orange

First melt the butter in a saucepan and add the onion, cover and cook gently until soft taking care not to brown the onion. Stir in the flour, add all the remaining ingredients except the orange. Bring to the boil then half cover and leave to simmer for 20 minutes; remove bay leaf.

Peel the orange thinly with a potato peeler. Snip this peel into needle shreds with scissors.

To finish, sieve or purée the soup, then reheat for 2 minutes with the orange rind before serving.

To freeze This soup freezes very well either before or after the addition of orange rind.
Note A handy use for orange or tangerine peel. If making a large quantity for the freezer you may want to omit orange rind for a basic tomato soup to serve in other ways.

Serves 4

Tomato soup

Cream of Mushroom Soup

Metric/Imperial	American
25 g/1 oz butter	2 tablespoons butter
1 large onion, sliced	1 large onion, sliced
25 g/1 oz flour	$\frac{1}{4}$ cup all-purpose flour
900 ml/1½ pints water	3¾ cups water
1 stock cube	1 bouillon cube
small sprig of rosemary	small sprig of rosemary
1 teaspoon salt	1 teaspoon salt
pepper	pepper
100 g/4 oz button mushrooms	1 cup button mushrooms
1 egg yolk	1 egg yolk
150 ml/¼ pint single cream	$\frac{2}{3}$ cup light cream
Garnish	**Garnish**
sliced raw mushrooms	sliced raw mushrooms
sprigs of parsley	sprigs of parsley

Melt the butter in a saucepan and add the sliced onion; cover and cook carefully until soft, without browning. Stir in the flour, remove from the heat and add first the water then the stock cube, rosemary and seasoning. Simmer for 15 minutes and then remove rosemary. (This stage may be completed 24 hours in advance.)

To finish, reduce to a purée in a liquidiser or sieve, adding the washed mushrooms, egg yolk and cream; reheat immediately, without quite boiling. Stir occasionally at first, then constantly as the soup becomes quite hot to give a creamy, velvety consistency. Serve garnished with sliced raw mushrooms and sprigs of parsley.

This soup does not freeze well, as the raw nutty flavour of the mushrooms would be spoilt.

Note   If mushrooms are liquidised too early the soup becomes a disappointing grey colour. If soup does boil and curdle at the end, tip into a tureen or bowl and whisk quickly to rectify.

Serves 4

Cream of mushroom soup

Sorrel and Spinach Soup

Metric/Imperial	American
2 handfuls sorrel	2 handfuls sorrel
225 g/8 oz spinach	½ lb fresh spinach
1 onion	1 onion
40 g/1½ oz butter	3 tablespoons butter
25 g/ 1 oz flour	$\frac{1}{4}$ cup all-purpose flour
900 ml/1½ pints water	3¾ cups water
1 chicken stock cube	1 chicken bouillon cube
1 teaspoon salt	1 teaspoon salt
½ teaspoon sugar	½ teaspoon sugar
pepper	pepper
pinch grated nutmeg	pinch grated nutmeg
1 teaspoon lemon juice	1 teaspoon lemon juice
4 tablespoons double cream	$\frac{1}{3}$ cup whipping cream

To prepare the sorrel and spinach, wash well and discard any coarse stems. Slice the onion and cook in the butter until soft and golden. Then chop the sorrel and spinach and add to the pan.

Cook for 4 minutes stirring from time to time. Sprinkle in the flour, stir well and add the water, stock cube and seasoning. Bring to the boil, simmer for 6 minutes, but do not overcook, and then purée in a liquidiser or sieve.

To serve, reheat and add lemon juice. Ladle into soup bowls and swirl a spoonful of cream into each.

To freeze   Prepare and freeze soup without cream, reheat and add cream when serving.

Note   Frozen spinach can also be used, in which case add it to the soup with the water and simmer until completely thawed. Spinach helps to improve the colour of this soup as sorrel turns brownish when cooked.

Serves 4

Parsley to garnish

Cream of Cauliflower Soup

Metric/Imperial
50 g/2 oz butter
1 large onion, sliced
25 g/1 oz flour
600 ml/1 pint milk
300 ml/½ pint water
1 bay leaf
0·5 kg/1 lb cauliflower
1 teaspoon salt
pepper
chopped parsley to garnish

American
¼ cup butter
1 large onion, sliced
¼ cup all-purpose flour
2½ cups milk
1¼ cups water
1 bay leaf
1 lb cauliflower
1 teaspoon salt
pepper
chopped parsley to garnish

Melt the butter in a large saucepan and add the sliced onion. Cover tightly and cook very slowly for 5 minutes without browning; stir in the flour. Remove from the heat and blend in the milk, add the water and bay leaf and bring to the boil.

Break the cauliflower into florets, add to the pan with the seasoning and simmer gently, uncovered, for 15 minutes until cauliflower is tender. Remove bay leaf.

To finish, purée in a liquidiser or sieve, reheat, garnish with the chopped parsley and serve.

This soup does not freeze well.

Note A proportion of leaves and stalks trimmed off cauliflower can be used in this soup to save wastage. Do not keep hot for a long time or the flavour of the soup will spoil. Make up to 6 hours in advance. For a special occasion serve with croûtons of diced bread fried golden in oil.

Cream of cauliflower soup

Serves 4

Pea and Lettuce Soup

Metric/Imperial	American
40 g/1½ oz butter	3 tablespoons butter
1 onion, sliced	1 onion, sliced
1 small lettuce	1 small head lettuce
0·5 kg/1 lb frozen peas	3 cups frozen peas
750 ml/1¼ pints boiling water	3 cups boiling water
2 teaspoons salt	2 teaspoons salt
1 teaspoon sugar	1 teaspoon sugar
pepper	pepper
2 sprigs of mint	2 sprigs of mint
2 tablespoons single cream	3 tablespoons light cream
1 tablespoon snipped chives	1 tablespoon snipped chives

Melt the butter and add the sliced onion to the pan, cover and cook gently for 5 minutes. Shred the lettuce and add to the pan with the peas, stir for 1 minute and add the water and seasoning. Simmer uncovered for 7 minutes until peas are tender.

Cool slightly, then reduce to a purée with the mint in a liquidiser or sieve. Reheat to serve. Swirl in the cream and garnish with the chives.

Note This quick and delicious soup should not be kept hot but can be cooked and then reheated. Lettuces which have bolted and gone to seed and any outside leaves can all be used.

Serves 4

Carrot Soup

Metric/Imperial	American
0·5 kg/1 lb carrots	1 lb carrots
1 small onion	1 small onion
40 g/1½ oz butter	3 tablespoons butter
750 ml/1¼ pints water	3 cups water
1 chicken stock cube	1 chicken bouillon cube
1 bay leaf	1 bay leaf
3 strips orange peel	3 strips orange peel
1 teaspoon salt	1 teaspoon salt
pepper	pepper
4 tablespoons soured or fresh cream	⅓ cup sour or fresh cream
1 tablespoon chopped parsley	1 tablespoon chopped parsley

Slice the carrots and onion. Cook gently in the butter in a covered pan for 10 minutes. Pour on the water and crumble in the stock cube. Add the bay leaf, strips of orange peel (remove with a potato peeler) and seasoning to the pan. Bring to the boil and simmer for 15 minutes. Remove bay leaf and orange peel; purée through a mouli, sieve or in a liquidiser. Reheat and serve adding a spoonful of cream and a pinch of chopped parsley to each soup bowl.

To freeze Make and freeze before adding cream and parsley. Reheat and add these when serving.
Note Do not include the white part of the orange skin as it gives a bitter flavour. The texture of this soup is best if very finely moulied or liquidised.

Variation
Celery Soup Substitute one head of celery, finely chopped, for the carrots. Omit the orange peel, reduce the quantity of water by 150 ml/¼ pint (US ⅔ cup) and substitute dry white wine. Taste for seasoning and garnish as above.

Serves 4

Celery soup

Watercress Soup

Metric/Imperial	American
350 g/12 oz potatoes	¾ lb potatoes
40 g/1½ oz butter	3 tablespoons butter
450 ml/¾ pint hot milk	2 cups hot milk
300 ml/½ pint chicken stock	1¼ cups chicken stock
1 teaspoon salt	1 teaspoon salt
pepper	pepper
small bunch watercress	small bunch watercress
2 tablespoons single cream	3 tablespoons light cream

Boil the potatoes in their skins. When tender drain and peel. Mash very thoroughly, beat in the butter and 3–4 tablespoons milk. Beat until smooth and creamy using a wooden spoon or whisk. Blend in the remaining milk and pour in the stock. Add salt and pepper and bring to the boil.

Remove any discoloured leaves from the watercress and chop finely. Add to the soup and simmer gently for 3 minutes. Stir in the cream and serve hot or cold.

Note The success of this soup lies in making a really creamy textured potato purée. To serve cold, stir occasionally during cooling then again just before serving.

Serves 4

Chilled vichyssoise

Chilled Vichyssoise

Metric/Imperial
0·5 kg/1 lb large leeks
1 medium potato
40 g/1½ oz butter
900 ml/1½ pints chicken stock
1 teaspoon salt
pepper
150 ml/¼ pint double cream
1 tablespoon chopped parsley

American
1 lb large leeks
1 medium potato
3 tablespoons butter
3¾ cups chicken stock
1 teaspoon salt
pepper
⅔ cup whipping cream
1 tablespoon chopped parsley

Discard bright and dark green parts of leeks; wash rest thoroughly. Slice trimmed leeks and peeled potato thinly. Melt the butter in a pan, add the vegetables and cover with foil or a tight-fitting lid. Cook very slowly for 7 minutes. The leeks should be soft but not coloured. Pour on the stock and season. Bring to the boil and simmer for 15 minutes.

Sieve the soup through a fine sieve or purée in a liquidiser until very smooth. When cold, whisk in the cream for 30 seconds then chill. Serve with parsley sprinkled on top.

To freeze   Freeze before adding cream. Thaw and whisk well, then add the cream and whisk for a further 30 seconds.
Note   The green part of the leek would discolour this soup, but it can be used in other mixed vegetable soups.

Serves 4

Gazpacho

Metric/Imperial
0·75 kg/1½ lb ripe tomatoes
½ onion
1 small green pepper
½ cucumber
1 clove garlic
2 slices white bread
100 ml/4 fl oz salad oil
50 ml/2 fl oz white wine
    vinegar
300 ml/½ pint chicken stock
    or 300 ml/½ pint water and
    1 stock cube
salt and freshly ground black
    pepper
cucumber slices to garnish

American
1½ lb ripe tomatoes
½ onion
1 small green pepper
½ cucumber
1 clove garlic
2 slices white bread
½ cup salad oil
¼ cup white wine vinegar

1¼ cups chicken stock or
    1¼ cups water and 1
    bouillon cube
salt and freshly ground black
    pepper
cucumber slices to garnish

Skin the tomatoes and cut in quarters; remove the pips. Peel and chop the onion. Remove the stem, seeds and white pith from the pepper. Peel and roughly chop the cucumber. Crush the garlic. Remove the crusts from the bread and cut in pieces.

Put all the ingredients except the cucumber slices into a large bowl and mix, then reduce to a purée in a liquidiser, in two batches. Turn into a bowl and leave to chill in the refrigerator for several hours.

Divide the soup into four bowls or dishes and garnish with cucumber slices.

Note   This classic soup from Spain improves by being kept overnight in the refrigerator to allow the flavours to blend. Serve, as they do in Spain, with side dishes of diced tomato, cucumber and fried bread croûtons.

Serves 4

Kipper Pâté

Metric/Imperial
283-g/10-oz packet buttered
    kipper fillets
175 g/6 oz unsalted butter
1 small clove garlic
2 tablespoons lemon juice
cayenne pepper

American
10-oz package buttered
    kipper fillets
¾ cup sweet butter
1 small clove garlic
3 tablespoons lemon juice
cayenne pepper

Cook the kipper fillets as directed on the packet, remove them from the bag, drain off the butter and reserve.

Remove all dark skin and bones from the fillets and place in the liquidiser with the reserved liquor from the bag. Melt two-thirds of the butter and crush the garlic; add to the kippers with lemon juice and cayenne to taste, and blend until smooth.

Divide the pâté between four individual ramekins. Melt the remaining butter and pour a little over each pot. Chill well and serve with fresh toast and butter.

Serves 4

Quick Chicken Liver Pâté

Metric/Imperial	American
1 small onion	1 small onion
75 g/3 oz butter	$\frac{1}{3}$ cup butter
225 g/8 oz chicken livers	$\frac{1}{2}$ lb chicken livers
1 tablespoon freshly chopped parsley	1 tablespoon freshly chopped parsley
salt and pepper	salt and pepper
2 tablespoons brandy	3 tablespoons brandy
1 teaspoon yeast extract (optional)	1 teaspoon yeast extract (optional)

Peel and finely chop the onion. Melt two-thirds of the butter in a small pan, add the onion and chicken livers and fry for 3–4 minutes. Sprinkle with the parsley and seasoning and cook for a further 2–3 minutes. Leave to cool, then put in the liquidiser and blend until smooth, or chop and mash for a coarser texture. Stir in the brandy and yeast extract (if used).

Turn into a small dish, melt the remaining butter and pour over the top. Chill.

Serve with fresh toast and butter, or piled on small biscuits for a party.

Serves 4–6

Stevenson's Sardine Pâté

Metric/Imperial	American
120-g/4$\frac{1}{4}$-oz can sardines in oil	4$\frac{1}{4}$-oz can sardines in oil
4 hard-boiled eggs	4 hard-cooked eggs
150 ml/$\frac{1}{4}$ pint mayonnaise	$\frac{2}{3}$ cup mayonnaise
150 ml/$\frac{1}{4}$ pint double cream	$\frac{2}{3}$ cup whipping cream
salt and pepper	salt and pepper
few drops Worcestershire sauce	few drops Worcestershire sauce

Drain the sardines and mash. Mash the eggs and place in a bowl with the sardines and mayonnaise.

Lightly whisk the cream until thick and holding a soft peak. Fold into the sardine and egg mixture. Season to taste with salt and pepper and Worcestershire sauce. Turn into a 750-ml/1$\frac{1}{4}$-pint (US 1$\frac{1}{2}$-pint) dish and leave in a cool place for several hours.

Serve with fresh toast and butter or as a special filling for sandwiches or rolls.

Note A quick recipe, inexpensive and full of flavour.

Serves 6

Taramasalata

Metric/Imperial	American
225 g/8 oz smoked cod's roe	$\frac{1}{2}$ lb smoked cod roe
2 small slices white bread without crusts	2 small slices white bread without crusts
2 tablespoons milk	3 tablespoons milk
1 clove garlic, crushed (optional)	1 clove garlic, crushed (optional)
100 ml/4 fl oz olive oil	$\frac{1}{2}$ cup olive oil
2 tablespoons lemon juice	3 tablespoons lemon juice
salt and pepper	salt and pepper
2 bay leaves to garnish	2 bay leaves to garnish

Remove the skin from the cod's roe. Place the roe in a mortar or bowl and pound it with a pestle or mash it with a fork until it is smooth. Soak the bread in the milk, then squeeze out as much milk as possible. Add the bread to the cod's roe and mash again. Add the crushed garlic, if liked. Add the oil 1 teaspoon at a time. Stir in the lemon juice and seasoning. Garnish with bay leaves and chill before serving with hot toast and butter.

Note If you have a liquidiser, use it to make this pâté. Should you have difficulty getting fresh smoked cod's roe, buy a jar instead. It cuts down the time and tastes just as good.

Serves 4

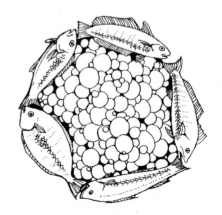

Quick chicken liver pâté   *opposite* Taramasalata

Smoked trout pâté

Smoked Trout Pâté

Metric/Imperial
1 large smoked trout
175 g/6 oz rich cream cheese
1 tablespoon creamed
    horseradish
1–2 tablespoons top of milk
salt and black pepper
pinch cayenne pepper
Garnish
8 prawns
sprigs of parsley

American
1 large smoked trout
¾ cup full-fat cream cheese
1 tablespoon creamed
    horseradish
2–3 tablespoons rich milk
salt and black pepper
pinch cayenne pepper
Garnish
8 prawns
sprigs of parsley

Carefully remove all skin and bones from the trout and purée in a liquidiser or mash with a fork until smooth. Add the remaining ingredients and blend until smooth. Turn into a small pudding basin and chill well. Turn out and garnish with prawns and sprigs of parsley.
    Serve with hot toast and butter.

Serves 4

Baked Grapefruit with Ginger

Metric/Imperial
2 grapefruit
stem ginger in syrup
4 teaspoons soft brown sugar

American
2 grapefruit
preserved ginger in syrup
4 teaspoons soft brown sugar

Cut the grapefruit in half. Divide into segments, removing as much of the membrane as possible. Pour 1 tablespoon of the ginger syrup over each grapefruit half, sprinkle with sugar and arrange thin slices of ginger around the edge. Fill the centre cavity with small pieces of ginger.
    Heat in a moderate oven (160°C, 325°F, Gas Mark 3) for 10–15 minutes until the sugar has melted.

Note   A very good way to use preserved ginger that you may have been given for Christmas. If you are not ginger addicts leave out the ginger and increase the sugar to heaped teaspoonfuls.

Serves 4

Salmon Mousse

Metric/Imperial	American
225 g/8 oz cooked boned salmon	½ lb boneless cooked salmon
200 ml/generous ¼ pint milk	¾ cup milk
1 bay leaf	1 bay leaf
1 slice onion	1 slice onion
100 g/4 oz butter	½ cup butter
25 g/1 oz flour	¼ cup all-purpose flour
1 teaspoon salt	1 teaspoon salt
few drops red food colouring	few drops red food coloring
4 tablespoons double cream	⅓ cup whipping cream
1 tablespoon sherry	1 tablespoon sherry
aspic jelly crystals	aspic jelly crystals
boiling water	boiling water

Skin the salmon and remove all small bones. Heat the milk in a pan with the bay leaf and onion – as it comes to the boil pour into a bowl and cover. Melt half the butter in a saucepan, remove from the heat, stir in the flour and then gradually strain and blend in the flavoured milk. When smooth bring sauce to the boil, season and simmer for 2 minutes. Cover well and cool.

Pound the salmon well with a pestle in a mortar or in a strong bowl using the end of a rolling pin. Gradually add the cold sauce and remaining butter which should be fairly soft. Alternatively blend the salmon, sauce and butter in a liquidiser. Colour the mousse a very light salmon pink with a little red food colouring. Add colouring a drop at a time by dipping a skewer into the colour so that only a little is added. (Never tip food colouring straight from the bottle and risk expensive mistakes.)

Lightly whip the cream and fold into the mousse with the sherry. Following the instructions on the packet of aspic jelly, put sufficient crystals in a bowl to make 4 tablespoons (US ⅓ cup) aspic. Pour on boiling water and stir until crystals dissolve. When jelly is cold fold into the salmon mousse and turn the mousse into a generous 1-litre/2-pint (US 2½-pint) mould; level the top. Chill to set. Turn out on a serving dish and accompany with assorted salads.

To freeze Prepare the mousse, turn into dish, level and freeze. Thaw overnight.

Note Fresh or canned salmon may be used for this recipe. If fresh is used buy 350 g/12 oz (US ¾ lb) fresh salmon to allow for weight loss due to shrinkage in cooking and removal of bone and skin. Wrap in foil and bake for 20–25 minutes in a moderate oven (160°C, 325°F, Gas Mark 3). This is a useful way of using up small pieces where a whole salmon has been cooked and served. If canned, choose pink, not red salmon, as there is no need to pay half as much again when you can add the colour yourself. Drain off any juice from the can first.

Serves 4–6

Danish Caviar Mousse

Metric/Imperial	American
7·5 g/¼ oz gelatine	2 teaspoons gelatin
50 ml/2 fl oz cold water	¼ cup cold water
150 ml/¼ pint double cream	⅔ cup whipping cream
150 ml/¼ pint soured cream	⅔ cup dairy sour cream
1 tablespoon very finely chopped onion	1 tablespoon very finely chopped onion
4 tablespoons mayonnaise	⅓ cup mayonnaise
juice of ½ lemon	juice of ½ lemon
salt and pepper	salt and pepper
100-g/3½-oz jar lump fish roe (caviar)	3½-oz jar lump fish roe (caviar)
lemon wedges to garnish	lemon wedges to garnish

Salmon mousse

Soak the gelatine in the water for 5 minutes then stand the bowl in a pan of simmering water and allow the gelatine to dissolve and become clear. Remove from the pan and leave to cool but not set.

Whisk the double cream until thick, stir in the soured cream, onion and mayonnaise. Add the lemon juice and a little salt and pepper with the gelatine and mix well. Finally stir in the caviar, leaving a little for decoration.

Turn into a shallow 600-ml/1-pint (US 1¼-pint) serving dish and chill in the refrigerator until set. Decorate with the remaining caviar and lemon wedges. Serve with thinly sliced brown bread and butter.

Serves 4

Egg mousse

Egg Mousse

Metric/Imperial
15 g/½ oz gelatine
2 tablespoons cold water
298-g/10½-oz can condensed
  consommé
6 hard-boiled eggs
150 ml/¼ pint double cream
150 ml/¼ pint mayonnaise
1–2 teaspoons curry powder
1 tablespoon mango chutney
  juice
salt and pepper
tomato, cucumber and
  watercress to garnish

American
4 teaspoons gelatin
3 tablespoons cold water
10½-oz can condensed
  consommé
6 hard-cooked eggs
⅔ cup whipping cream
⅔ cup mayonnaise
1–2 teaspoons curry powder
1 tablespoon mango chutney
  juice
salt and pepper
tomato, cucumber and
  watercress to garnish

Put the gelatine in a small bowl with the water and leave to stand for 5 minutes. Place the bowl in a pan of simmering water and stir until the gelatine has dissolved. Place the consommé in a measure and stir in the gelatine.

Chop the eggs. Whisk the cream until thick.

Mix together the eggs, cream, mayonnaise, curry powder and mango chutney juice and stir in three-quarters of the consommé. Check the seasoning then pour the mixture into eight individual serving dishes or ramekins. Leave to set.

Garnish each mousse attractively with the tomato, cucumber and watercress, then spoon over the remaining consommé. Chill until set.

To freeze   This mousse (ungarnished) freezes well. Cover each dish with foil, label and freeze. Thaw overnight in the refrigerator.

Serves 8

Prawn Cocktail

Metric/Imperial
150 ml/¼ pint mayonnaise
1 teaspoon tomato purée
¼ teaspoon castor sugar
few drops Worcestershire
  sauce
few drops chilli sauce
1 tablespoon lemon juice
2 tablespoons double cream
freshly ground black pepper
1 lettuce
225 g/8 oz peeled prawns
Garnish
paprika
lemon wedges
4 whole prawns

American
⅔ cup mayonnaise
1 teaspoon tomato paste
¼ teaspoon sugar
few drops Worcestershire
  sauce
few drops hot chili sauce
1 tablespoon lemon juice
3 tablespoons whipping cream
freshly ground black pepper
1 head lettuce
1 cup peeled shrimp
Garnish
paprika
lemon wedges
4 whole shrimp

Mix the mayonnaise, tomato purée, sugar, Worcestershire sauce, chilli sauce, lemon juice, cream and pepper together.

Finely shred the lettuce leaves and place a good tablespoonful in the bottoms of four glasses. Divide the prawns between the glasses, spoon over the sauce, sprinkle with paprika and serve each garnished with a lemon wedge and a prawn.

Serves 4

Prawn cocktail

Moules Marinières

Metric/Imperial	American
3·5 litres/6 pints fresh mussels	7½ pints fresh mussels
25 g/1 oz butter	2 tablespoons butter
1 large onion	1 large onion
4 stalks parsley	4 stalks parsley
2 sprigs fresh thyme or	2 sprigs fresh thyme or
¼ teaspoon dried thyme	¼ teaspoon dried thyme
1 bay leaf	1 bay leaf
freshly ground black pepper	freshly ground black pepper
300 ml/½ pint dry white wine	1¼ cups dry white wine
salt	salt
chopped parsley	chopped parsley
Beurre manié	**Beurre manié**
25 g/1 oz creamed soft butter	2 tablespoons creamed soft butter
15 g/½ oz flour	2 tablespoons all-purpose flour

Scrape and clean each mussel with a strong knife, removing every trace of seaweed, mud and beard. Wash in several changes of water, discarding any which are badly chipped or cracked or that do not close tightly. Mussels which remain open are dead and should not be used. Drain the mussels in a colander.

Melt the butter in a large pan over a low heat. Peel and chop the onion, add to the pan and fry until soft but not coloured. Add the herbs, pepper, wine and the mussels. Cover the pan with a tight-fitting lid and cook quickly, shaking the pan constantly until the mussels open, about 5–6 minutes. Lift the mussels out, discard the empty half of the shell and keep hot in a covered dish. Reduce the liquor to about 300 ml/½ pint (US 1¼ cups). Remove the fresh thyme, parsley stalks and bay leaf.

Blend the butter and flour for the beurre manié to a smooth paste. Drop the beurre manié into the simmering stock 1 teaspoon at a time and whisk until the stock is smooth and has thickened. Add more pepper and salt if necessary. Pour the stock over the mussels and scatter with plenty of chopped parsley.

Serve with French bread and butter. Finger bowls are a help, as picking up mussels is a messy process. You will need a dish for the empty shells.

Note Allow approx. 450–600 ml/¾–1 pint (US 2–2½ cups) of mussels per person. It is essential that they be really fresh, so only buy ones that are tightly closed. The winter months are the best time to buy mussels.

Beurre manié is the best way to thicken the sauce that goes with the mussels.

Variation
Moules Provençale Halve the quantity of wine used, and add instead eight tomatoes, chopped. Substitute fresh or dried basil for the thyme.

Serves 6

Coquilles St Jacques

Metric/Imperial
6 scallops
25 g/1 oz butter
1 shallot
1 stick celery
1 sprig fresh thyme
1 bay leaf
300 ml/½ pint dry white wine
salt and pepper
Sauce
25 g/1 oz butter
25 g/1 oz flour
300 ml/½ pint cooking liquor
  from scallops
Topping
milk
15 g/½ oz butter
0·5 kg/1 lb potatoes, boiled
  and mashed
few crisp breadcrumbs
Garnish
lemon wedges
sprig of parsley

American
6 large scallops
2 tablespoons butter
1 shallot
1 stalk celery
1 sprig fresh thyme
1 bay leaf
1¼ cups dry white wine
salt and pepper
Sauce
2 tablespoons butter
¼ cup all-purpose flour
1¼ cups cooking liquor from
  scallops
Topping
milk
1 tablespoon butter
1 lb potatoes, boiled and
  mashed
few crisp bread crumbs
Garnish
lemon wedges
sprig of parsley

Clean six scallop shells. Cook the scallops: melt the butter in a pan, peel and chop the shallot, chop the celery and add to the pan with the thyme and bay leaf and fry until the shallot is soft but not coloured. Add the wine and simmer for 2 minutes. Season with salt and pepper, add the scallops and simmer them gently for 5 minutes. Remove the scallops from the pan and strain the liquor into a measure.

Make a white sauce with butter, flour and the cooking liquor from the scallops. Bring it to boiling point and simmer until the sauce is thick and smooth. Season with salt and pepper. Add the scallops cut in 2·5-cm/1-inch pieces and reheat them for 1 minute.

Add enough milk and butter to the mashed potatoes to give a soft piping consistency. Season with salt and pepper, put into a large piping bag with a large rose nozzle and decorate the edge of each scallop shell with potato. Fill the centres of the shells with the scallops and sauce, top with the breadcrumbs then brown under the grill.

Garnish with lemon wedges and parsley and serve piping hot.

Note These may be made 12 hours or so in advance, put in the refrigerator, then reheated at 200°C (400°F, Gas Mark 6) for 15 minutes.

When buying scallops from the fishmonger ask for the deep half of the shell so that you can use it as the serving dish; keep these afterwards as next time you might well be buying frozen scallops that come without shells.

Serves 6

Asparagus

Fresh asparagus is a splendid starter for a summer dinner party. A (0·5-kg/1-lb) bundle will serve 2–3 persons.

Trim off the white and jagged ends of the asparagus and cut all the sticks to an average length. Scrape off the rough skin near the cut end with a sharp knife. Wash well in cold water to get rid of any sandy grit.

Boil in salted water for 12–15 minutes until just tender, then lift the asparagus out carefully and drain. A fish slice is a useful utensil for this. Serve hot with melted butter or Hollandaise sauce or cold with French dressing (see page 25).

Globe Artichokes

These are the buds of a large plant flowering in middle to late summer in northern climates. However, because of imports from more southern areas the season has been greatly extended and artichokes are now available from April to November. They not only make an unusual starter but they keep everyone busy too!

Allow one artichoke for each person. Wash the artichokes well in salted water and cut off any stalk to level the base.

Cook in boiling salted water for 45 minutes or until a leaf can be easily pulled out. Drain well. Serve hot with Hollandaise sauce or melted butter, or cold with French dressing (see page 25). When serving cold, the centre of the vegetable, called the choke, is pulled out leaving a cup which is then filled with the dressing.

Mushrooms in Garlic Butter

Metric/Imperial	American
50 g/2 oz butter	¼ cup butter
1 clove garlic	1 clove garlic
salt and pepper	salt and pepper
1 tablespoon chopped parsley	1 tablespoon chopped parsley
225 g/8 oz button mushrooms	2 cups button mushrooms
juice of ½ lemon	juice of ½ lemon

Cream the butter until soft. Crush the garlic to a very smooth paste and beat into the butter with the salt, pepper and chopped parsley. Cover the bowl and leave in a cool place until ready for use.

Wash the mushrooms, drain well and trim the stalks. Melt the garlic butter in a frying pan, add the mushrooms and cook quickly for about 5 minutes or until just cooked. Add the lemon juice, mix well and serve piled into individual ramekin dishes. Serve hot with brown bread and butter.

Note Use very small fresh mushrooms for this recipe.

Serves 2

Salade Niçoise

Metric/Imperial	American
3 tomatoes	3 tomatoes
½ cucumber	½ cucumber
225 g/8 oz French beans, cooked	½ lb green beans, cooked
1 small green pepper (optional)	1 small green pepper (optional)
1 small onion	1 small onion
1 clove garlic	1 clove garlic
1 cos lettuce	1 head romaine lettuce
150 ml/¼ pint French dressing (see page 25)	⅔ cup French dressing (see page 25)
57-g/2-oz can anchovy fillets	2-oz can anchovy fillets
50 g/2 oz stuffed green or black olives	⅓ cup stuffed green or black olives
198-g/7-oz can tuna	7-oz can tuna
2 hard-boiled eggs	2 hard-cooked eggs
2 tablespoons chopped parsley (optional)	3 tablespoons chopped parsley (optional)

Quarter the tomatoes. Slice the cucumber. Cut the French beans into 3·5-cm/1½-inch lengths. Quarter the pepper, if using, remove the seeds and slice thinly. Peel and finely chop the onion. Crush the garlic. Wash the lettuce and tear into strips; arrange in the bottom of a salad bowl or serving dish.

Add the garlic to the French dressing followed by the prepared vegetables. Drain the anchovies and add with the sliced olives. Place on top of the lettuce. Drain and flake the tuna and place on top of the salad. Cut the eggs in half lengthwise and add with the chopped parsley if used.

Toss the salad lightly to mix the ingredients and serve immediately.

Note Take care not to overblend the mixture or the appearance will be messy and the salad will taste fishy.

Serves 4

Salade niçoise

Mild Curried Eggs

Metric/Imperial	American
4 hard-boiled eggs	4 hard-cooked eggs
4 tablespoons mayonnaise	$\frac{1}{3}$ cup mayonnaise
2 teaspoons lemon juice	2 teaspoons lemon juice
1 tablespoon mango chutney juice	1 tablespoon mango chutney juice
$\frac{1}{2}$–1 teaspoon curry powder	$\frac{1}{2}$–1 teaspoon curry powder
salt and pepper	salt and pepper
sprigs of cress to garnish	sprigs of cress to garnish

Cut the eggs in half lengthwise and arrange them on a serving dish. Blend together the mayonnaise, lemon juice, chutney juice, curry powder and seasoning. Spoon the curried mayonnaise over the eggs and decorate with sprigs of cress.

Serves 4

London Pots

Metric/Imperial	American
1 small clove garlic	1 small clove garlic
175 g/6 oz cream cheese	$\frac{3}{4}$ cup cream cheese
425-g/15-oz can consommé	15-oz can consommé
1 tablespoon sherry	1 tablespoon sherry
1 teaspoon curry powder	1 teaspoon curry powder
few chives to garnish	few chives to garnish

Crush the clove of garlic and place with all the ingredients into a liquidiser and mix well until smooth. Pour into six individual ramekins or dishes and leave to set in a cool place. Just before serving sprinkle the top of each dish with a few finely snipped chives.

Note If a liquidiser is not available put all the ingredients together in a large bowl and beat thoroughly with a wooden spoon until smooth.

Serves 6

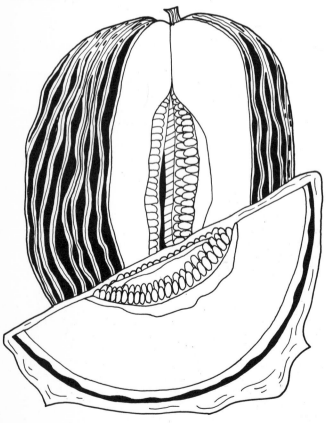

Parma Ham with Melon

Metric/Imperial	American
175 g/6 oz Parma ham, very thinly sliced	6 oz Parma ham, very thinly sliced
1 small ripe melon	$\frac{1}{2}$ honeydew melon
lemon wedges to garnish	lemon wedges to garnish

Arrange the Parma ham on four plates. Cut the melon into six slices, remove the seeds and put a slice on each plate.
    Garnish with wedges of lemon.

Note You can buy Parma ham at a good delicatessen. It also comes in 170-g/6-oz cans. Various kinds of smoked ham are available from different countries, so try a different one if you cannot get Parma ham. Sereno from Spain is excellent.

Variation
Melon and Ham Cornets Thinly sliced shoulder of ham is ideal for this dish. Halve a small ripe melon, scoop out the seeds and dice the flesh. Mix with a small carton of natural yogurt, season lightly to taste and carefully fill 12 ham cornets. Secure with wooden cocktail sticks and garnish with whole prawns, sprigs of parsley and tomato quarters.

Serves 6

Rillettes (pâté of pork)

Metric/Imperial	American
1 kg/2 lb belly pork	2 lb fresh picnic shoulder
300 ml/½ pint water	1¼ cups water
2 cloves garlic	2 cloves garlic
2 teaspoons salt	2 teaspoons salt
pepper	pepper
½ teaspoon ground ginger	½ teaspoon ground ginger
pinch cayenne pepper	pinch cayenne pepper
2 teaspoons sage	2 teaspoons sage
½ teaspoon chopped savory (optional)	½ teaspoon chopped savory (optional)
2 teaspoons lemon juice	2 teaspoons lemon juice
75 g/3 oz lard to seal	⅓ cup shortening to seal

Cut the pork into 2·5-cm/1-inch cubes, discard skin but not the bones. Place the pork in a pan and heat gently until the fat of the meat runs. Raise the heat and brown meat lightly, stirring occasionally. Pour on the water and add the sliced garlic, salt, pepper, ginger and cayenne. Bring to the boil then lower the heat and simmer very slowly for 3 hours.

When cooked most of the water should be evaporated and mainly fat and meat will remain. Next check over all the pieces of meat, removing all bones and gristle. Mash the meat with a fork or potato masher very thoroughly, or purée in a liquidiser. For a finer texture, pound. Season to taste, add the herbs and lemon juice. Leave the mixture to cool and as it begins to thicken and solidify, stir well and press into a 750-ml/1¼-pint (US 1½-pint) pâté dish and level the surface.

Rillettes may be used straight away or thoroughly covered with melted lard to seal the surface. Once sealed it will keep in the refrigerator for up to 1 month. Serve accompanied by toast and lemon wedges or olives.

To freeze Freeze for up to 3 months, preferably in the container in which it was made for easy serving.
Note Add more water during long cooking if water evaporates too early. If the meat cooks only in its fat it will become hard.

below Oeufs aurore

Variation
Country Pâté with Olives Omit water and lard. Mince raw pork with one clove garlic and stir in half the given amounts of ginger, sage and lemon juice along with the remaining ingredients. Add ten sliced stuffed green olives, a small finely chopped onion, 5 (US 6) tablespoons milk and 50 g/2 oz (US 1 cup) breadcrumbs; mix well and press into a 0·5-kg/1-lb loaf tin. Cover with foil, place in a bain-marie and cook in a moderate oven (160°C, 325°F, Gas Mark 3) for 2 hours. Leave to cool in the tin, turn out and serve sliced with French bread.

Serves 6–8   Country pâté with olives

Oeufs Aurore

Metric/Imperial	American
1 bunch cress	1 bunch cress
4 hard-boiled eggs	4 hard-cooked eggs
150 ml/¼ pint well seasoned mayonnaise	⅔ cup well seasoned mayonnaise
2 teaspoons tomato purée	2 teaspoons tomato paste
1 teaspoon lemon juice	1 teaspoon lemon juice
pinch sugar	pinch sugar
salt and black pepper	salt and black pepper
paprika	paprika

Arrange the sprigs of cress on a serving dish. Cut the eggs in half lengthwise and arrange them cut side down on the dish. Blend together the mayonnaise, tomato purée, lemon juice, sugar and seasoning and just before serving coat the eggs with the sauce and sprinkle with paprika.

Note Do not boil eggs for too long. Cook for 10–11 minutes, plunge into cold water to prevent further cooking, then crack the shells and leave to finish cooling; this will prevent a dark ring forming round the yolk.

Variation For a more substantial starter, fold 100 g/4 oz (US ⅔ cup) peeled prawns into 175 g/6 oz (US 1 cup) cooked long-grain rice. Season to taste and pile into four dishes. Place the whole eggs on top, spoon over the Aurore sauce and garnish with cress.

Serves 4

Hollandaise sauce

Hollandaise Sauce

Metric/Imperial	American
50 ml/2 fl oz wine or malt vinegar	$\frac{1}{4}$ cup wine or malt vinegar
6 peppercorns	6 peppercorns
$\frac{1}{2}$ bay leaf	$\frac{1}{2}$ bay leaf
1 blade mace	1 blade mace
3 egg yolks	3 egg yolks
100 g/4 oz butter, softened	$\frac{1}{2}$ cup butter, softened
$\frac{1}{4}$ teaspoon salt	$\frac{1}{4}$ teaspoon salt
pinch pepper	pinch pepper

Liquidiser method

Put the vinegar, peppercorns, bay leaf and mace in a pan and simmer until the vinegar is reduced to 1 tablespoon. Put the egg yolks in a liquidiser, add the strained vinegar and blend on maximum speed for a few seconds. Just before serving bring the butter to boiling point in a pan, switch liquidiser to maximum speed for a few seconds and slowly pour on the boiling butter; blend until thick, add seasoning, pour into a warmed sauce boat and serve at once.

Classic method

Put the vinegar, peppercorns, bay leaf and mace in a pan and simmer until the vinegar is reduced to 1 tablespoon. Put the egg yolks in a small bowl, blend in the strained vinegar and mix well. Put the bowl on top of a pan of hot, but not boiling, water and beat in the butter a knob at a time, whisking well over the heat after each addition until the sauce has thickened. Remove the bowl from the heat if the sauce thickens too quickly. When finished the sauce should just form very soft peaks. Add salt and pepper. Keep warm by standing in a bowl over warm water until needed.

Note   There are two *musts* for success with this sauce. One is to make it in a basin over hot, not boiling, water and to whisk continually while it is cooking. The other is to keep it warm by standing it in a bowl over warm water – if the water is too hot the sauce will continue to cook and turn into scrambled egg. It is easy if you take care.

This sauce is especially good served with fish or asparagus.

Serves 4

French Dressing

Metric/Imperial	American
$\frac{1}{2}$ clove garlic, crushed	$\frac{1}{2}$ clove garlic, crushed
$\frac{1}{2}$ teaspoon dry mustard	$\frac{1}{2}$ teaspoon dry mustard
$\frac{1}{2}$ teaspoon salt	$\frac{1}{2}$ teaspoon salt
pinch freshly ground black pepper	pinch freshly ground black pepper
1 teaspoon very finely chopped onion	1 teaspoon very finely chopped onion
1 teaspoon castor sugar	1 teaspoon sugar
150 ml/$\frac{1}{4}$ pint olive, vegetable or corn oil	$\frac{2}{3}$ cup olive, vegetable or corn oil
4–6 tablespoons cider or white wine vinegar	$\frac{1}{3}$–$\frac{1}{2}$ cup cider or white wine vinegar

Blend the first six ingredients together in a bowl. Mix in the oil slowly with a whisk or spoon. Stir in the vinegar. Taste and adjust seasoning if necessary.

Any of the following may be added to the basic French dressing to give it a new subtle flavour:

1 heaped teaspoon chopped parsley or watercress;
$\frac{1}{2}$ teaspoon chopped fresh herbs, e.g. tarragon or chervil;
2 teaspoons chopped capers or gherkins;
2 teaspoons chopped mint and an extra teaspoon sugar;
2–3 tablespoons tomato ketchup and pinch cayenne pepper.

Makes 300 ml/$\frac{1}{2}$ pint (US 1$\frac{1}{4}$ cups)

Mayonnaise

Metric/Imperial	American
2 egg yolks	2 egg yolks
$\frac{1}{2}$ teaspoon made mustard	$\frac{1}{2}$ teaspoon prepared mustard
$\frac{1}{2}$ teaspoon salt	$\frac{1}{2}$ teaspoon salt
pinch pepper	pinch pepper
$\frac{1}{2}$ teaspoon castor sugar	$\frac{1}{2}$ teaspoon sugar
300 ml/$\frac{1}{2}$ pint olive, vegetable or corn oil	1$\frac{1}{4}$ cups olive, vegetable or corn oil
1 tablespoon lemon juice	1 tablespoon lemon juice
1 tablespoon white wine or malt vinegar	1 tablespoon white wine or malt vinegar

Stand a bowl on a damp cloth to prevent it slipping on the table. Put the egg yolks, mustard, salt, pepper and sugar into the bowl and mix thoroughly.

Add the oil drop by drop, beating constantly with a whisk until the sauce is thick and smooth. In order to add the oil a drop at a time, put into the bottle neck a cork from which a small wedge has been cut out. Add the lemon juice and vinegar. This makes a traditional thick mayonnaise. For a thinner mixture add a little cream or top of the milk.

Note   Should the sauce curdle because the oil has been added to the egg yolks too quickly, take a fresh yolk and start again, adding the curdled mayonnaise to it very slowly the way the oil should have been added to the original egg yolks.

Makes approx. 350 ml/12 fl oz (US 1$\frac{1}{2}$ cups)

Mayonnaise ingredients

Salads and vegetables

Salad can add a welcome touch of freshness to a meal, whether a simple tomato and onion or a hearty potato, celery and apple combination. And you can enjoy salads all year round by choosing seasonal or canned ingredients, or by using rice as a base instead of lettuce.

Vegetables should be treated with consideration, too, and can be served either on their own as a light lunch — try marrow and tomato casserole — or as an accompaniment to meat or fish dishes. Old favourites are included in this chapter, such as baked leeks mornay, as well as interesting new ideas for potatoes, onions, carrots and celery. With these suggestions to guide you, don't be afraid to apply a new treatment to whatever vegetables you have in the pantry — you may be surprised at the warm reception they receive from your family or guests.

Winter Salad

Metric/Imperial	American
1 iceberg lettuce	1 head iceberg lettuce
2 sticks celery	2 stalks celery
1 red dessert apple	1 red dessert apple
100 g/4 oz green grapes	½ cup white grapes
25 g/1 oz walnut pieces	¼ cup walnut pieces
Dressing	**Dressing**
100 ml/4 fl oz corn or vegetable oil	½ cup corn or vegetable oil
2 tablespoons lemon juice	3 tablespoons lemon juice
salt and pepper	salt and pepper
½ teaspoon dry mustard	½ teaspoon dry mustard
½ teaspoon castor sugar	½ teaspoon sugar
Garnish	**Garnish**
1 red dessert apple	1 red dessert apple
few black grapes	few purple grapes

Wash and drain the lettuce, then shred and place in the bottom of a large salad bowl. Slice the celery. Peel, core and slice the apple and add to the lettuce with the celery.

Remove any pips from the grapes, skin and add to the bowl with the walnut pieces.

Mix all the dressing ingredients together and pour over the salad. Garnish attractively with thinly sliced apple and whole grapes.

Serves 6–8

Winter salad

Coleslaw

Metric/Imperial	American
1 small (0·75 kg/1½ lb) hard white cabbage	1 small head (1½ lb) white cabbage
4 tablespoons French dressing (see page 25)	⅓ cup French dressing (see page 25)
salt and pepper	salt and pepper
1 small onion	1 small onion
2 carrots	2 carrots
50 g/2 oz seedless raisins	⅓ cup seedless raisins
1 teaspoon made mustard	1 teaspoon prepared mustard
4 tablespoons mayonnaise	⅓ cup mayonnaise

Cut the cabbage into quarters and trim away the hard stalk, then finely slice into strips. Place in a mixing bowl with the French dressing, salt and pepper and very finely chopped onion; toss. Leave to stand in a cool place for 3–4 hours or overnight in the refrigerator.

Peel and coarsely grate the carrots, add with the raisins to the cabbage. Stir the mustard into the mayonnaise and add to the bowl. Toss well until the salad is mixed and turn into a serving dish. Leave to stand for 1 hour before serving.

Variation Omit the carrots from the coleslaw, and add instead two sticks celery, finely chopped, and two dessert apples, peeled, cored and chopped. Toss to mix and serve with a plate of cold meats.

Serves 6

Coleslaw

Hot curried rice

Curried Rice

Metric/Imperial	American
175 g/6 oz long-grain rice	¾ cup long-grain rice
3 tablespoons salad cream	¼ cup mayonnaise
1 teaspoon curry powder	1 teaspoon curry powder
1 tablespoon mango chutney juice	1 tablespoon mango chutney juice
salt	salt
sprig of parsley to garnish	sprig of parsley to garnish

Cook the rice in boiling salted water until tender, about 12 minutes; rinse and drain well.

Put the salad cream, curry powder and chutney juice in a bowl and blend well. Stir in the rice and add salt to taste.

Place in a serving dish and leave to become quite cold. Garnish with a sprig of parsley and serve.

Note Use bottled mayonnaise or salad cream if you do not want to make up home-made mayonnaise (see page 25). This salad goes very well with cold meats or poultry.

Variation
Hot Curried Rice Add 1–2 teaspoons curry powder to the boiling salted water, and cook the rice until tender, separating the grains with a fork. Drain well and toss with slivered almonds.

Serve immediately to accompany a main dish.

Serves 4

Sweetcorn and Soured Cream

Metric/Imperial
312-g/11-oz can sweetcorn
 kernels, well drained
2–3 spring onions
142-g/5-oz carton soured
 cream
salt and pepper

American
11-oz can corn kernels, well
 drained
2–3 scallions
5-oz carton dairy sour cream

salt and pepper

Put the well drained sweetcorn in a bowl, finely chop the spring onions and add to the corn with the soured cream and plenty of salt and pepper. Turn the salad into a serving dish and serve at once.

Note It is essential to drain the corn really well beforehand and to add the cream just before serving so there will not be a lot of watery liquid floating in the dish, which spoils the salad.

If you have some cooked peas left over from a previous meal they may be added to the salad.

Variation
Sweetcorn and Rice Salad Mix 100 g/4 oz (US $\frac{2}{3}$ cup) cooked long-grain rice with drained canned sweetcorn, peeled chopped tomatoes and lightly boiled sliced courgettes. Finely chop an onion, fry until soft, cool, then toss into the rice salad with French dressing, chopped mixed herbs and seasoning to taste. Mix well and serve.

Serves 4

Sweetcorn and rice salad

Dressed rice salad

Sunshine Rice Salad

Metric/Imperial	American
100 g/4 oz patna rice	½ cup long-grain rice
4 tablespoons sweetcorn kernels	⅓ cup corn kernels
4 pineapple rings	4 pineapple rings
50 ml/2 fl oz corn oil	¼ cup corn oil
1 tablespoon wine or cider vinegar	1 tablespoon wine or cider vinegar
salt and pepper	salt and pepper
25 g/1 oz butter	2 tablespoons butter
25 g/1 oz flaked almonds	¼ cup flaked almonds
1 hard-boiled egg, sliced, to garnish	1 hard-cooked egg, sliced, to garnish

Cook the rice in plenty of boiling salted water until tender, rinse and drain well. Place in a bowl with sweetcorn, chop three pineapple rings and add to the rice.

Blend the oil, vinegar and salt and pepper together and stir into the rice; leave on one side until the rice becomes quite cold.

Melt the butter in a pan, add the almonds and fry until golden brown; drain on kitchen paper.

Pile the rice on to a serving dish and garnish with the remaining pineapple ring cut into wedges and the sliced egg. Sprinkle with almonds and serve.

Variation

Dressed Rice Salad Mix the cooked rice with quartered tomatoes, diced cucumber and chopped mixed herbs. Toss in the dressing and leave to cool. Crumble 50 g/2 oz (US ½ cup) blue cheese into 100 ml/4 fl oz (US ½ cup) soured cream, spoon over the salad and garnish with cucumber slices and sprigs of dill.

Serves 4

Potato, Apple and Celery Salad

Metric/Imperial	American
0·5 kg/1 lb potatoes, boiled	1 lb potatoes, boiled
100 ml/4 fl oz French dressing (see page 25)	½ cup French dressing (see page 25)
1 small head celery	1 small bunch celery
1 large dessert apple	1 large dessert apple
150 ml/¼ pint mayonnaise	⅔ cup mayonnaise
salt and pepper	salt and pepper
1 tablespoon snipped chives	1 tablespoon snipped chives

Slice the hot potatoes into a bowl. Blend in the French dressing and leave on one side until the potatoes are cold.

Wash and chop the celery. Quarter, core and dice the apple and add to the potatoes with the mayonnaise and seasoning and most of the chives. Stir well, cover the bowl and leave in a cold place until the salad is required. Turn into a serving dish and sprinkle with the remaining chives.

Note This salad is best if the French dressing is mixed with the potatoes and left to soak in overnight. Next day add the celery and peeled or unpeeled apple (as liked) with the mayonnaise.

Serves 6

Tomato and Onion Salad

Metric/Imperial	American
0·5 kg/1 lb firm tomatoes	1 lb firm tomatoes
2 medium onions	2 medium onions
4 tablespoons French dressing (see page 25)	⅓ cup French dressing (see page 25)
salt and freshly ground black pepper	salt and freshly ground black pepper
1 tablespoon chopped spring onion to garnish	1 tablespoon chopped scallion to garnish

Plunge the tomatoes into a pan of boiling water for 10 seconds, drain and rinse under cold water. Remove the skins and cut the tomatoes in slices.

Peel and slice the onions very finely. Arrange the tomato and onion slices in neat layers in a serving dish, finishing with a layer of tomato. Spoon over the French dressing and season well. Leave in a cool place until required. Just before serving sprinkle with the chopped spring onion.

Note Make this salad when tomatoes are at their cheapest. Firm tomatoes will cut into neater slices.

Serves 4

French Dressed Mushrooms

Metric/Imperial	American
100 ml/4 fl oz corn or vegetable oil	½ cup corn or vegetable oil
2 tablespoons lemon juice	3 tablespoons lemon juice
salt and pepper	salt and pepper
½ teaspoon dry mustard	½ teaspoon dry mustard
½ teaspoon castor sugar	½ teaspoon sugar
225 g/8 oz button mushrooms	2 cups button mushrooms
1 tablespoon chopped parsley to garnish	1 tablespoon chopped parsley to garnish

Mix the oil, lemon juice, seasoning, mustard and sugar together. Wash and dry the mushrooms, trim the stalks and slice very finely. Place in a dish and pour over the dressing; toss well. Leave to stand in a cool place for at least 2 hours before serving. Turn into a serving dish, sprinkle with parsley and serve.

Serves 4–6

Garlic Baked Potatoes

Metric/Imperial	American
0·75 kg/1½ lb large potatoes	1½ lb large potatoes
1 large clove garlic	1 large clove garlic
50 g/2 oz butter	¼ cup butter
chopped parsley to garnish	chopped parsley to garnish

Peel the potatoes and cut roughly into 1·5-cm/¾-inch squares. Place in a pan, cover with cold water and bring to the boil; cook for about 5 minutes and drain well.

Crush the garlic, place with the butter in an ovenproof dish in a warm oven and leave until melted. Add the potatoes and stir well so they are thoroughly coated with the garlic butter. Bake in a moderately hot oven (190°C, 375°F, Gas Mark 5), stirring occasionally, until a pale golden brown, about 40 minutes. Serve sprinkled with chopped parsley.

Note These potatoes are delicious served with roast meat – bake them alongside the joint and adjust heat and cooking time as necessary.

Serves 4

Tomato and onion salad

Baked Aubergines and Tomatoes

Metric/Imperial	American
350–450 g/¾–1 lb aubergines	¾–1 lb eggplant
salt	salt
225 g/8 oz tomatoes	½ lb tomatoes
butter	butter
pepper	pepper
1 tablespoon chopped parsley	1 tablespoon chopped parsley

Slice the aubergines and cook in boiling salted water for 5 minutes; drain thoroughly. Place the tomatoes in a bowl, cover with boiling water and leave to stand for 1 minute, drain, peel and slice.

Well butter a shallow ovenproof dish and layer the aubergines and tomatoes in the dish, seasoning well between each layer. Sprinkle with the parsley, dot with a little butter and cover the dish with foil. Bake in a moderately hot oven (190°C, 375°F, Gas Mark 5) until the aubergines are tender, about 40–45 minutes. Serve with grilled or roast meat, poultry or simple fish dishes.

Note This recipe makes a few aubergines go a long way and is a very good way of using up soft tomatoes.

Serves 4–6

Oven baked potatoes and onions

Oven Baked Potatoes and Onions

Metric/Imperial
1 kg/2 lb medium potatoes
225 g/8 oz onions
salt
75 g/3 oz butter
pepper
50 g/2 oz fresh white
  breadcrumbs
sprig of parsley to garnish

American
2 lb medium potatoes
½ lb onions
salt
⅓ cup butter
pepper
1 cup fresh white bread
  crumbs
sprig of parsley to garnish

Peel and slice the potatoes and onions very finely. Put them in a pan, cover with cold water, add 1 teaspoon salt and bring to boiling point. Boil for 1 minute then drain in a colander.

Well grease a 1·5-litre/2½-pint (US 3-pint) straight sided oven-proof dish, using some of the butter.

Place the sliced onion and potato in the buttered dish, adding salt and pepper to taste with each spoonful. Top with a layer of potato slices and sprinkle with breadcrumbs. Dot with the remaining butter.

Bake in a moderately hot oven (190°C, 375°F, Gas Mark 5) for 1½–2 hours, until golden brown and tender. Add a little extra butter during cooking if necessary. Garnish with parsley sprig before serving.

Note By blanching the potatoes and onions this dish may be prepared in advance.

Serves 6

Baked Leeks Mornay

Metric/Imperial
4 medium leeks
4 (50-g/2-oz) slices ham
Mornay sauce
25 g/1 oz butter
15 g/½ oz flour

300 ml/½ pint milk
75 g/3 oz hard cheese, grated
1 rounded teaspoon made
  mustard
½ teaspoon salt
pepper
4 mushroom caps and lemon
  slice to garnish

American
4 medium leeks
4 slices cooked or cured ham
Mornay sauce
2 tablespoons butter
2 tablespoons all-purpose
  flour
1¼ cups milk
¾ cup grated hard cheese
1 rounded teaspoon prepared
  mustard
½ teaspoon salt
pepper
4 mushroom caps and lemon
  slice to garnish

Cut the coarse green leaves off the leeks. Cut a deep slit through all the green and half the white part of the leeks and open up, keeping the green end down. Hold under running cold water to wash thoroughly. Wrap each leek in a slice of ham. Pack closely in an open generous 1-litre/2-pint (US 2½-pint) oven-proof dish.

To prepare the sauce, melt the butter in a saucepan. Stir in the flour and cook gently for 1 minute, remove from the heat and blend in the milk. Return to the heat and bring to the boil, stirring well. Remove from the heat and add two-thirds of the cheese, the mustard and seasoning. Spoon the sauce over the leeks and sprinkle with the remaining grated cheese. Bake uncovered in a moderate oven (180°C, 350°F, Gas Mark 4) for 1–1¼ hours or until leeks are tender when pierced in the thickest part with the point of a knife. Garnish and serve.

Note If frozen leeks are used the cooking may be cut to 30–40 minutes depending on size.

Serves 4

opposite Baked leeks mornay

Quick casserole of potatoes and mushrooms

Quick Casserole of Potatoes and Mushrooms

Metric/Imperial	American
175 g/6 oz button mushrooms	1½ cups button mushrooms
25 g/1 oz butter	2 tablespoons butter
40 g/1½ oz flour	⅓ cup all-purpose flour
450 ml/¾ pint milk	2 cups milk
salt and pepper	salt and pepper
538-g/1 lb 3-oz can new potatoes	20-oz can new potatoes
grated nutmeg	grated nutmeg

Wash the mushrooms and trim but do not remove the stalks (this helps the mushrooms keep their shape).

Melt the butter and toss the mushrooms in it for 3 minutes. Stir in the flour, add the milk and seasoning, bring to the boil and simmer for 2 minutes.

Drain the potatoes and add to the sauce; simmer for 5 minutes. Turn into a serving dish and sprinkle with nutmeg.

Note This dish keeps hot well. For a summertime variation, omit the white sauce and mix cubed boiled potatoes with thin slices of mushroom and toss well with salt, pepper and French dressing. Sprinkle with chopped parsley.

Serves 4

Braised Celery

Metric/Imperial	American
2 heads celery	2 bunches celery
salt	salt
1 small onion	1 small onion
1 carrot	1 carrot
300 ml/½ pint stock	1¼ cups stock
black pepper	black pepper
7 g/¼ oz butter	1½ teaspoons butter
7 g/¼ oz flour	1 tablespoon all-purpose flour
chopped parsley to garnish	chopped parsley to garnish

Trim the roots off the celery and remove any damaged stalks and the green leafy tops. Scrub well and cut each head in half lengthwise. Place in a pan of boiling salted water and cook for 10 minutes; drain very thoroughly.

Place the celery in a large shallow pan. Peel and slice the onion and carrot and add to the pan with the stock, more salt and pepper. Cover the pan and cook over a low heat until tender, about 40 minutes. Remove the celery carefully and arrange in a warm serving dish.

Cream the butter and flour together and whisk into the stock in the pan, bring to the boil and simmer for 2 minutes. Check seasoning and strain over the celery. Sprinkle with a little chopped parsley and serve.

Serves 4

Cauliflower Polonaise

Metric/Imperial	American
1 medium cauliflower	1 medium cauliflower
40 g/1½ oz butter	3 tablespoons butter
25 g/ 1 oz fresh white breadcrumbs	½ cup fresh white bread crumbs
1 tablespoon chopped parsley	1 tablespoon chopped parsley
1 hard-boiled egg to garnish	1 hard-cooked egg to garnish

Remove all the tough outside leaves and hard stalk from the cauliflower and wash well. Cook whole in boiling salted water for 10–15 minutes or until tender. Drain thoroughly and place on a warm serving dish; keep warm.

Melt the butter in a pan, add the breadcrumbs and fry quickly for 2–3 minutes until golden brown. Remove from the heat, stir in the parsley and spoon over the cauliflower.

Cut the egg in half, sieve the yolk and chop the white. Garnish the dish with some of the yolk and white and arrange the remainder attractively on top of the cauliflower.

Serves 4

Leeks in Soured Cream

Metric/Imperial	American
0·5 kg/1 lb leeks	1 lb leeks
salt and freshly ground black pepper	salt and freshly ground black pepper
142-g/5-oz carton soured cream	5-oz carton dairy sour cream
grated nutmeg	grated nutmeg

Wash the leeks thoroughly and cut across their width into thin slices. Place in a pan, cover with boiling water, add a little salt and cook until just tender, about 6–8 minutes.

Drain very thoroughly and return to the pan, add the pepper and soured cream and stir well. Turn into a warm serving dish and sprinkle with nutmeg.

Note This is a very easy way to serve leeks and makes a nice change from white sauce.

Serves 4

Salad vegetables

Marrow and Tomato Casserole

Metric/Imperial	**American**
1 small (450-g/1-lb) marrow	1 lb summer squash
4 tomatoes	4 tomatoes
1 small onion	1 small onion
butter	butter
salt and pepper	salt and pepper

Peel the marrow then cut in half and scoop out the seeds. Cut in 1-cm/½-inch cubes. Skin, slice and deseed the tomatoes and finely chop the onion.

Thoroughly butter an ovenproof casserole and put the marrow, tomatoes and onion in alternate layers in the dish. Season each layer, finishing with a layer of marrow. Dot with butter, cover with a tight-fitting lid or piece of foil and bake in a moderate oven (180°C, 350°F, Gas Mark 4) for 45 minutes until marrow is just cooked.

Serve with roast meat, chops or sausages.

Note It is not necessary to add any liquid to the vegetables as they cook in their own moisture.

Serves 4

Baked Onions

Metric/Imperial	**American**
25 g/1 oz butter	2 tablespoons butter
4 medium onions	4 medium onions
salt and pepper	salt and pepper

Grease the bottom of a small heavy ovenproof casserole with half the butter. Peel the onions, put them whole in the casserole and top each with a small piece of the remaining butter. Sprinkle the onions with a little salt and pepper, cover with a lid and bake in a moderate oven (180°C, 350°F, Gas Mark 4) until tender, about 1½ hours.

Serves 4

Vichy Carrots in the Oven

Metric/Imperial	**American**
0·75 kg/1½ lb carrots	1½ lb carrots
300 ml/½ pint water	1¼ cups water
25 g/1 oz butter	2 tablespoons butter
1½ teaspoons castor sugar	1½ teaspoons sugar
salt and pepper	salt and pepper

Peel or scrape the carrots and slice lengthwise in thin strips. Put in a generous 1-litre/2-pint (US 2½-pint) ovenproof casserole. Add the water, butter, sugar and plenty of salt and pepper.

Cover the casserole with a well fitting lid or piece of foil and cook in a moderate oven (180°C, 350°F, Gas Mark 4) for 1¼–1½ hours or until the carrots are tender. Serve the carrots with a little of the cooking liquor or drain.

Serves 6

below Ratatouille

above Peas and ham

Vichy carrots in the oven

Ratatouille

Metric/Imperial
2 small aubergines
2 courgettes
150 ml/¼ pint olive or
    vegetable oil
2 medium onions
1 small green and 1 small red
    pepper
1 clove garlic
225 g/8 oz tomatoes
salt and pepper
1 tablespoon chopped parsley

American
2 small eggplant
2 zucchini
⅔ cup olive or vegetable oil
2 medium onions
1 small green and 1 small red
    pepper
1 clove garlic
½ lb tomatoes
salt and pepper
1 tablespoon chopped parsley

Cut the scrubbed, unpeeled aubergines and courgettes into
5-mm/¼-inch slices. Sprinkle with salt and leave them to drain
on kitchen paper for about 30 minutes.

Heat the oil in a large heavy pan. Peel and slice the onions
and add to the pan; cook slowly until they are soft but not
coloured. Dry the aubergines and courgettes and add them to
the pan. Remove the seeds from the peppers and slice thinly,
crush the garlic and add both to the pan. Cover and simmer for
30 minutes, stirring occasionally.

Skin the tomatoes and slice, add to the pan with plenty of
seasoning, cover and cook for a further 10 minutes or until the
vegetables are tender. Sprinkle over the parsley.

Serve hot as a vegetable or cold as an hors d'œuvre.

Note Frozen ratatouille is well worth trying when these
vegetables are expensive, or you might buy 225 g/8 oz (US ½ lb)
courgettes and add them to the frozen mixture.

Serves 6

Peas and Courgettes

Metric/Imperial
225 g/8 oz courgettes
salt
340 g/12 oz frozen peas
butter

American
½ lb zucchini
salt
1½ cups frozen peas
butter

Top and tail the courgettes. Do not peel. If they are very small
cut into 5 mm/¼ inch thick slices, if larger cut into cubes. Put
them into a pan of boiling salted water with the peas. Cover and
simmer for 5 minutes or until just tender. Drain thoroughly.
Return to the pan, add the butter and toss over a low heat until
the vegetables are warm and evenly coated.

Note This is a very good way to stretch a small amount of
courgettes when they are expensive.

Variation
Peas and Ham If courgettes are not available, try adding a
couple of slices of cooked ham, cut into thin strips, and a small
onion, thinly sliced or chopped. Cook in butter over a low heat
until the onion is soft, then mix well. Serve with crisp fried
bread croûtons.

Serves 4

Savoury quiches

For the small amount of effort involved, there must be no more rewarding dish to make than any of the savoury quiches included in this chapter. There is something about a freshly baked flan, full of the goodness of cheese and eggs, bacon or tomatoes, that arouses the appetite of even the most particular of eaters, especially at buffet parties or picnics.

Once the basic method is mastered, variations on the theme are endless. Start with a Spanish quiche, tuna and tomato or ham and mushroom. Then begin to incorporate your favourite vegetables, herbs and fish into shortcrust flans that will delight your family and give you an easy solution to the problem of unexpected guests.

Spanish Quiche

Metric/Imperial	American
Shortcrust pastry	Basic pie dough
175 g/6 oz plain flour	1½ cups all-purpose flour
pinch salt	pinch salt
50 g/2 oz butter	¼ cup butter
25 g/1 oz lard	2 tablespoons shortening
approx. 25 ml/1 fl oz cold water	approx. 2 tablespoons cold water
Filling	Filling
2 small onions	2 small onions
25 g/1 oz butter	2 tablespoons butter
175 g/6 oz streaky bacon	8–9 slices bacon
12 Spanish stuffed green olives, sliced	12 Spanish stuffed green olives, sliced
300 ml/½ pint single cream	1¼ cups light cream
2 large eggs	2 large eggs
salt and pepper	salt and pepper

Heat the oven to moderately hot (200°C, 400°F, Gas Mark 6) and place a baking tray in the centre of the oven.

Make the shortcrust pastry: sift the flour and salt into a bowl. Rub the butter and lard into the flour until well blended. Gradually add sufficient of the water to form a dough. Roll it out on a lightly floured surface and line a shallow 23-cm/9-inch fluted flan tin.

Finely chop the onions and fry in the butter until soft but not browned. Remove the rind from the bacon and cut into small pieces, add to the onions and cook until brown, drain and place with the sliced olives in the flan case. Mix together the cream, eggs and seasoning and pour on top of the bacon.

Place in the oven on the hot baking tray and cook for 15 minutes, then reduce the heat to moderate (180°C, 350°F, Gas Mark 4) and cook for a further 20–25 minutes until the filling is just set and a pale golden brown. Serve hot or cold.

Serves 6

Cheese and Pepper Quiche

Metric/Imperial	American
Pastry	Pastry
175 g/6 oz plain flour	1½ cups all-purpose flour
pinch salt	pinch salt
50 g/2 oz butter	¼ cup butter
25 g/1 oz lard	2 tablespoons shortening
approx. 25 ml/1 fl oz cold water	approx. 2 tablespoons cold water
Filling	Filling
½ green pepper	½ green pepper
75–100 g/3–4 oz Cheddar cheese, grated	¾–1 cup grated Cheddar cheese
300 ml/½ pint single cream	1¼ cups light cream
2 large eggs	2 large eggs
salt and pepper	salt and pepper

Heat the oven to moderately hot (200°C, 400°F, Gas Mark 6) and place a baking tray in the centre of the oven.

Make the shortcrust pastry in the usual way. Roll it out on a lightly floured surface and line a shallow 23-cm/9-inch fluted flan tin.

Remove stalk and seeds from the pepper and cut into small dice. Place in a small saucepan, cover with cold water and bring to the boil; drain well. Mix the cheese with the pepper and place in the flan case. Mix together the cream, eggs and seasoning and pour on top.

Place in the oven on the hot baking tray and cook for 15 minutes, then reduce the heat to moderate (180°C, 350°F, Gas Mark 4) and cook for a further 20–25 minutes until the filling is set and a pale golden brown. Serve hot.

Serves 6

Cheese and Onion Quiche

Metric/Imperial
Pastry
175 g/6 oz plain flour
pinch salt
50 g/2 oz butter
25 g/1 oz lard
approx. 25 ml/1 fl oz cold
  water
Filling
40 g/1½ oz butter
225 g/8 oz onions
2 large eggs
300 ml/½ pint single cream
salt and pepper
75–100 g/3–4 oz Cheddar
  cheese, grated

American
Pastry
1½ cups all-purpose flour
pinch salt
¼ cup butter
2 tablespoons shortening
approx. 2 tablespoons cold
  water
Filling
3 tablespoons butter
½ lb onions
2 large eggs
1¼ cups light cream
salt and pepper
¾–1 cup grated Cheddar
  cheese

Heat the oven to moderately hot (200°C, 400°F, Gas Mark 6) and place a baking tray in the centre of the oven.

Make the shortcrust pastry in the usual way. Roll it out on a lightly floured surface and line a shallow 23-cm/9-inch fluted flan tin.

Melt the butter for the filling in a small pan. Finely slice the onions, add to the pan and cook for 5 minutes, until soft but not browned; place in the flan case. Mix together the eggs, cream and seasoning and pour over the onions. Sprinkle with cheese.

Place in the oven on the hot baking tray and cook for 15 minutes, then reduce the heat to moderate (180°C, 350°F, Gas Mark 4) and cook for a further 20–25 minutes until the filling is set and a pale golden brown. Serve hot or cold.

Serves 6

Crab Quiche

Metric/Imperial
Pastry
175 g/6 oz plain flour
pinch salt
50 g/2 oz butter
25 g/1 oz lard
approx. 25 ml/1 fl oz cold
  water
Filling
92-g/3¼-oz can crabmeat
1 tablespoon chopped parsley
300 ml/½ pint single cream
2 large eggs
salt and pepper

American
Pastry
1½ cups all-purpose flour
pinch salt
¼ cup butter
2 tablespoons shortening
approx. 2 tablespoons cold
  water
Filling
3¼-oz can crabmeat
1 tablespoon chopped parsley
1¼ cups light cream
2 large eggs
salt and pepper

Heat the oven to moderately hot (200°C, 400°F, Gas Mark 6) and place a baking tray in the centre of the oven.

Make the shortcrust pastry in the usual way. Roll it out on a lightly floured surface and line a shallow 23-cm/9-inch fluted flan tin.

Flake the crabmeat and remove any pieces of bone, spread over the base of the flan and sprinkle with parsley. Mix the cream, eggs and seasoning together and pour over the crabmeat.

Place in the oven on the hot baking tray and cook for 15 minutes, then reduce the heat to moderate (180°C, 350°F, Gas Mark 4) and cook for a further 20–25 minutes until the filling is just set and a golden brown. Serve hot or cold. This quiche is delicious served as a first course at a dinner party.

Serves 6

Cheese and Chive Quiche

Metric/Imperial	American
Pastry	**Pastry**
175 g/6 oz plain flour	1½ cups all-purpose flour
pinch salt	pinch salt
50 g/2 oz butter	¼ cup butter
25 g/1 oz lard	2 tablespoons shortening
approx. 25 ml/1 fl oz cold water	approx. 2 tablespoons cold water
Filling	**Filling**
100 g/4 oz Emmenthal or Gruyère cheese	¼ lb Emmenthal, Gruyère or other Swiss cheese
4 rashers streaky bacon	4 slices bacon
300 ml/½ pint single cream	1¼ cups light cream
2 large eggs	2 large eggs
1 tablespoon chopped parsley	1 tablespoon chopped parsley
2 teaspoons snipped chives	2 teaspoons snipped chives
salt and pepper	salt and pepper

Heat the oven to moderately hot (200°C, 400°F, Gas Mark 6) and place a baking tray in the centre of the oven.

Make the shortcrust pastry in the usual way. Roll it out on a lightly floured surface and line a shallow 23-cm/9-inch fluted flan tin.

Slice the cheese and arrange in the base of the flan case. Remove the rind from the bacon and fry the rashers very lightly for 1–2 minutes. Cut each in half and arrange on top of the cheese. Mix together the cream, eggs, herbs and seasoning and pour into the flan case.

Place in the oven on the hot baking tray and cook for 15 minutes, then reduce the heat to moderate (180°C, 350°F, Gas Mark 4) and cook for a further 20–25 minutes until the filling is just set and a pale golden brown. Serve hot or cold.

To freeze All quiches freeze well and may be reheated straight from the freezer.
Note For an 18-cm/7-inch flan use pastry made with 100 g/ 4 oz (US 1 cup) flour and half the filling.

Serves 6

Asparagus Quiche

Metric/Imperial	American
Pastry	**Pastry**
175 g/6 oz plain flour	1½ cups all-purpose flour
pinch salt	pinch salt
50 g/2 oz butter	¼ cup butter
25 g/1 oz lard	2 tablespoons shortening
approx. 25 ml/1 fl oz cold water	approx. 2 tablespoons cold water
Filling	**Filling**
283-g/10-oz can asparagus tips	10-oz can asparagus tips
300 ml/½ pint single cream	1¼ cups light cream
2 large eggs	2 large eggs
salt and pepper	salt and pepper
2 stuffed green olives to garnish (optional)	2 stuffed green olives to garnish (optional)

Heat the oven to moderately hot (200°C, 400°F, Gas Mark 6) and place a baking tray in the centre of the oven.

Make the shortcrust pastry in the usual way. Roll it out on a lightly floured surface and line a shallow 23-cm/9-inch fluted flan tin.

Thoroughly drain the asparagus, reserve eight whole tips for decoration and cut the remainder into 2·5-cm/1-inch lengths; arrange in the base of the flan. Mix together the cream, eggs and seasoning and pour into the flan case over the asparagus.

Place in the oven on the hot baking tray and cook for 15 minutes, then reduce the heat to moderate (180°C, 350°F, Gas Mark 4) and cook for a further 20–25 minutes until the filling is just set and a pale golden brown. Remove from the oven and arrange the whole asparagus tips on top. Serve hot or cold.

Note The same amount of pastry can be used to line six 5 × 10-cm/2 × 4-inch patty tins, which should be baked in a moderately hot oven (190°C, 375°F, Gas Mark 5) for 20 minutes.

Serves 6

Bacon and sweetcorn quiche

Bacon and Sweetcorn Quiche

Metric/Imperial
Pastry
175 g/6 oz plain flour
pinch salt
50 g/2 oz butter
25 g/1 oz lard
approx. 25 ml/1 fl oz cold
 water
Filling
6 rashers streaky bacon
25 g/1 oz butter
198-g/7-oz can sweetcorn
 kernels
300 ml/½ pint single cream
2 large eggs
salt and pepper

American
Pastry
1½ cups all-purpose flour
pinch salt
¼ cup butter
2 tablespoons shortening
approx. 2 tablespoons cold
 water
Filling
6 slices bacon
2 tablespoons butter
7-oz can corn kernels

1¼ cups light cream
2 large eggs
salt and pepper

Heat the oven to moderately hot (200°C, 400°F, Gas Mark 6) and place a baking tray in the centre of the oven.

Make the shortcrust pastry in the usual way. Roll it out on a lightly floured surface and line a shallow 23-cm/9-inch fluted or plain flan tin.

Derind and finely chop the bacon and fry in the butter until just cooked, about 5 minutes. Drain and place in the base of the flan. Drain the corn well and spread over the bacon. Mix together the cream, eggs and seasoning and pour into the flan case.

Place in the centre of the oven on the hot baking tray and cook for 15 minutes, then reduce the heat to moderate (180°C, 350°F, Gas Mark 4) and cook for a further 20–25 minutes until the filling is just set and a pale golden brown. Serve hot or cold.

Note A small chopped green pepper can be added with the corn for a more colourful quiche.

Serves 6

Ham and Mushroom Quiche

Metric/Imperial
Pastry
175 g/6 oz plain flour
pinch salt
50 g/2 oz butter
25 g/1 oz lard
approx. 25 ml/1 fl oz cold
   water
Filling
100 g/4 oz button mushrooms
25 g/1 oz butter
100 g/4 oz ham, diced
300 ml/½ pint single cream
2 large eggs
salt and pepper
large mushroom to garnish

American
Pastry
1½ cups all-purpose flour
pinch salt
¼ cup butter
2 tablespoons shortening
approx. 2 tablespoons cold
   water
Filling
1 cup button mushrooms
2 tablespoons butter
½ cup chopped cooked ham
1¼ cups light cream
2 large eggs
salt and pepper
large mushroom to garnish

Heat the oven to moderately hot (200°C, 400°F, Gas Mark 6) and place a baking tray in the centre of the oven.

Make the shortcrust pastry in the usual way. Roll it out on a lightly floured surface and line a shallow 23-cm/9-inch fluted flan tin.

Wash and slice the mushrooms. Melt the butter in a small pan, cook the mushrooms for 2 minutes and place in the base of the flan. Add the ham to the mushrooms. Mix the cream, eggs and seasoning together and pour into the flan case.

Place in the oven on the hot baking tray and cook for 15 minutes, then reduce the heat to moderate (180°C, 350°F, Gas Mark 4) and cook for a further 20–25 minutes until set. Serve hot or cold, garnished with a large mushroom cap.

Variation
Ham, Mushroom and Tomato Quiche Add three peeled, sliced tomatoes to the cream and egg mixture, reserving a few slices for the garnish.

Serves 6

Smoked Salmon Quiche

Metric/Imperial
Pastry
175 g/6 oz plain flour
pinch salt
50 g/2 oz butter
25 g/1 oz lard
approx. 25 ml/1 fl oz cold
   water
Filling
75–100 g/3–4 oz smoked
   salmon pieces
few sprigs of watercress
300 ml/½ pint single cream
2 large eggs
salt and pepper

American
Pastry
1½ cups all-purpose flour
pinch salt
¼ cup butter
2 tablespoons shortening
approx. 2 tablespoons cold
   water
Filling
¼ lb smoked salmon pieces

few sprigs of watercress
1¼ cups light cream
2 large eggs
salt and pepper

Heat the oven to moderately hot (200°C, 400°F, Gas Mark 6) and place a baking tray in the centre of the oven.

Make the shortcrust pastry in the usual way. Roll it out on a lightly floured surface and line a shallow 23-cm/9-inch fluted flan tin.

Cut the smoked salmon into thin strips and lay in the base of the flan. Cover with a few small sprigs of watercress. Beat the cream, eggs and seasoning together, using pepper sparingly, and pour into the flan case.

Place in the oven on the hot baking tray and cook for 15 minutes, then reduce the heat to moderate (180°C, 350°F, Gas Mark 4) and cook for a further 20–25 minutes until the filling is just set and a pale golden brown. Serve hot for lunch or as a first course for dinner.

Serves 6

Ham, mushroom and tomato quiche

Tuna and Tomato Quiche

Metric/Imperial
Pastry
175 g/6 oz plain flour
pinch salt
50 g/2 oz butter
25 g/1 oz lard
approx. 25 ml/1 fl oz cold
    water
Filling
198-g/7-oz can tuna
300 ml/½ pint single cream
2 large eggs
salt and pepper
2 tomatoes, sliced
whole prawns and sprigs of
    dill to garnish

American
Pastry
1½ cups all-purpose flour
pinch salt
¼ cup butter
2 tablespoons shortening
approx. 2 tablespoons cold
    water
Filling
7-oz can tuna
1¼ cups light cream
2 large eggs
salt and pepper
2 tomatoes, sliced
whole shrimp and sprigs of
    dill to garnish

Heat the oven to moderately hot (200°C, 400°F, Gas Mark 6) and place a baking tray in the centre of the oven.

Make the shortcrust pastry in the usual way. Roll it out on a lightly floured surface and line a shallow 23-cm/9-inch fluted flan tin.

Thoroughly drain the tuna, flake and spread over the base of the flan. Mix together the cream, eggs and seasoning and pour into the flan case.

Place in the oven on the hot baking tray and cook for 15 minutes, then reduce the heat to moderate (180°C, 350°F, Gas Mark 4) and cook for a further 20 minutes. Arrange the tomato slices on top and cook for 5 minutes further. The filling should be set and a pale golden brown. Garnish with the whole prawns and dill.

Serves 6

Fish dishes

Fish can provide a nourishing and attractive meal, and there is a wide variety available, either fresh, frozen or canned, from which to choose. Fish is an excellent source of protein, and it is also low in calories.

Included in this chapter are recipes for each of the main types — white, oily, shellfish and freshwater fish. Be sure whatever fish you buy is fresh — and this applies especially to shellfish. To make up a tasty stock, just ask your fishmonger for a few fish trimmings. Simmer them in water, plus a little dry white wine, with a few slices of onion, herbs, salt and peppercorns for about 30 minutes and strain before using.

Try any of these delicious recipes, such as plaice with taramasalata, pickled herrings or prawns in curry sauce, and see whether you can convert any doubtfuls in your family to the varied delights of fish.

Grilled Cod with Tomato and Onion Sauce

Metric/Imperial	American
0·5 kg/1¼ lb cod fillet	1¼ lb cod fillet
seasoned flour	seasoned all-purpose flour
75 g/3 oz butter	⅓ cup butter
100 g/4 oz onions	¼ lb onions
1 small clove garlic	1 small clove garlic
350 g/12 oz tomatoes	¾ lb tomatoes
1 tablespoon vinegar	1 tablespoon vinegar
1 rounded teaspoon tomato purée	1 rounded teaspoon tomato paste
½ teaspoon castor sugar	½ teaspoon sugar
1 rounded tablespoon chopped parsley	1 rounded tablespoon chopped parsley
salt and pepper	salt and pepper

Cut the fish into convenient size portions and coat in the seasoned flour. Melt two-thirds of the butter in the grill pan, add the fish, baste with the butter and grill under a moderate heat for about 15 minutes or until tender. Set aside and keep warm.

Melt the remaining butter in a pan, peel and slice the onions, crush the garlic and add to the pan; cover and cook for about 10 minutes or until the onions are soft but not brown.

Place the tomatoes in a bowl, cover with boiling water and leave for 1 minute; drain, peel and quarter. Add to the pan with the vinegar, tomato purée, sugar and parsley; cover and cook for a further 3 minutes. Season to taste and serve with the grilled cod.

Variation
Cod Portugaise Substitute four cod cutlets and place in a buttered shallow ovenproof dish with equal amounts of wine vinegar and water to come halfway up the cutlets. Cover and bake in a moderate oven (180°C, 350°F, Gas Mark 4) for 30–35 minutes and serve with the tomato and onion sauce.

Serves 4

Cod portugaise

Bert's Pride

Metric/Imperial
175 g/6 oz long-grain rice
salt
4 frozen cod cutlets, thawed
25 g/1 oz butter
25 g/1 oz flour
300 ml/½ pint milk
pepper
225 g/8 oz tomatoes
100 g/4 oz cheese, grated

American
¾ cup long-grain rice
salt
4 frozen cod cutlets, thawed
2 tablespoons butter
¼ cup all-purpose flour
1¼ cups milk
pepper
½ lb tomatoes
1 cup grated cheese

Cook the rice in rapidly boiling salted water for about 12 minutes or until tender. Rinse and drain thoroughly.

Well butter a large shallow ovenproof dish and place the rice around the edge of the dish. Put the cod cutlets in the centre.

Melt the butter in a small pan, add the flour and cook for 2–3 minutes. Add the milk and bring to the boil, stirring; simmer for 2 minutes and season well. Pour the sauce over the cod.

Slice the tomatoes thickly and arrange on top of the rice around the edge of the dish. Sprinkle the grated cheese over all.

Bake for 30 minutes in the centre of a moderately hot oven (200°C, 400°F, Gas Mark 6) until the cheese is golden brown and the fish tender.

Variation
Cheesy Cod and Bacon Grill For a quick but tasty cod dinner, grill the cod cutlets on both sides until nearly cooked, then top with the grated cheese mixed with 1 teaspoon lemon juice and 1 teaspoon made mustard. Melt the cheese and top with fried bacon rashers. Garnish with sprigs of parsley.

Serves 4

Baked Stuffed Plaice

Metric/Imperial
Stuffing
50 g/2 oz fresh white
  breadcrumbs
1 tablespoon chopped
  parsley
1 tablespoon grated onion
grated rind of 1 lemon
salt and pepper
1 egg

2 (350-g/12-oz) whole
  plaice

butter
1 tomato

American
Stuffing
1 cup fresh white bread
  crumbs
1 tablespoon chopped parsley

1 tablespoon grated onion
grated rind of 1 lemon
salt and pepper
1 egg

2 (¾-lb) whole flounder or
  other suitable flat white
  fish
butter
1 tomato

Place the breadcrumbs in a bowl with the parsley, onion, lemon rind and seasoning; lightly beat the egg and stir into the breadcrumbs, and mix well.

Remove the head and gut from the fish. Trim the fins and tails with scissors. Place each fish, dark-skinned side down, on a board and with a sharp knife make a cut through the white skin along the backbone to within 1·5 cm/¾ inch of the head and tail. Ease the flesh away from either side of the bone so that two large pockets are formed. Fill with stuffing.

Well butter a flat ovenproof dish, lay the fish on it and dot with a little more butter, cover with a piece of greaseproof paper and bake for 30 minutes in a moderate oven (180°C, 350°F, Gas Mark 4). Slice the tomato, place on top of the stuffing and return to the oven for a further 10 minutes.

Serves 2

Plaice with Taramasalata

Metric/Imperial	American
2 large or 4 small plaice fillets	2 large or 4 small flounder or other suitable flat white fish fillets
85-g/3-oz jar taramasalata (smoked cod's roe pâté)	3-oz jar taramasalata (smoked cod's roe pâté)
300 ml/½ pint milk	1¼ cups milk
0·75 kg/1¼ lb potatoes, boiled and mashed	1¼ lb potatoes, boiled and mashed
25 g/1 oz butter	2 tablespoons butter
25 g/1 oz flour	¼ cup all-purpose flour
2–3 tablespoons single cream	¼ cup light cream
butter	butter
salt and pepper	salt and pepper
sprigs of parsley and few mushrooms to garnish	sprigs of parsley and few mushrooms to garnish

Remove any dark skin from the fillets of plaice and spread the skin side of each fillet with the taramasalata and roll up with the filling inside. Place in a shallow pan, pour over the milk, cover and gently poach until cooked, about 15 minutes.

Meanwhile pipe or fork the hot mashed potato to make a border around the edge of a shallow ovenproof dish and keep warm.

Remove the fillets from the pan, drain (reserving the cooking liquor) and arrange in the centre of the potato; keep warm.

Melt the butter in a small pan, stir in the flour and cook for 2 minutes. Add the cooking liquor from the fish and bring to the boil, stirring; cook for 2 minutes to thicken the sauce. Without boiling, add the cream, a knob of butter and salt and pepper to taste. Spoon over the fish and garnish with sprigs of parsley and slices of mushroom.

Plaice with taramasalata

Variation For a special occasion omit the mashed potato border and add 2 tablespoons (us 3 tablespoons) Grand Marnier liqueur to the sauce with the cream. Serve fresh fruit for dessert. If you have the time, make your own taramasalata (see page 14).

Serves 2

Pickled herrings

Kedgeree

Metric/Imperial	American
175 g/6 oz long-grain rice	¾ cup long-grain rice
salt	salt
2 hard-boiled eggs	2 hard-cooked eggs
350 g/12 oz smoked haddock fillet	¾ lb smoked haddock fillet
50 g/2 oz butter	¼ cup butter
1 tablespoon lemon juice	1 tablespoon lemon juice
cayenne pepper	cayenne pepper
sprigs of parsley to garnish	sprigs of parsley to garnish

Cook the rice in plenty of boiling salted water for 12 minutes or until tender; rinse well and drain. Keep warm.

Peel and roughly chop the eggs, reserving a few slices.

Poach the smoked haddock in a little water for about 10 minutes. Drain and remove all skin and bones and flake the fish.

Melt the butter in a large pan, add the rice, eggs and fish and heat through slowly; stir in the lemon juice and add salt and cayenne pepper to taste. Pile into a warm dish and serve garnished with parsley sprigs and slices of egg.

Serves 4

opposite Kedgeree

Pickled Herrings

Metric/Imperial	American
4 herrings	4 herrings
salt and pepper	salt and pepper
1 small onion	1 small onion
2 teaspoons mixed pickling spice	2 teaspoons mixed pickling spice
300 ml/½ pint mixed red wine vinegar and water	1¼ cups mixed red wine vinegar and water
3–4 small bay leaves	3–4 small bay leaves

Cut the heads off the herrings using a sharp knife. Scrape the skin with a round-bladed knife from tail to head to remove any loose scales and rinse under running water. Cut along the underside of each fish from head to tail, remove roe and gut and scrape away any blood vessels. Open the fish and place skin side up on a board. Press firmly all the way along the centre back of the fish to loosen the backbone. Turn the fish over and ease away the backbone from the flesh, starting at the head end, and cut off tail. Slice into 2·5-cm/1-inch pieces. Season the fish with salt and pepper.

Peel and finely slice the onion. Place half the onion with half the pickling spice in an ovenproof dish and arrange the fish pieces close together on top. Pour over the vinegar and water, add the remaining pickling spice, onion and bay leaves. Cover with foil and bake in a moderate oven (180°C, 350°F, Gas Mark 4) for 45 minutes, remove and leave to cool in the dish.

Serves 4

Hot Smoked Haddock Soufflé

Metric/Imperial	American
212-g/7½-oz packet buttered smoked haddock fillets	7½-oz package buttered smoked haddock fillets
milk	milk
25 g/1 oz butter	2 tablespoons butter
25 g/1 oz flour	¼ cup all-purpose flour
salt and pepper	salt and pepper
cayenne pepper	cayenne pepper
50 g/2 oz Cheddar cheese, grated	½ cup grated Cheddar cheese
4 eggs	4 eggs

Cook the smoked haddock as directed on the packet then drain off the butter into a measure. Flake the haddock and remove any dark skin and bones. Make the butter liquid up to 250 ml/ just under ½ pint (US 1 cup) with milk.

Melt the butter in a saucepan and stir in the flour, cook for 1 minute, gradually stir in the milk and fish mixture and bring to the boil; cook for 2 minutes to thicken. Season to taste with salt, pepper and a little cayenne. Stir in the cheese and flaked fish, remove from the heat and leave to cool for about 5 minutes.

Thoroughly butter a generous 1-litre/2-pint (US 2½-pint) oven-proof soufflé dish. Separate the eggs and beat the yolks into the sauce, one at a time. Whisk the egg whites until stiff and gently fold into the sauce using a metal spoon. Turn into the dish and bake for 30–35 minutes in the centre of a moderately hot oven (190°C, 375°F, Gas Mark 5) until well risen and golden brown. Serve at once with a green salad.

Serves 4

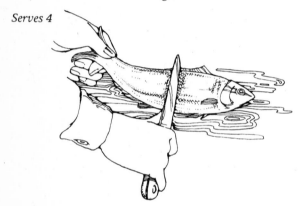

Hot smoked haddock soufflé

Baked Herrings with Mustard Sauce

Metric/Imperial	American
4 herrings, filleted, with tails on	4 herrings, filleted, with tails on
50 g/2 oz fresh white breadcrumbs	1 cup fresh white bread crumbs
1 stick celery, chopped	1 stalk celery, chopped
1 heaped teaspoon chopped parsley	1 heaped teaspoon chopped parsley
grated rind of ½ lemon	grated rind of ½ lemon
1 teaspoon lemon juice	1 teaspoon lemon juice
½ teaspoon thyme	½ teaspoon thyme
salt and pepper	salt and pepper
25 g/1 oz butter	2 tablespoons butter
Sauce	**Sauce**
25 g/1 oz butter	2 tablespoons butter
25 g/1 oz flour	¼ cup all-purpose flour
300 ml/½ pint milk	1¼ cups milk
salt and pepper	salt and pepper
3–4 teaspoons made mustard	3–4 teaspoons prepared mustard
1 tablespoon cider or malt vinegar	1 tablespoon cider or malt vinegar
2 teaspoons castor sugar	2 teaspoons sugar
slice of lemon to garnish	slice of lemon to garnish

Wash the herrings and dry thoroughly on kitchen paper. Put the breadcrumbs in a bowl with the celery, parsley, lemon rind and juice and seasoning. Melt the butter and stir into the bread-crumbs to bind the mixture, which should be moist and crumbly. Divide the stuffing between the herrings and press the fish back into shape. Slash the skin twice on each side.

Well butter a shallow ovenproof dish and lay the fish in it. Cover with a lightly buttered piece of greaseproof paper and bake for 25–30 minutes in a moderately hot oven (200°C, 400°F, Gas Mark 6).

Meanwhile prepare the sauce: melt the butter in a pan, stir in the flour and cook for 1 minute. Gradually stir in the milk and bring to the boil, stirring well until the sauce is quite smooth. Add the remaining ingredients to the sauce and simmer for 3 minutes. Arrange the herrings on a serving dish and serve the sauce separately, with new potatoes and peas. Garnish with a slice of lemon.

Serves 4

opposite Baked herrings with mustard sauce

Herrings in Oats

Metric/Imperial	American
4 herrings, filleted	4 herrings, filleted
50 g/2 oz quick cook oats	⅓ cup quick cook oats
1 teaspoon salt	1 teaspoon salt
oil	oil
lemon wedges and parsley to garnish	lemon wedges and parsley to garnish

Wash the herrings, dry them thoroughly on kitchen paper, and open flat.

Mix the oats with the salt and thoroughly coat the herrings. Heat the oil in a frying pan and fry the fish until golden brown on both sides, turning once, for about 10 minutes. Drain on kitchen paper, arrange on a serving dish and garnish with lemon wedges and sprigs of parsley.

Serves 4

Herrings in oats

Trout with Almonds

Metric/Imperial	American
4 trout	4 trout
50 g/2 oz whole shelled almonds	⅓ cup whole shelled almonds
seasoned flour	seasoned all-purpose flour
75 g/3 oz butter	⅓ cup butter
lemon wedges and parsley to garnish	lemon wedges and parsley to garnish

Wash the trout under running water to remove any loose blood. If the trout have not been cleaned, slit them along the belly with a sharp knife and remove the gut; wash thoroughly and remove the eyes.

Place the almonds in a small basin, cover with boiling water and leave for 2 minutes. Drain, remove the skins and shred finely.

Coat the trout in flour. Melt two-thirds of the butter in a large frying pan and fry the fish for 7–8 minutes, turning once. Remove from the pan and arrange on a warm serving dish.

Add the remaining butter to the pan with the almonds and fry quickly until golden brown. Pour the almond and butter sauce over the trout and garnish with lemon wedges and parsley.

Serves 4

Prawns in Curry Sauce

Metric/Imperial	American
2 small onions	2 small onions
1 tablespoon salad oil	1 tablespoon salad oil
1 rounded teaspoon curry powder	1 rounded teaspoon curry powder
15 g/½ oz flour	2 tablespoons all-purpose flour
300 ml/½ pint chicken stock	1¼ cups chicken stock
1 rounded teaspoon tomato purée	1 rounded teaspoon tomato paste
1 rounded tablespoon mango chutney	1 rounded tablespoon mango chutney
juice of ½ lemon	juice of ½ lemon
25 g/1 oz butter	2 tablespoons butter
225 g/8 oz peeled prawns	1⅓ cups peeled shrimp
150 ml/¼ pint single cream	⅔ cup light cream

Peel and finely chop one onion. Heat the oil in a saucepan, add the onion, cover and cook over a low heat for 5–8 minutes until the onion is soft but not brown. Stir in the curry powder and fry gently for 3–4 minutes, stir in the flour and cook for 1 minute more. Stir in the stock and bring to the boil. Add the tomato purée, chutney and lemon juice and simmer for 5 minutes, then strain through a sieve.

Peel and finely chop the remaining onion. Heat the butter in a large frying pan, add the onion and fry gently until soft, add the prawns, stir in the curry sauce and bring to the boil. Remove from the heat and stir in the cream. Serve with plain boiled rice.

Serves 4

Baked Stuffed Mackerel in Foil

Metric/Imperial
3 mackerel
3 rounded teaspoons creamed
   horseradish
salt and pepper
butter
lemon slice and parsley to
   garnish

American
3 mackerel
3 rounded teaspoons creamed
   horseradish
salt and pepper
butter
lemon slice and parsley to
   garnish

Cut off the heads of the mackerel using a sharp knife. Cut along
the underside of each fish from head to tail and remove any roe
and gut. Wash under cold running water and pat dry on kitchen
paper.

Place 1 teaspoon of creamed horseradish inside each fish and
spread; season well with salt and pepper.

Butter three pieces of foil large enough to wrap each fish in;
place a fish in the centre of each piece, top each with small pieces
of butter and seal in the foil.

Put on a baking tray and bake in a moderately hot oven (190°C,
375°F, Gas Mark 5) for 30–40 minutes, depending on size.

Either serve the fish in their parcels or remove and place on
a bed of rice tossed with chopped onion, mushrooms and herbs.
Garnish with lemon and a sprig of parsley.

Serves 3

51

Fried Whitebait

Metric/Imperial
0·5 kg/1 lb whitebait

seasoned flour
deep fat or oil for frying
sprigs of parsley to garnish

American
1 lb whitebait, sprats or
sardines
seasoned all-purpose flour
deep fat or oil for frying
sprigs of parsley to garnish

Wash and drain the fish and dry in a clean cloth. Place the seasoned flour in a bag, put in some of the whitebait and shake well until the fish are coated with flour. Place in a wire basket, shake off the surplus flour and cook the fish in the deep fat or oil for 2–3 minutes. Keep the basket moving around while frying. Drain on kitchen paper. Continue in this way until all the fish have been coated in flour and fried.

Pile on to a warm serving dish and garnish with sprigs of parsley which have been lightly fried in the oil until crisp. Serve with crusty white bread and butter.

Serves 4

Holiday Fish Pie

Metric/Imperial
212-g/7½-oz packet frozen
cod fillets or steaks
212-g/7½-oz packet smoked
haddock fillets
283-g/10-oz can condensed
celery soup
368-g/13-oz packet frozen
puff pastry, thawed
1 tablespoon chopped parsley
milk
sprig of parsley to garnish

American
7½-oz package frozen cod
fillets or steaks
7½-oz package smoked
haddock fillets
10-oz can condensed celery
soup
13-oz package frozen puff
paste, thawed
1 tablespoon chopped parsley
milk
sprig of parsley to garnish

Cook the fish as directed on the packets and then flake and remove any skin and bones, put in a bowl and stir in the soup; mix well.

Cut the pastry into two pieces, one slightly bigger than the other. Roll out the larger piece of pastry into a circle and use to line a shallow ovenproof dish. Spoon in the fish mixture, sprinkle with parsley and spread flat. Moisten the edge of the pastry with a little cold water. Roll out the remaining pastry to a circle to fit the top of the pie, press edges firmly together and decorate with a fork or a knife. Roll out the trimmings, cut into leaves and use to decorate the pie.

Brush the top with a little milk and make two slits in the top. Bake in a hot oven (220°C, 425°F, Gas Mark 7) for 25–30 minutes until well risen and golden brown. Garnish with parsley sprig.

Note   Vary this pie by using another variety of soup or using a can of tuna or salmon in place of the smoked fish. Or add 75 g/3 oz (US ¾ cup) chopped mushrooms and 225 g/8 oz (US ½ lb) roughly chopped tomatoes to the fish and soup mixture.

Serves 6

opposite Fried whitebait   *above* Holiday fish pie

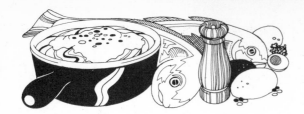

Trawler's Pie

Metric/Imperial	American
25 g/1 oz butter	2 tablespoons butter
0·75 kg/1½ lb cod fillet	1½ lb cod fillet
salt and pepper	salt and pepper
Sauce	**Sauce**
40 g/1½ oz butter	3 tablespoons butter
40 g/1½ oz flour	⅓ cup all-purpose flour
approx. 300 ml/½ pint milk	approx. 1¼ cups milk
2 teaspoons anchovy essence	2 teaspoons anchovy extract
3 hard-boiled eggs	3 hard-cooked eggs
salt and pepper	salt and pepper
0·5 kg/1 lb potatoes, boiled and mashed, for topping	1 lb potatoes, boiled and mashed, for topping
1 tomato, chopped to garnish	1 tomato, chopped to garnish

Spread a 1·5-litre/2½-pint (US 3½-pint) ovenproof serving dish with half of the butter, put the cod in the dish and season. Put the rest of the butter, cut in very small pieces, on top. Cover and cook in a moderate oven (160°C, 325°F, Gas Mark 3) for 20–30 minutes, until fish flakes easily. Strain the liquor from the dish into a measuring jug. Remove skin and any small bones from the fish.

Melt the butter for the sauce in a pan, blend in the flour and cook for 1 minute to make a roux. Add enough milk to the cooking liquor to make up to 450 ml/¾ pint (US 2 cups), blend with the roux to make a smooth sauce. Bring to the boil and simmer for 2 minutes, stirring. Blend in the anchovy essence. Chop the eggs and add, seasoning well. Add the flaked fish to the sauce and turn back into the ovenproof dish.

Spread the potato over the fish and mark with a fork, making a pattern. Increase the oven temperature to 200°C (400°F, Gas Mark 6) and reheat the pie for about 20 minutes, until it is piping hot and the top is golden brown. Garnish with chopped tomato.

Note Sliced boiled potatoes sprinkled with 25 g/1 oz (US ¼ cup) finely grated Cheddar cheese can be used instead of mashed potatoes to encircle the fish mixture. After reheating, brown the potato and cheese under the grill before serving garnished with the chopped tomato.

Serves 4

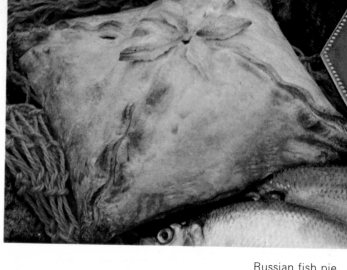

Russian fish pie

Russian Fish Pie

Metric/Imperial	American
368-g/13-oz packet frozen cod fillets or 350 g/12 oz cod, filleted	13-oz package frozen cod fillets or ¾ lb fresh cod, filleted
25 g/1 oz margarine	2 tablespoons margarine
25 g/1 oz flour	¼ cup all-purpose flour
300 ml/½ pint milk	1¼ cups milk
1 tablespoon chopped parsley	1 tablespoon chopped parsley
salt and pepper	salt and pepper
1–2 teaspoons lemon juice	1–2 teaspoons lemon juice
50 g/2 oz peeled prawns	⅓ cup peeled shrimp
368-g/13-oz packet frozen puff pastry, thawed	13-oz package frozen puff paste, thawed
beaten egg or milk to glaze	beaten egg or milk to glaze

Cook the fish by frying, grilling or poaching; leave to cool, then remove all dark skin and bones and flake.

Melt the margarine in a pan, stir in the flour and cook for 2 minutes; add the milk, bring to the boil stirring and continue cooking to thicken the sauce. Add the parsley, seasoning and lemon juice and mix well. Remove from the heat and stir in the flaked fish and prawns; leave to cool.

Roll out the pastry on a floured surface to a 33-cm/13-inch square and trim the edges. Place the filling in the centre, damp the edges of the pastry and bring the four corners to the centre forming an envelope. Seal edges firmly. Decorate with pastry leaves, brush with egg or milk and place on a baking tray in a hot oven (220°C, 425°F, Gas Mark 7). Cook until well risen and golden brown, about 25 minutes.

Serves 4

Trawler's pie

Salmon rice bake

Salmon and Noodle Bake

Metric/Imperial	American
75 g/3 oz lasagne or egg noodles	3 oz lasagne or egg noodles
salt	salt
25 g/1 oz margarine	2 tablespoons margarine
25 g/1 oz flour	$\frac{1}{4}$ cup all-purpose flour
450 ml/$\frac{3}{4}$ pint milk	2 cups milk
212-g/7$\frac{1}{2}$-oz can pink salmon	7$\frac{1}{2}$-oz can salmon
75 g/3 oz Cheddar cheese, grated	$\frac{3}{4}$ cup grated Cheddar cheese
1 rounded tablespoon chopped parsley	1 rounded tablespoon chopped parsley
pepper	pepper
2 tablespoons fresh white breadcrumbs for topping	3 tablespoons fresh white bread crumbs for topping

Cook the lasagne in 1·75 litres/3 pints (us 4 pints) boiling salted water for about 8 minutes or until tender. Drain in a colander, refresh with cold water, then arrange on a clean damp tea towel so that the pieces do not stick together.

Melt the margarine in a pan, add the flour and cook for 2 minutes, stir in milk and bring to the boil; cook for 2 minutes to thicken.

Drain the liquid from the can of salmon and add it to the sauce. Remove the black skin and bones from the salmon and flake. Stir into the sauce with two-thirds of the cheese, parsley and seasoning to taste.

Layer the noodles and sauce in a generous 1-litre/2-pint 2$\frac{1}{2}$-pint) shallow ovenproof dish starting with a layer of pasta and finishing with a layer of sauce. Sprinkle the top with the remaining cheese and breadcrumbs and bake in a moderately hot oven (190°C, 375°F, Gas Mark 5) for about 40 minutes until golden brown. Serve with a green salad.

Variation

Salmon Rice Bake Substitute 225 g/8 oz (us 1 cup) long-grain rice, boiled with salt until tender, for the lasagne. Toss a small drained can of mixed vegetables with the flaked salmon and rice, top with sauce and bake as above for 30–40 minutes.

Serves 4

Meat dishes

As it is the traditional basis for most meals, different methods for preparing meat will always be of interest to both the housewife and the busy working cook. In this chapter are delicious recipes for beef — varying from elegant steak diane to familiar steak and kidney pudding — as well as lamb, pork, veal, chicken, pigeon, rabbit, gammon and offal. Whether you try quick-to-make meatballs in spicy tomato sauce, traditional raised pork pie, exotic chicken tetrazzini or tempting lamb with apricots, you will find your family and guests will enjoy your meals tremendously.

From wine to apples and chestnuts to olives, the assortment of flavourful additions in these easy-to-follow recipes will increase the scope of your cooking, even with old favourites. Remember, though, when cooking a casserole, that the liquid must simmer and not boil vigorously — this can be done either in the oven or on top of the cooker. If you are adding cream to a dish, it should usually be stirred in at the end so that the sauce is hot when served but the cream does not curdle.

Steak Diane

Metric/Imperial
Brown sauce
1 large onion
1 carrot
50 g/2 oz butter
15 g/½ oz flour

450 ml/¾ pint beef stock
1 bay leaf
3 parsley stalks
pinch thyme
1 tablespoon tomato purée
1 teaspoon salt
pepper

25 g/1 oz butter
4 fillet steaks, wrapped in
    strips of fat
2 tablespoons brandy or
    sherry
1 tablespoon Worcestershire
    sauce
1 tablespoon chopped parsley
    to garnish

American
Brown sauce
1 large onion
1 carrot
¼ cup butter
2 tablespoons all-purpose
    flour
2 cups beef stock
1 bay leaf
3 parsley stems
pinch thyme
1 tablespoon tomato paste
1 teaspoon salt
pepper

2 tablespoons butter
4 filet mignon steaks, wrapped
    in strips of fat
3 tablespoons brandy or
    sherry
1 tablespoon Worcestershire
    sauce
1 tablespoon chopped parsley
    to garnish

Finely dice the onion and carrot. Melt the butter in a saucepan and fry the onion and carrot slowly until dry and slightly shrivelled but not brown. Stir with a metal spoon occasionally. Add the flour and continue cooking until flour and vegetables are a rich brown. Pour on the stock and add all the remaining sauce ingredients. Stir well, bring to the boil and simmer gently for 30 minutes until reduced by half. Strain but do not sieve, then cover the sauce and set aside until required.

To complete the dish just before serving, have all the ingredients ready and the guests assembled.

Use one large or two medium frying pans and heat until very hot. Drop in the butter and then the steaks to brown on each side. Pour over the brandy or sherry and cook for 2–3 minutes more; the vapours may be ignited if you wish with a match or gas flame. Put all the steaks in one pan if two were used. Pour over the brown sauce and Worcestershire sauce, bring to the boil, sprinkle with parsley and serve.

To freeze   The brown sauce freezes well and is a useful base for a variety of dishes. Steaks should always be cooked just before serving.
Note   The success of this dish lies in the quality of the brown sauce; use a good stock if possible and make up the sauce very carefully. It can be prepared well in advance. Serve with a bowl of cooked rice with a can of drained mandarin oranges added.

Serves 4

Hot Salt Brisket with Mustard Sauce

Metric/Imperial	**American**
1·5-kg/3-lb piece boned and rolled salt brisket	3-lb piece boneless rolled corned beef brisket
225 g/8 oz small carrots	½ lb small carrots
225 g/8 oz small onions	½ lb small onions
50 g/2 oz butter	¼ cup butter
50 g/2 oz flour	½ cup all-purpose flour
300 ml/½ pint milk	1¼ cups milk
1 tablespoon dry mustard	1 tablespoon dry mustard
1 tablespoon brown sugar	1 tablespoon brown sugar
3 tablespoons vinegar	¼ cup vinegar
salt and pepper	salt and pepper

Wash the meat in cold water. Place in a large saucepan, cover with cold water and bring to the boil. Peel the carrots and onions and leave whole. Cover the pan with a lid and simmer very gently, allowing 35 minutes per 0·5 kg/1 lb and 35 minutes over. Add the vegetables to the pan for the last hour of cooking time. Lift the meat on to a warm serving dish and place the vegetables around; keep warm.

Melt the butter in a small pan, add the flour and cook for 2 minutes. Stir in the milk and 300 ml/½ pint (US 1¼ cups) of the cooking liquor, bring to the boil and simmer for 2 minutes to thicken the sauce. Blend the mustard with the sugar and vinegar and stir into the sauce. Season to taste and serve with the meat.

Note It is very important to *simmer* the meat, as rapid boiling causes shrinkage and toughens meat fibres.

Serves 6–8

Steak Diane

Beef Wellington

Metric/Imperial	American
0·75 kg/1½ lb beef fillet	1½ lb rump or sirloin steak
50 g/2 oz butter	¼ cup butter
2 large onions	2 large onions
100 g/4 oz mushrooms	1 cup mushrooms
1 tablespoon chopped parsley	1 tablespoon chopped parsley
pinch thyme	pinch thyme
½ teaspoon salt	½ teaspoon salt
pepper	pepper
368-g/13-oz packet frozen puff pastry	13-oz package frozen puff paste
1 egg yolk to glaze	1 egg yolk to glaze

Trim the fillet of beef of any coarse skins, or the butcher could do this for you. Melt the butter in a frying pan and brown the meat quickly, turning occasionally to seal in the juices on all sides. Remove from the pan and cool.

Slice the onions, add to the pan and cook for about 10 minutes until golden. Meanwhile slice the mushrooms thickly, add them and cook quickly for 5 minutes until dry; add the chopped parsley, thyme and seasoning. Leave to cool.

Thaw the pastry and roll out thinly to an oblong 35 × 40 cm/ 14 × 16 inches. Set the fillet of beef in the middle and put the mushroom mixture on top. Cut a 3·5-cm/1½-inch square from each corner of the pastry and set on one side. Fold up the pastry round the meat, turning up the ends first and then the sides which should just overlap to cover the meat thoroughly. Moisten the pastry with water wherever it overlaps so that it sticks together well in cooking. Turn over, set on a baking tray and brush with egg yolk. With a round pastry cutter cut half moon shapes from the pastry trimmings. Use these to decorate the top. Brush decorations with egg yolk. Bake in a hot oven (220°C, 425°F, Gas Mark 7) for 1 hour and serve immediately if you like the beef pink in the centre.

Note   Not suitable for freezing as juices running out from the meat on thawing make the pastry soggy underneath. Make sure the mushroom mixture is fairly dry and that most of it is on top of the meat to help prevent this tendency. The beef can be covered with pastry and chilled for up to 18 hours in advance. Keep covered with cling film or polythene in the refrigerator.

Serves 5

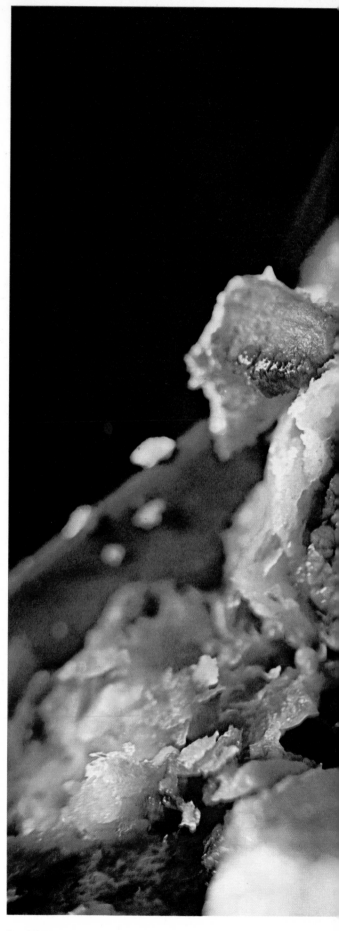

Beef Wellington

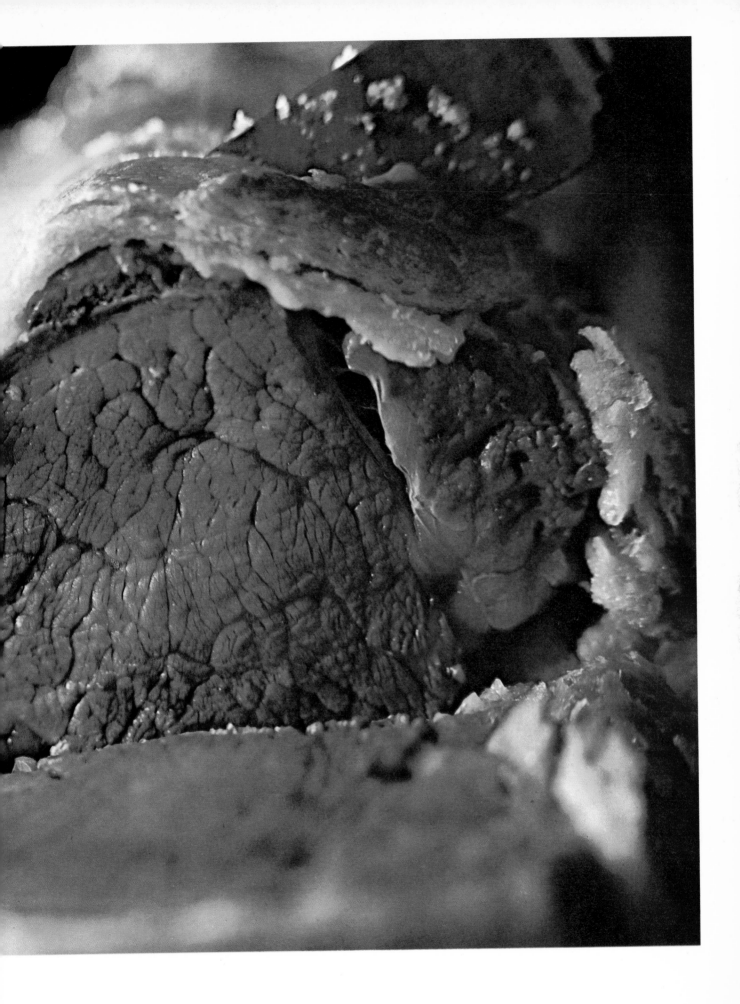

Salcombe Beef

below Pepperpot beef with ginger

opposite Boeuf bourguignon

Metric/Imperial	American
0·75 kg/1½ lb braising steak	1½ lb flank steak
225 g/8 oz onions	½ lb onions
225 g/8 oz carrots	½ lb carrots
1 red pepper	1 red pepper
25 g/1 oz dripping	2 tablespoons drippings
900-ml/1½-pint packet oxtail soup	3¾-cup package thick beef soup mix
600 ml/1 pint water	2½ cups water
salt	salt
1 orange	1 orange
8 cloves	8 cloves

Cut the steak into 2·5-cm/1-inch cubes. Peel and slice the onions and carrots. Deseed and cut the red pepper into strips.

Melt the dripping in a large saucepan and fry the onions and meat for 3–4 minutes. Stir in the contents of the packet of soup and the water and bring to the boil, stirring. Add the carrots, pepper strips and salt.

Carefully remove some peel from the orange and cut into thin strips; reserve for garnish. Cut orange in half and place four cloves in each half; add to the pan, cover and simmer until the meat is tender, about 2 hours. Remove the orange and squeeze any juice back into the pan. Adjust seasoning and garnish with orange strips. Serve with creamed potatoes and green beans.

Note An unusual recipe well worth trying, this makes an inexpensive and easy dish for entertaining.

Serves 4–6

Salcombe beef

Pepperpot Beef with Ginger

Metric/Imperial	American
1 kg/2 lb braising steak	2 lb flank steak
2 onions	2 onions
25 g/1 oz flour	¼ cup all-purpose flour
1 teaspoon salt	1 teaspoon salt
pinch pepper	pinch pepper
½ teaspoon ground ginger	½ teaspoon ground ginger
50 g/2 oz lard or dripping	¼ cup shortening or drippings
Sauce	**Sauce**
1 teaspoon chilli sauce	1 teaspoon hot chili sauce
227-g/8-oz can tomatoes	8-oz can tomatoes
100 g/4 oz mushrooms, sliced	1 cup sliced mushrooms
1 tablespoon Worcestershire sauce	1 tablespoon Worcestershire sauce
25 g/1 oz soft brown sugar	2 tablespoons soft brown sugar
2 tablespoons wine vinegar	3 tablespoons wine vinegar
2 cloves garlic, crushed	2 cloves garlic, crushed
1 bay leaf	1 bay leaf
1 small red pepper	1 small red pepper
1 small swede	1 small rutabaga
425-g/15-oz can red kidney beans	15-oz can red kidney beans
8–10 stuffed green olives	8–10 stuffed green olives
150 ml/¼ pint soured cream	⅔ cup dairy sour cream

Cut the beef into 2·5-cm/1-inch cubes and chop the onions. Mix together the flour, seasoning and ginger and use to coat the beef. Heat the lard in a large pan, add the beef and onions and fry quickly until browned, turning once. Drain on kitchen paper, then transfer to a 1·75-litre/3-pint (US 4-pint) ovenproof dish. Combine all the ingredients for the sauce except the pepper, swede, beans and olives, and pour over the meat. Cover the casserole and cook in a moderate oven (160°C, 325°F, Gas Mark 3) until the meat is tender, about 2 hours.

Remove the seeds and white pith from the pepper and cut in strips. Peel and dice the swede. Drain the can of beans and add to the meat with the pepper, swede and olives for the last 30 minutes of cooking time. Stir in the soured cream just before serving.

Serves 6

Boeuf Bourguignon

Metric/Imperial
0·75 kg/1½ lb chuck steak or
  top leg of beef
175 g/6 oz streaky bacon
25 g/1 oz bacon fat or
  dripping
15 g/½ oz flour

300 ml/½ pint water
1 beef stock cube
150 ml/¼ pint cheap red wine
1 bay leaf
½ teaspoon dried mixed herbs
sprig of parsley
½ teaspoon salt
pinch pepper
12 small white onions
175 g/6 oz button mushrooms

American
1½ lb chuck steak

6–8 slices bacon
2 tablespoons bacon fat or
  drippings
2 tablespoons all-purpose
  flour
1¼ cups water
1 beef bouillon cube
⅔ cup cheap red wine
1 bay leaf
½ teaspoon dried mixed herbs
sprig of parsley
½ teaspoon salt
pinch pepper
12 small white onions
1½ cups button mushrooms

Cut the steak into 3·5-cm/1½-inch cubes. Derind and chop the bacon. Melt the fat or dripping in a large pan and fry the bacon in it until crisp. Remove the bacon and place in a 1·75-litre/3-pint (US 4-pint) ovenproof casserole. Fry the steak in the fat remaining in the pan until it is golden brown. Add to the bacon in the casserole.

Blend in the flour and cook until browned, then stir in the water, stock cube and wine. Bring to the boil and simmer until thickened, then stir in the bay leaf, herbs, parsley and seasoning. Pour this liquor over the meat, cover and cook for 1½ hours in a moderate oven (160°C, 325°F, Gas Mark 3).

Peel the onions, add to the casserole with the mushrooms and cook for a further hour or until the meat is really tender. Add more seasoning if necessary. Skim off any excess fat and remove bay leaf before serving. This dish freezes well. Serve with boiled potatoes.

Note If fresh small white onions are unobtainable use a small can of onions.

Serves 4–6

Carbonnade of beef

Carbonnade of Beef

Metric/Imperial
0·75 kg/1½ lb chuck steak
2 medium onions
25 g/1 oz butter
2 tablespoons salad oil
15 g/½ oz flour

300 ml/½ pint beer
150 ml/¼ pint water
pinch thyme
1 bay leaf
1 teaspoon sugar
1 teaspoon salt
freshly ground black pepper

American
1½ lb chuck steak
2 medium onions
2 tablespoons butter
3 tablespoons salad oil
2 tablespoons all-purpose
  flour
1¼ cups beer
⅔ cup water
pinch thyme
1 bay leaf
1 teaspoon sugar
1 teaspoon salt
freshly ground black pepper

Cut beef into 3·5-cm/1½-inch cubes. Peel and chop the onions.

Melt the butter in a pan with the oil and brown the meat quickly on all sides and remove from the pan; add the onions to the fat and fry until golden brown.

Blend in the flour and cook for 1 minute. Remove the pan from the heat, add the beer and water and stir until smooth. Return to the heat, bring to the boil, and simmer until the sauce has thickened.

Add the meat, thyme, bay leaf and sugar with the salt and pepper. Cover the pan and simmer over a low heat for 2 hours, or until the meat is tender. Check seasoning, remove bay leaf and serve with boiled potatoes.

Serves 6

Swiss Steak

Metric/Imperial	American
4 slices (0·75 kg/1½ lb) topside of beef	4 slices (1½ lb) bottom round of beef
40 g/1½ oz flour	⅓ cup all-purpose flour
1 teaspoon salt	1 teaspoon salt
¼ teaspoon pepper	¼ teaspoon pepper
40 g/1½ oz lard	3 tablespoons shortening
2 onions	2 onions
2 sticks celery (optional)	2 stalks celery (optional)
227-g/8-oz can tomatoes	8-oz can tomatoes
2 teaspoons tomato purée	2 teaspoons tomato paste
½ teaspoon Worcestershire sauce	½ teaspoon Worcestershire sauce
150 ml/¼ pint water	⅔ cup water
1 tablespoon chopped parsley to garnish	1 tablespoon chopped parsley to garnish

Cut the steak into eight pieces. Mix together the flour, salt and pepper. Toss the meat in the flour mixture, pressing it in so that all the flour is used. Melt the lard in a pan and fry the meat quickly on all sides until it is brown, then transfer to an oven-proof casserole.

Finely slice the onions, chop the celery if used and add to the fat remaining in the pan. Fry until pale golden brown then add to the meat in the casserole with the tomatoes and juice from the can, tomato purée, Worcestershire sauce and water. Cover and cook in a cool oven (150°C, 300°F, Gas Mark 2) until the meat is tender, about 2½ hours. Garnish with chopped parsley.

Serves 4

left Swiss steak
below Chilli con carne

Chilli con Carne

Metric/Imperial	American
2 medium onions	2 medium onions
2 sticks celery	2 stalks celery
2 cloves garlic	2 cloves garlic
100 g/4 oz bacon trimmings	¼ lb bacon trimmings
0·75 kg/1½ lb stewing steak	1½ lb flank meat or brisket
25 ml/1 fl oz salad oil	2 tablespoons salad oil
25 g/1 oz butter	2 tablespoons butter
63-g/2¼-oz can tomato purée	2¼-oz can tomato paste
450 ml/¾ pint water	2 cups water
salt and pepper	salt and pepper
1 teaspoon chilli powder	1 teaspoon chili powder
425-g/15-oz can red kidney beans (optional)	15-oz can red kidney beans (optional)

Finely chop the onions, slice the celery and crush the garlic. Cut the bacon trimmings into 1-cm/½-inch pieces and the steak into 1·5-cm/¾-inch cubes.

Heat the oil in a pan, add the butter and fry the onions, celery and garlic until soft and a pale golden brown. Remove from the pan and put aside. Add the meat and bacon to the pan and fry until lightly browned.

Replace the onions and garlic in the pan and add the tomato purée, water, seasoning and chilli powder. Bring to the boil, cover and simmer for 2 hours. Add the kidney beans, if used, for the last 10 minutes of cooking time. Adjust seasoning and serve with green peas and rice.

Note Chilli powder varies considerably in spiciness among different brands, so check carefully and adjust if necessary. If you have difficulty getting kidney beans use a can of baked beans in tomato sauce instead. Minced beef can be substituted for the stewing steak, if preferred, and chopped green pepper added.

Serves 4–6

Meatballs in spicy tomato sauce

Meatballs in Spicy Tomato Sauce

Metric/Imperial	American
2 slices brown bread	2 slices brown bread
150 ml/¼ pint hot water	⅔ cup hot water
0·5 kg/1 lb minced steak	1 lb ground lean beef
1 onion	1 onion
½ teaspoon thyme	½ teaspoon thyme
½ teaspoon salt	½ teaspoon salt
½ teaspoon grated lemon rind	½ teaspoon grated lemon rind
25 g/1 oz butter	2 tablespoons butter
2 tablespoons salad oil	3 tablespoons salad oil
Sauce	**Sauce**
1 onion	1 onion
25 g/1 oz butter	2 tablespoons butter
1 tablespoon paprika	1 tablespoon paprika
15 g/½ oz flour	2 tablespoons all-purpose flour
300 ml/½ pint water mixed with 1 stock cube	1¼ cups water mixed with 1 bouillon cube
100 g/4 oz mushrooms	1 cup mushrooms
2 teaspoons tomato purée	2 teaspoons tomato paste
2 teaspoons vinegar	2 teaspoons vinegar
1 teaspoon sugar	1 teaspoon sugar
½ teaspoon salt	½ teaspoon salt

Remove crusts from bread and put the bread in a bowl. Pour on hot water and leave to cool. Place the meat in a large bowl and add the very finely chopped, minced or grated onion, thyme, salt and lemon rind. Work well together using one hand or a beater. Gradually work in the bread and water mixture. The meat mixture will remain firm and not become sloppy if sufficiently worked.

Roll the meat mixture into small balls the size of an egg yolk, using wet hands. Melt the butter and oil in a large pan. Fry the meatballs quickly to lightly brown, about 10–15 at a time. Lift out carefully into a bowl when done. Brown the next batch.

Chop the onion for the sauce and melt the butter in the pan when all the meatballs are browned. Cook the onion for 1 minute to just colour, then stir in the paprika pepper and flour. Remove from the heat and pour in the stock. Slice the mushrooms and add with the remaining sauce ingredients and stir well. Return to the heat and bring to the boil. Tip the meatballs into the sauce, cover the pan and simmer gently for 20 minutes. Serve with noodles or pasta shells.

To freeze   Meatballs freeze well.
Note   Choose best quality mince or even minced veal for this dish as meatballs require a short cooking time in order to be light. For a special occasion dot with spoonfuls of soured cream just before serving.

Serves 4–5

Steak and kidney pudding

Steamed Beef and Bacon Pudding

Metric/Imperial	American
225 g/8 oz streaky bacon	10–12 slices bacon
25 g/1 oz fresh white breadcrumbs	½ cup fresh white bread crumbs
½ lemon	½ lemon
1 tablespoon chopped parsley	1 tablespoon chopped parsley
½ teaspoon thyme	½ teaspoon thyme
0.5 kg/1 lb minced steak	1 lb ground lean beef
1 tablespoon Worcestershire sauce	1 tablespoon Worcestershire sauce
1 teaspoon salt	1 teaspoon salt
pepper	pepper

Oil a 1-litre/2-pint (US 2½-pint) pudding basin. Derind and chop the bacon very finely. Place in a bowl with the breadcrumbs. Add the grated rind and juice of ½ lemon, the herbs finely chopped and all the remaining ingredients. Work the ingredients very thoroughly until they bind together in a ball. Turn into the prepared basin and cover well with double foil or greaseproof paper, turning the paper under the rim of the bowl. Tie a cloth over if greaseproof paper is used.

Place the bowl in a large saucepan with 5 cm/2 inches of boiling water at the bottom. Simmer very gently for 1½ hours or until cooked, topping up with boiling water if necessary. When cooked remove the bowl from the pan. Leave covered to cool, then chill before serving.

To serve slip a knife round the top edge of the bowl. Dip the bowl in hot water for 10 seconds and turn the contents out on to a plate. Cut in slices to serve with a variety of salads.

To freeze Unmould, wrap and freeze.
Note To make a firmer pudding for slicing more thinly, place a saucer with a weight on top on the meat pudding when it is cooked. Leave to press overnight. Chill before serving.

Variation
Steamed Bacon and Tomato Pudding Make up suet crust pastry and use to line a pudding basin (see above). Omit the minced steak, double the quantity of bacon and add four tomatoes, sliced. Make up and steam as for the steak and kidney pudding.

Serves 5

Steak and Kidney Pudding

Metric/Imperial	American
0.5 kg/1 lb stewing steak	1 lb flank meat or brisket
100 g/4 oz ox kidney	¼ lb beef kidney
25 g/1 oz seasoned flour	¼ cup seasoned all-purpose flour
1 onion	1 onion
100 g/4 oz mushrooms	1 cup mushrooms
Suet crust pastry	**Suet crust pastry**
225 g/8 oz self-raising flour	2 cups all-purpose flour sifted with 2 teaspoons baking powder
½ teaspoon salt	½ teaspoon salt
100 g/4 oz shredded suet	½ cup chopped suet
approx. 150 ml/¼ pint cold water	approx. ⅔ cup cold water

Cut the steak into 2.5-cm/1-inch cubes, remove skin and core from the kidney and cut into 1-cm/½-inch pieces. Coat the steak with seasoned flour. Chop the onion.

Sieve the flour and salt for the pastry into a bowl. Stir in the suet, then add enough water to make a fairly soft dough. Roll out two-thirds of the pastry to a circle large enough to line a greased 1-litre/2-pint (US 2½-pint) pudding basin. Roll out the remaining pastry to a circle the size of the top of the basin.

Put the steak, kidney, mushrooms and onion in alternate layers in the basin, then add sufficient water to come within 2.5 cm/1 inch of the top of the basin. Moisten edges of the pastry lid and press firmly on top. Cover with a lid of greaseproof paper, then cover with foil, both pleated to allow for expansion. Steam or boil for 4½ hours, topping up with boiling water as necessary.

Serves 4

Steamed bacon and tomato pudding

Beef and rice hot pot

Devon Farmhouse Hot Pot

Metric/Imperial	American
1 kg/2 lb potatoes	2 lb potatoes
225 g/8 oz swede	½ lb rutabaga
1 small onion	1 small onion
0·5 kg/1 lb stewing steak	1 lb flank meat or brisket
25 g/1 oz flour	¼ cup all-purpose flour
1 teaspoon salt	1 teaspoon salt
pepper	pepper
1 stock cube	1 bouillon cube
600 ml/1 pint hot water	2½ cups hot water
25 g/1 oz dripping	2 tablespoons drippings

Peel the potatoes, slice two and cut the remainder with the swede into small pieces. Slice the onion. Cut the steak into 1-cm/½-inch cubes and toss in the flour and seasoning. Arrange the potato and swede pieces, sliced onion and meat in layers in a casserole or large ovenproof dish. Reserve sliced potatoes for the top.

Crumble the stock cube in the water and pour over. Cover with sliced potato. Dot with dripping, cover with a lid and bake in a moderate oven (160°C, 325°F, Gas Mark 3) for 1½ hours. Remove the lid and bake for a further 30 minutes in a hot oven (220°C, 425°F, Gas Mark 7) to crisp and brown the top.

This dish is *not* suitable for freezing.

Variation

Beef and Rice Hot Pot Omit the potatoes and swede and substitute 100 g/4 oz (US ¾ cup) peas, four skinned sliced tomatoes, ½ small cauliflower broken into florets and two sliced leeks, all of which should be arranged in layers with the floured meat cubes and sliced onion. Add stock cube and water, cover with a lid and bake in a moderate oven as above for 1 hour. Sprinkle on 100 g/4 oz (US ½ cup) long-grain rice, stirring to ensure it is covered by the cooking liquid, and bake, covered, at the same temperature for a further 30 minutes.

Serves 4–5

Lamb Chops Provençale

Metric/Imperial	American
4 lamb chops	4 lamb chops
25 g/1 oz butter	2 tablespoons butter
½ teaspoon mixed dried herbs	½ teaspoon mixed dried herbs
Ratatouille	**Ratatouille**
2 large green peppers	2 large green peppers
2 medium onions	2 medium onions
50 g/2 oz butter	¼ cup butter
1 small aubergine	1 small eggplant
1 clove garlic	1 clove garlic
227-g/8-oz can tomatoes	8-oz can tomatoes
salt and pepper	salt and pepper
mustard and cress to garnish	mustard and cress to garnish

Remove the rack from the grill pan and place the chops in the pan. Dot with butter and sprinkle with herbs. Cook the chops under a medium grill turning once, for 15 minutes or until tender.

Meanwhile prepare the ratatouille: cut the peppers in half, remove the seeds and cut into 1 cm/½ inch wide strips. Chop the onions coarsely. Melt the butter in a pan and fry the peppers and onions for about 5 minutes or until soft and the onion is a pale golden brown. Remove stalk from the aubergine and cut into 5 mm/¼ inch thick slices. Crush the garlic and add with the aubergine and tomatoes to the pan; cook for a further 10 minutes.

Season the ratatouille with salt and pepper, turn it on to a serving dish and arrange the chops on top. Garnish with mustard and cress.

To freeze Ratatouille freezes very well and may be either reheated slowly to serve as a vegetable or thawed and served cold as a first course (see page 37).

Serves 4

Crispy Lamb Chops

Metric/Imperial	American
75 g/3 oz cooked ham, chopped	$\frac{1}{3}$ cup chopped cooked ham
25 g/1 oz fresh white breadcrumbs	$\frac{1}{2}$ cup fresh white bread crumbs
$\frac{1}{2}$ teaspoon salt	$\frac{1}{2}$ teaspoon salt
25 g/1 oz flour	$\frac{1}{4}$ cup all-purpose flour
1 egg	1 egg
1 egg yolk	1 egg yolk
8 lamb cutlets, trimmed	8 rib lamb chops
1 teaspoon salad oil	1 teaspoon salad oil
75 g/3 oz butter	$\frac{1}{3}$ cup butter
0·5 kg/1 lb tomatoes	1 lb tomatoes
1 teaspoon sugar	1 teaspoon sugar
$\frac{1}{2}$ teaspoon salt	$\frac{1}{2}$ teaspoon salt
pepper	pepper

Mix the very finely chopped ham with the breadcrumbs and salt on a plate. Place the flour on a second plate and the egg and yolk on a third. Beat the egg well with a fork to mix thoroughly. Holding a cutlet by the bone, dip first in the flour, shaking off surplus. Dip next in the egg, using a pastry brush to coat the meat evenly. Hold up to drain a moment then coat with the ham and breadcrumb mixture. Press this on firmly with the side of a palette knife. Set on one side and repeat with the remaining cutlets holding each by the bone during the entire process.

Heat the oil in a frying pan. If only half the cutlets will fit in the pan add 25 g/1 oz (US 2 tablespoons) butter, if all will fit in add double the amount. Fry the cutlets over a moderate heat for 7 minutes until golden, then turn over and cook for a further 7 minutes. Place in a warm oven to keep hot while the remainder of the cutlets are fried. If necessary add a further 25 g/1 oz (US 2 tablespoons) butter to the pan.

Meanwhile peel the tomatoes by plunging in boiling water for 10 seconds and then removing their skins. Slice thickly. Melt the remaining butter in a frying pan, and when beginning to turn brown add the tomatoes, sugar and seasoning. Cook very quickly, shaking the pan, for 1 minute. Turn into a dish and serve with the crispy cutlets.

Note Crumb coating can separate from meat so prepared cutlets cannot be frozen. The first side of a cutlet to be fried browns most evenly, so make sure the cutlets all face the same way in the pan. That way they can be arranged attractively in a dish to serve.

Variation Omit the ham and coat the cutlets in breadcrumbs. Serve on a bed of cooked spaghetti and garnish with tomato ketchup or preferably the tomato sauce and a sprig of parsley.

Serves 4

below Crispy lamb chops   *above* Irish stew

Irish Stew

Metric/Imperial	American
1·25 kg/2$\frac{1}{2}$ lb middle neck of lamb	2$\frac{1}{2}$ lb lamb neck slices
2 large onions	2 large onions
225 g/8 oz carrots (optional)	$\frac{1}{2}$ lb carrots (optional)
0·5 kg/1 lb potatoes	1 lb potatoes
salt and pepper	salt and pepper
chopped parsley to garnish	chopped parsley to garnish

Cut the lamb in neat pieces and remove the spinal cord. Peel and slice the onions, carrots and potatoes. Alternate layers of meat with layers of each vegetable in a 1·75-litre/3-pint (US 4-pint) ovenproof casserole, seasoning each layer with salt and pepper and finishing with a layer of potato.

Pour in just enough water to come halfway up the casserole. Cover with a lid and cook in a moderate oven (160°C, 325°F, Gas Mark 3) for 2$\frac{1}{2}$ hours or until the meat is nearly tender.

Remove the lid, increase the oven temperature to 180°C (350°F, Gas Mark 4) and cook for a further 30 minutes or until the top layer of potato is golden brown. Place in a serving dish and garnish with parsley.

Note In true Irish stew the carrots are served separately, but I put them in the stew for colour and to save washing up an extra dish. For quickness cut onions in quarters and leave potatoes whole. Place in the ovenproof casserole and cook as above, without removing the lid.

Serves 4

Lamb with apricots

Lamb with Apricots

Metric/Imperial
1·25 kg/2½ lb fillet end leg of lamb
2 onions
2 teaspoons paprika
25 g/1 oz flour
300 ml/½ pint water or stock
1 teaspoon salt
pepper
1 teaspoon sugar
1 tablespoon vinegar
225 g/8 oz apricots
1 small packet frozen peas

American
2½ lb leg of lamb

2 onions
2 teaspoons paprika
¼ cup all-purpose flour
1¼ cups water or stock
1 teaspoon salt
pepper
1 teaspoon sugar
1 tablespoon vinegar
½ lb apricots
1 small package frozen peas

Cut lamb off the bone and into 5-cm/2-inch cubes. Put fat side down in a large pan and cook over a moderate heat for 5 minutes, then turn to brown the other side for a further 5 minutes. Chop the onions and add to the pan with the paprika and cook gently for 2 minutes; stir in the flour.

Remove from the heat and blend in the water, add salt, pepper, sugar and vinegar and bring to the boil. Simmer for 1 hour.

Stone and slice the apricots, add to the lamb, then cook for a further 30 minutes. Add the peas 15 minutes before the end of the cooking time.

Serve with noodles or pasta shells, tossed in fresh or soured cream, or with baked potatoes.

This dish freezes well.

Note When fresh apricots are out of season use canned. Half the juice can be used in the recipe to make up with water to 300 ml/½ pint (US 1¼ cups). Omit the sugar. Dried apricots soaked overnight in water can also be used.

Serves 4

67

Hungarian Lamb

Metric/Imperial	American
25 g/1 oz lard	2 tablespoons shortening
1 kg/2 lb middle neck of lamb, cut into joints	2 lb lamb neck slices, cut into joints
1 onion	1 onion
1 clove garlic	1 clove garlic
2 tablespoons paprika	3 tablespoons paprika
425-g/15-oz can tomatoes	15-oz can tomatoes
1 bay leaf	1 bay leaf
salt and pepper	salt and pepper
½ teaspoon sugar	½ teaspoon sugar
0.5 kg/1 lb new potatoes	1 lb new potatoes
1 tablespoon chopped parsley to garnish (optional)	1 tablespoon chopped parsley to garnish (optional)

Melt the lard in a pan and brown the pieces of lamb on both sides for about 5 minutes. Remove meat from the pan and put in an ovenproof casserole. Chop the onion and fry in the fat remaining in the pan until soft, crush the garlic and add with paprika, and cook for a further minute. Add the tomatoes with their juice, the bay leaf, salt, pepper and sugar. Bring the mixture to the boil and pour over the meat.

Cover the casserole and cook for 1 hour in a moderate oven (160°C, 325°F, Gas Mark 3). Remove from the oven, allow the fat to settle then skim off.

Peel the potatoes and cut into 1·5-cm/¾-inch cubes. Place on top of the casserole, put on the lid and cook for a further hour, removing the lid for the last 30 minutes. Remove bay leaf. Scatter chopped parsley over the potatoes and serve.

Note If new potatoes are small they can be left whole.

Serves 4

Sweet and Sour Chops

Metric/Imperial	American
4 pork chops	4 pork chops
4 tablespoons clear honey	¼ cup clear honey
2 tablespoons soya sauce	3 tablespoons soy sauce
1 tablespoon tomato ketchup	1 tablespoon tomato ketchup
1 tablespoon wine vinegar	1 tablespoon wine vinegar
1 tablespoon tomato purée	1 tablespoon tomato paste
salt and pepper	salt and pepper
few drops Tabasco sauce	few drops Tabasco sauce
juice of 1 small orange	juice of 1 small orange
225 g/8 oz patna rice	1 cup long-grain rice
¼ teaspoon saffron powder (optional)	¼ teaspoon saffron powder (optional)
parsley to garnish	parsley to garnish

Remove any excess fat from the chops and place in a shallow ovenproof dish.

Blend all the ingredients, except the rice and saffron powder, and pour over the chops. Bake uncovered in a moderately hot oven (190°C, 375°F, Gas Mark 5), basting occasionally, until tender, about 30–40 minutes.

Cook the rice in boiling salted water with the saffron powder, if used, for 12–15 minutes until tender, drain well and place on a serving dish. Arrange the chops on top and serve any extra sauce separately. Garnish with parsley.

Serves 4

above Hungarian lamb

Sweet and sour chops

Pork Barbecue Style

Metric/Imperial	American
4 pork chops	4 pork chops
½ teaspoon each salt and pepper	½ teaspoon each salt and pepper
½ teaspoon castor sugar	½ teaspoon sugar
½ teaspoon ground ginger	½ teaspoon ground ginger
25 g/1 oz butter	2 tablespoons butter
Barbecue sauce	**Barbecue sauce**
1–2 teaspoons chilli sauce	1–2 teaspoons hot chili sauce
1 tablespoon mushroom ketchup	1 tablespoon mushroom ketchup
1 tablespoon Worcestershire sauce	1 tablespoon Worcestershire sauce
2 teaspoons sugar	2 teaspoons sugar
2 tablespoons vinegar	3 tablespoons vinegar
2 tablespoons tomato ketchup	3 tablespoons tomato ketchup
1 teaspoon soya sauce	1 teaspoon soy sauce
2 cloves garlic, crushed	2 cloves garlic, crushed
2 bay leaves	2 bay leaves
4 sprigs of parsley to garnish	4 sprigs of parsley to garnish

Trim pork chops carefully. Mix together the salt, pepper, sugar and ginger and rub over the chops. Heat butter in a heavy meat tin and add the chops. Brown in the oven, turning once to brown on both sides.

Meanwhile mix together all the ingredients for the sauce. When the chops are brown pour off all the fat from the baking tin, pour over the sauce and cover with a lid of foil. Bake for 20–30 minutes in a moderately hot oven (190°C, 375°F, Gas Mark 5), basting occasionally, until tender. Arrange the chops on a serving dish and spoon over the sauce, removing the bay leaves. Garnish with parsley.

Variation
Cider Pork Chops Omit the sugar and ginger from the initial preparation and, after the chops are browned, pour over a sauce made as follows: deseed and cut into strips ½ green and ½ red pepper, core and slice one eating apple, and mix with 150 ml/¼ pint (US ⅔ cup) dry cider and ½ teaspoon fresh rosemary. Continue as above. You can omit the parsley garnish as the rosemary looks quite attractive.

Serves 4

Pork with Red Wine and Prunes

Metric/Imperial	American
2 tablespoons salad oil	3 tablespoons salad oil
0·75 kg/1½ lb pork tenderloin fillet	1½ lb pork tenderloin
0·5 kg/1 lb pickling onions or 3 medium onions	1 lb small or 3 medium onions
2 cloves garlic	2 cloves garlic
300 ml/½ pint red wine	1¼ cups red wine
1 teaspoon salt	1 teaspoon salt
pepper	pepper
213-g/7½-oz can prunes	7½-oz can prunes
20 g/¾ oz flour	3 tablespoons all-purpose flour
Garnish	**Garnish**
8 slices French bread	8 slices French bread
oil for frying	oil for frying
1 tablespoon chopped parsley	1 tablespoon chopped parsley

Heat the oil in a large frying pan with a lid. Do not cut up the pork but quickly brown it whole in hot oil until golden. Lift the meat out of the pan and set on one side. Leave peeled pickling onions whole, or quarter medium onions. Lower the heat, add the onions and brown gently for about 10 minutes. Slice or crush the garlic and add to the pan, cook slowly for 1 minute

with the onions, then pour on the red wine. Boil the wine quickly for 1 minute to evaporate alcohol. Lower the heat and return the pork to the pan, season, cover and simmer very slowly for 20 minutes.

Remove stones from the prunes and blend the prune juice and flour to a smooth paste. Remove pan from the heat and cut the pork into slices 2·5 cm/1 inch thick. Pour in the flour and prune juice and stir quickly to make a smooth red wine sauce. Add the prunes, return pan to the boil and simmer very gently for a further 5 minutes. If the sauce has reduced too much in simmering and is too thick, add a little water to give a light coating sauce.

Fry slices of French bread until golden brown in hot oil. Drain on kitchen paper. Turn the pork on to a serving dish, surround with French bread, sprinkle with chopped parsley and serve.

To freeze Prepare and cook pork dish, without French bread, and freeze. Thaw in refrigerator overnight and reheat.
Note Do not overcook or reheat for too long as pork tenderloin is prone to excessive shrinkage.

Serves 4

Stuffed Pork Chops

Metric/Imperial	American
4 loin pork chops	4 loin pork chops
1 pig's kidney	1 pork kidney
1 onion	1 onion
25 g/1 oz butter	2 tablespoons butter
15 g/½ oz fresh white breadcrumbs	¼ cup fresh white bread crumbs
½ teaspoon thyme	½ teaspoon thyme
½ teaspoon salt	½ teaspoon salt
pepper	pepper
oil	oil
Sauce	**Sauce**
3 tomatoes	3 tomatoes
1 teaspoon flour	1 teaspoon all-purpose flour
200 ml/generous ¼ pint water	¾ cup water
1 teaspoon tomato purée	1 teaspoon tomato paste
1 tablespoon Worcestershire sauce	1 tablespoon Worcestershire sauce
½ teaspoon salt	½ teaspoon salt
pepper	pepper

Trim excess fat from the chops and then insert the tip of a sharp knife into the fat side of the chop and cut inwards to make a large pocket in the meat. Finely dice the kidney, discarding the core, chop the onion finely and cook both quickly in the butter until golden, about 5 minutes. Remove from the heat and stir in the breadcrumbs, thyme and seasoning. Cool the stuffing, divide into four portions and fill the chops using a teaspoon. Press to flatten slightly without loosening filling.

Brush the chops with oil and place under a preheated grill for 8–10 minutes on each side, depending on size. Keep warm. Meanwhile peel and cut the tomatoes into small wedges. Tip sediment and juices from the grill pan into a saucepan, blend in the flour, stir in the water and bring to the boil. Add the tomato purée, Worcestershire sauce and seasoning. Add the tomatoes to the sauce and pour over the meat to serve.

To freeze Pockets may be cut in chops when meat is half frozen. Stuffed meat should not be frozen.
Note If the pork chops are rather small, have them cut thicker. After making the pocket, bat out thinner with a cutlet bat or rolling pin.

Variation Omit the sauce. Slice the onion and fry in juices from the chops. Serve with the chops and garnish with prunes and sliced tomatoes. Serve with a mixed salad.

Serves 4   *opposite* Stuffed pork chops

Casserole of pork normande

Casserole of Pork Normande

Metric/Imperial	American
1 tablespoon salad oil	1 tablespoon salad oil
0·75 kg/1½ lb thick end belly of pork	1½ lb salt pork
2 medium onions	2 medium onions
1 cooking apple	1 baking apple
20 g/¾ oz flour	3 tablespoons all-purpose flour
150 ml/¼ pint dry cider	⅔ cup dry cider
250 ml/scant ½ pint water	1 cup water
1 teaspoon salt	1 teaspoon salt
2 tablespoons single cream	3 tablespoons light cream
Garnish	**Garnish**
2 Cox's apples	2 eating apples
25 g/1 oz butter	2 tablespoons butter
25 g/1 oz castor sugar	2 tablespoons sugar

Heat the oil in a metal casserole, skin the pork and remove bones. Cut into 5-cm/2-inch cubes and brown in the pan 5–6 at a time. Take out of the pan when golden and set on one side. When all the meat is browned, add the peeled, sliced onions and apple to the pan. Cook gently for 5 minutes stirring occasionally. Sprinkle in the flour and blend, then remove pan from the heat. Add the cider, water and salt, stirring well so that the flour is evenly blended. Return to the heat and bring to the boil, stirring

to give a smooth sauce. Return meat to pan. Cover and place the pan in a moderate oven (160°C, 325°F, Gas Mark 3) for 1½ hours. Prick meat with a fork to check that it is tender.

Cut each Cox's apple into 4–5 rings; do not remove peel. Cut out the centre core using an apple corer, small pastry cutter or knife. Heat the butter in a frying pan and quickly dip apple rings in sugar before frying over a moderate heat until golden on each side. Turn once only. Fry the remaining apple, taking care not to overbrown. Keep warm on an oiled plate for no more than 30 minutes.

Remove casserole of pork from the oven. Boil over a quick heat if there is too much sauce. Stir in the cream. Garnish with fried apple rings arranged overlapping round the top.

To freeze Prepare and cook casserole but not apple rings. Freeze pork then thaw and reheat. Prepare apple rings just before serving.

Note If a metal casserole is not available, start dish in a frying pan and transfer to an ovenproof casserole for putting in the oven.

When Cox's apples are out of season replace with a floury rather than a juicy eating apple.

Variation Apples can be omitted and three sticks of celery, sliced, added with the onions. Garnish with chopped parsley and serve with buttered noodles.

Serves 4

72

Raised pie

Raised Pie

Metric/Imperial	**American**
Hot water crust pastry	Hot water pie crust
275 g/10 oz plain flour	2½ cups all-purpose flour
100 g/4 oz lard	½ cup shortening
1 teaspoon salt	1 teaspoon salt
150 ml/¼ pint water	⅔ cup water
Filling	Filling
0·75 kg/1½ lb lean pork	1½ lb lean pork
1 teaspoon sage	1 teaspoon sage
1 teaspoon salt	1 teaspoon salt
pinch ground mace	pinch ground mace
pinch pepper	pinch pepper
1 stock cube	1 bouillon cube
150 ml/¼ pint hot water	⅔ cup hot water
2 hard-boiled eggs	2 hard-cooked eggs
1 egg yolk	1 egg yolk
1 teaspoon powdered gelatine	1 teaspoon powdered gelatin

Put the flour into a bowl, then put the lard, salt and water in a pan and bring to the boil. Pour immediately on to the flour and mix .quickly with a wooden spoon until a smooth dough is obtained. Leave the dough to stand until hand hot but not cold.

To prepare the filling cut the pork into 1-cm/½-inch cubes and add sage to the meat with the salt, mace and pepper. Dissolve the stock cube in the water and add 3 tablespoons (US ¼ cup) of this stock to the meat mixture.

To assemble the pie first grease a 15-cm/6-inch loose bottom cake tin, then take three-quarters of the warm dough, keeping the remainder warm. Pat out on a flat surface to a 23-cm/9-inch circle then drop into the prepared tin. With the finger tips draw the dough up the sides to evenly cover base and sides. Chill for 5 minutes. When the dough is firm, pack tightly with half the meat mixture. Place the eggs on top and cover, packing round with the remaining meat. Damp top pastry edge with water. Roll out the remaining dough and cover the pie. Press edges together to seal. Trim off surplus pastry and shape into leaves for decoration. Brush the pie with egg yolk, make a hole in the centre and decorate with pastry leaves. Brush again with egg yolk then chill for 10 minutes. Cook for 30 minutes in a hot oven (220°C, 425°F, Gas Mark 7), then reduce the heat for a further 2 hours (160°C, 325°F, Gas Mark 3). Cover with paper after 30 minutes if too brown. Remove from the oven and set aside to chill. When nearly cold sprinkle gelatine on the remaining stock, warm to dissolve and pour carefully into the pie to top up. Freezing is not recommended as pastry loses its crispness.

Note Remove from tin when pie is thoroughly chilled and the jellied stock is set. This pie can also be made using a special raised pie mould.

Variation Omit eggs and substitute one apple, peeled, cored and sliced.

Serves 4

Pork Fillet with Apples

Metric/Imperial	American
0·75 kg/1½ lb pork fillet or boned loin of pork	1½ lb pork tenderloin or boneless loin roast
350 g/12 oz onions	¾ lb onions
75 g/3 oz butter	¼ cup butter
350 g/12 oz tart cooking apples	¾ lb baking apples
100 ml/4 fl oz water	½ cup water
1 rounded tablespoon demerara sugar	1 rounded tablespoon light brown sugar
63-g/2¼-oz can tomato purée	2¼-oz can tomato paste
½ teaspoon thyme	½ teaspoon thyme
salt and pepper	salt and pepper

Cut the pork into 2·5-cm/1-inch cubes and peel and chop the onions. Melt the butter in a pan and fry the pork lightly for 2–3 minutes; transfer to a 1·75-litre/3-pint (US 4-pint) ovenproof casserole. Add the onions to the butter remaining in the pan and fry for 5 minutes or until golden brown; add to the pork.

Peel, core and slice the apples, put in a saucepan with the water and sugar and cook for about 5 minutes or until just soft. Add to the casserole with the tomato purée, thyme and seasoning. Cover with a well fitting lid or piece of foil and cook in the centre of a moderate oven (180°C, 350°F, Gas Mark 4) until tender. Serve with new potatoes and green beans.

Note   This recipe will not freeze well.

Serves 4

Blanquette de Veau

Metric/Imperial	American
0·75 kg/1½ lb boned shoulder or knuckle of veal	1½ lb boneless veal shoulder or knuckle
2 onions	2 onions
2 large carrots	2 large carrots
3 bay leaves	3 bay leaves
1 tablespoon lemon juice	1 tablespoon lemon juice
salt and pepper	salt and pepper
175 g/6 oz button mushrooms	1½ cups button mushrooms
40 g/1½ oz butter	3 tablespoons butter
40 g/1½ oz flour	⅓ cup all-purpose flour
1 egg yolk	1 egg yolk
142-g/5-oz carton single cream	5-oz carton light cream
sprig of parsley to garnish	sprig of parsley to garnish

Cut the veal into 3·5-cm/1½-inch pieces. Put in a pan, cover with cold water and bring to boiling point, then strain the veal into a colander and rinse off scum. Peel and quarter the onions and slice the carrots. Replace the veal pieces in the pan with the onions and carrots, add the bay leaves, lemon juice and plenty of salt and pepper. Add a generous litre/2 pints (US 2½ pints) water, bring to boiling point, then cover and simmer for 1½ hours or until tender. Thirty minutes before the end of cooking time add the whole mushrooms.

Melt the butter in a small pan, blend in the flour and cook over a low heat for 1 minute without letting it brown. Arrange the cooked veal and vegetables in a serving dish and keep warm. Reduce the cooking liquor to 600 ml/1 pint (US 2½ cups) by boiling rapidly. Strain the liquor into the pan containing the butter and flour. Stir the sauce constantly until it is smooth, then bring to boiling point and simmer for 5 minutes. Add more seasoning if necessary. Blend the egg yolk and cream together, remove sauce from the heat and stir in the egg mixture. Return the pan to the heat and reheat the mixture but do *not* allow it even to simmer. Pour the sauce over the veal. Garnish with parsley.

Pork hongroise

To freeze   Freeze the veal and sauce without adding the egg yolk and cream mixture. Reheat slowly until piping hot, remove from the heat and stir in the egg yolk and cream. Reheat but do not allow to boil.
Note   The blended egg yolk and cream must be added carefully. If the sauce boils or becomes too hot, it will curdle.

Serves 4–6

Pork Hongroise

Metric/Imperial	American
0·75 kg/1½ lb pork fillet or boned loin of pork	1½ lb pork tenderloin or boneless loin roast
2 tablespoons salad oil	3 tablespoons salad oil
25 g/1 oz butter	2 tablespoons butter
1 onion	1 onion
1 tablespoon paprika	1 tablespoon paprika
15 g/½ oz flour	2 tablespoons all-purpose flour
300 ml/½ pint water	1¼ cups water
1 beef stock cube	1 beef bouillon cube
5 tablespoons sherry	6 tablespoons sherry
1 teaspoon tomato purée	1 teaspoon tomato paste
salt and pepper	salt and pepper
175 g/6 oz small button mushrooms	1½ cups small button mushrooms
15 g/½ oz cornflour	2 tablespoons cornstarch
2 tablespoons water	3 tablespoons water
142-g/5-oz carton soured cream	5-oz carton dairy sour cream

Cut the pork into 3·5-cm/1½-inch pieces. Heat the oil in a pan, add the butter and fry the pork pieces quickly until they are just beginning to turn brown. Remove from the pan and drain on kitchen paper.

Chop the onion and fry in the pan with the paprika for 2 minutes. Blend in the flour and cook for a further minute. Remove from the heat and stir in the water and stock cube. Add the sherry and tomato purée, return to the heat and simmer until thick. Season with salt and pepper, then add the meat. Cover and simmer for 30–40 minutes or until the pork is tender.

At the end of cooking time add the whole mushrooms to the pan. Blend the cornflour to a smooth paste with cold water and add to the pan. Return to the boil and just before serving blend in the soured cream.

To freeze   Freeze the pork and sauce without adding the cream. Reheat slowly and stir in the cream just before serving.
Note   Garnish with crisp fried bread triangles and sprigs of parsley to serve.

Variation
Chicken Hongroise   Use four chicken joints instead of pork and increase the cooking time to 40–50 minutes. Serve on a bed of rice, garnished with lightly fried mushrooms.

Serves 4–6

Chicken hongroise

Italian Veal

Metric/Imperial
0·75 kg/1½ lb boneless shin
   or pie veal
3 carrots
2 sticks celery
1 onion
1 clove garlic
1 tablespoon salad oil
15 g/½ oz butter
15 g/½ oz flour

150 ml/¼ pint dry white wine
300 ml/½ pint stock or
   1 chicken stock cube and
   300 ml/½ pint water
425-g/15-oz can tomatoes
sprig of parsley
1 bay leaf
salt and pepper
1 tablespoon chopped parsley
   to garnish

American
1½ lb boneless veal shank

3 carrots
2 stalks celery
1 onion
1 clove garlic
1 tablespoon salad oil
1 tablespoon butter
2 tablespoons all-purpose
   flour
⅔ cup dry white wine
1¼ cups stock or 1 chicken
   bouillon cube and 1¼ cups
   water
15-oz can tomatoes
sprig of parsley
1 bay leaf
salt and pepper
1 tablespoon chopped parsley
   to garnish

Cut the meat into 3·5 cm/1½ inch thick pieces. Peel and thinly slice the carrots, slice the celery, chop the onion and crush the garlic. Heat the oil in a heavy frying pan, add the butter and fry half the meat at a time over a moderate heat, turning once until it is a golden brown. Drain the meat on kitchen paper then put it in a 1·75-litre/3-pint (US 4-pint) ovenproof casserole.

Fry the vegetables lightly in the pan for 5 minutes. Add the flour and continue to cook until it has browned, stirring constantly. Blend in the wine, stock and tomatoes, and add the parsley, bay leaf, salt and pepper. Bring the mixture to boiling point.

Pour the sauce on to the meat. Cover the casserole with a lid or foil and cook in a moderate oven (160°C, 325°F, Gas Mark 3) for about 2½ hours or until the veal is very tender. Remove parsley and bay leaf before serving. Garnish with chopped parsley and serve with mixed vegetables.

Variation   Red wine can be used instead of white wine.

Serves 4–6

Italian veal

Spanish veal rolls

Spanish Veal Rolls

Metric/Imperial	American
100 g/4 oz butter	½ cup butter
1 medium onion	1 medium onion
100 g/4 oz mushrooms	1 cup mushrooms
50 g/2 oz Spanish stuffed green olives (optional)	⅓ cup Spanish stuffed green olives (optional)
50 g/2 oz fresh white breadcrumbs	1 cup fresh white bread crumbs
1 beaten egg	1 beaten egg
salt and pepper	salt and pepper
4 veal escalopes, beaten thin	4 veal cutlets, pounded thin
40 g/1½ oz flour	⅓ cup all-purpose flour
150 ml/¼ pint chicken stock or 1 stock cube and 150 ml/ ¼ pint water	⅔ cup chicken stock or 1 bouillon cube and ⅔ cup water
1 orange	1 orange
1 tablespoon sherry	1 tablespoon sherry
150 ml/¼ pint single cream	⅔ cup light cream

Melt half the butter in a pan, chop the onion and mushrooms, fry the onion until cooked but not coloured, and add the mushrooms and cook for 2 minutes. Chop half the olives and add to the pan with the breadcrumbs and egg; season to taste. Spread the mixture over the veal escalopes, roll up and secure with string or wooden cocktail sticks. Melt the rest of the butter in a frying pan and fry the rolls until golden and cooked through. Put into a serving dish and keep hot; remove string if used.

Stir the flour into the fat remaining in the pan and add the stock slowly, stirring to blend. Cut thin strips of orange rind for garnish, squeeze the juice and add to the stock with the sherry. Season and bring to the boil, stirring; remove from heat and stir in the cream. Serve some of the sauce over the rolls and the remainder in a sauce boat. Garnish the veal with the remaining olives cut into halves and sprinkle strips of orange rind on top.

Variation Omit the orange and add 2 tablespoons (us 3 tablespoons) tomato purée to the sauce. For a more economical dish, omit the cream. Garnish with chopped parsley and serve with duchess potatoes.

Serves 4

Orange Tarragon Chicken

Metric/Imperial	American
40 g/1½ oz butter	3 tablespoons butter
2 tablespoons salad oil	3 tablespoons salad oil
4 chicken quarters	4 chicken quarters
1 large onion	1 large onion
5 tablespoons frozen orange juice concentrate	6 tablespoons frozen orange juice concentrate
1 chicken stock cube	1 chicken bouillon cube
4 sprigs of fresh tarragon, chopped or 1 tablespoon dried tarragon	4 sprigs of fresh tarragon, chopped or 1 tablespoon dried tarragon
15 g/½ oz cornflour	2 tablespoons cornstarch
2 tablespoons water	3 tablespoons water
142-g/5-oz carton soured cream	5-oz carton dairy sour cream

Melt the butter and oil in a flameproof casserole dish and brown the chicken quarters thoroughly on all sides. Remove from dish and, if desired, skin the chicken; put aside.

Chop the onion finely and cook gently for 2–3 minutes. Make the orange juice up to 300 ml/½ pint (US 1¼ cups) with water and add to the pan with the stock cube and tarragon. Bring to the boil and add the chicken. Cover with a lid or foil and bake in a moderate oven (180°C, 350°F, Gas Mark 4) for 30 minutes until the chicken is tender. Baste occasionally with orange sauce.

Remove the chicken and place down the centre of an oval serving dish. Skim off excess fat from the sauce. Blend the cornflour with the water to make a paste and add to the sauce. Return to the boil and cook for 2–3 minutes, stirring continuously. Cool slightly and stir in the soured cream. Pour over the chicken and garnish with fresh tarragon.

Serves 4

Orange tarragon chicken

Chicken Tetrazzini

Metric/Imperial	American
4 chicken legs	4 chicken legs
1 teaspoon rosemary	1 teaspoon rosemary
1 teaspoon salt	1 teaspoon salt
900 ml/1½ pints water	3¾ cups water
100 g/4 oz pasta shells	1 cup shell macaroni
50 g/2 oz butter	¼ cup butter
40 g/1½ oz flour	⅓ cup all-purpose flour
100 g/4 oz mushrooms	1 cup mushrooms
pepper	pepper
75 g/3 oz split almonds	¾ cup slivered almonds
50 ml/2 fl oz single cream	¼ cup light cream
Potato purée	**Mashed potatoes**
0·5 kg/1 lb potatoes	1 lb potatoes
25 g/1 oz butter	2 tablespoons butter
2–3 tablespoons milk	3–4 tablespoons milk
½ teaspoon salt	½ teaspoon salt
pepper	pepper

Put the chicken in a pan with the rosemary, salt and water, bring to the boil and simmer gently for 45 minutes.

Cook the pasta shells separately in boiling water for about 10 minutes until nearly tender.

Boil and drain the potatoes for the potato purée.

When the chicken is ready tip the contents of the chicken pan into a bowl. Rinse out the pan and melt the butter in this, add the flour and cook slowly for 1 minute. Remove from the heat and blend in 450 ml/¾ pint (US 2 cups) stock strained from the chicken. Cut the mushrooms in quarters and add these and the drained pasta shells to the sauce. Season with pepper, bring to the boil and simmer for 5 minutes. Cut the chicken from the bones in large pieces and stir into the sauce with the almonds and cream. Turn into a generous 1-litre/2-pint (US 2½-pint) pie dish.

Thoroughly mash the potatoes, adding butter, milk and seasoning. Using a large piping bag and star nozzle, pipe potato round the edges of the dish. Place under a hot grill for 5 minutes to brown the potatoes.

To freeze Freeze completed dish before browning, without adding almonds. Thaw, then reheat and brown in the oven, adding the almonds before serving.

Note Nuts lose their crispness if added too soon.

Serves 4–6

Chicken Escalopes Holstein

Metric/Imperial	American
4 chicken wings and breasts	4 chicken wings and breasts
25 g/1 oz flour	¼ cup all-purpose flour
½ teaspoon salt	½ teaspoon salt
1 tablespoon salad oil	1 tablespoon salad oil
75 g/3 oz butter	⅓ cup butter
Garnish	**Garnish**
4 anchovy fillets	4 canned anchovy fillets, drained
2 hard-boiled eggs	2 hard-cooked eggs
1 lemon	1 lemon
12 Spanish stuffed green olives	12 Spanish stuffed green olives

Remove wing tips and cut all bones from chicken using a small sharp knife. Work with a scraping action to remove meat. Cut off skin. Spread out breast meat and slip each piece into a wet polythene bag. Bat out very thin with a meat bat or rolling pin.

Mix the flour and salt and toss the chicken in this. Heat the oil in a large frying pan, add the butter and cook the chicken escalopes for 4 minutes on each side. Meanwhile split the anchovies in half lengthwise, chop the eggs, and cut the lemon into wedges. Arrange the escalopes on a dish with two anchovy fillets crossed on top and pile chopped egg, lemon wedges and olives on the side. Pour any butter left from cooking over the top.

Note Much larger escalopes can be made if cut from the whole chicken, not chicken joints. The chicken legs may be used in casseroles or chicken tetrazzini and the carcass used for stock.

Serves 4

Sauté of Chicken with Mushrooms

Metric/Imperial	American
50 g/2 oz butter	½ cup butter
4 chicken joints	4 chicken joints
1½ tablespoons sherry	2 tablespoons sherry
100 g/4 oz button mushrooms	1 cup button mushrooms
15 g/½ oz flour	2 tablespoons all-purpose flour
300 ml/½ pint creamy milk	1¼ cups rich milk
1 teaspoon salt	1 teaspoon salt
pepper	pepper

Melt half the butter in a sauté pan (frying pan with lid), lay the chicken joints skin side down in the pan, and brown over a very gentle heat for 7 minutes. Then turn the joints over, pour on the sherry and cover the pan tightly. Cook very gently for 35 minutes, then add the quartered mushrooms (or whole if small). Cover the pan tightly and cook for a further 5 minutes. Meanwhile prepare the sauce.

Melt the remaining butter in a separate pan and stir in the flour over the heat. Remove from the heat and blend in the creamy milk; add seasoning. Bring to the boil, stirring well. With scissors remove the wing tips and the knuckle from drumsticks. Pour the sauce over the chicken joints. Simmer the chicken very slowly for 5 minutes, uncovered to reduce the sauce slightly, stirring occasionally to prevent sticking. Serve with noodles and green vegetables.

To freeze Complete and freeze. To serve, thaw and reheat slowly in a covered casserole in the oven.
Note For an easy dish to cook and serve make the white sauce earlier in the day – cover to prevent skin forming. For an easy supper party dish to serve larger numbers, double the recipe and cook in a foil-covered roasting tin in the oven.

Variation
Chicken and Mushrooms in a Rice Ring Remove the cooked chicken from the joints and cut into bite-size pieces. Stir into the sauce with the mushrooms and keep hot. Cook 100 g/4 oz (US ½ cup) long-grain rice, drain and place in a ring mould, pressing down firmly. Stand for 10 minutes, before turning out. Carefully pile the chicken in the centre and garnish with whole button mushrooms and sprigs of parsley.

Serves 4

Orange Baked Chicken

Metric/Imperial	American
15 g/½ oz butter	1 tablespoon butter
2 tablespoons salad oil	3 tablespoons salad oil
4 chicken joints	4 chicken joints
1 large onion	1 large onion
170-g/6-oz can frozen orange juice concentrate	6-oz can frozen orange juice concentrate
1 chicken stock cube	1 chicken bouillon cube
150 ml/¼ pint water	⅔ cup water
salt and pepper	salt and pepper
1–2 tablespoons snipped chives to garnish	2–3 tablespoons snipped chives to garnish

Melt the butter and oil in a large frying pan. Add the chicken joints and fry until brown all over. Remove from pan and place in an ovenproof casserole.

Peel and chop the onion and add to the fat remaining in the pan; fry for 2–3 minutes. Stir in the orange juice concentrate, stock cube and water. Bring to the boil and pour over the chicken. Season, cover the casserole and place in a moderate oven (160°C, 325°F, Gas Mark 3). Cook for 40–45 minutes or until tender. Sprinkle with chives and serve.

Note The sauce will be thin as there is no thickening.

Variation The sauce can be served separately with spatch-cock of chicken (split along the back so it can be opened out flat); garnish with orange slices and leaves of lime peel.

Serves 4

Chicken in Wine

Metric/Imperial
225 g/8 oz pickling onions
2 sticks celery (optional)
6 chicken joints
40 g/1½ oz butter
1 tablespoon salad oil
100-g/4-oz piece smoked
   streaky bacon
1 clove garlic, crushed
25 g/1 oz flour
300 ml/½ pint cheap Burgundy
300 ml/½ pint water or
   chicken stock
1 bay leaf
sprig of fresh thyme or ½
   teaspoon dried thyme
salt and pepper
175 g/6 oz mushrooms
chopped parsley to garnish

American
½ lb small onions
2 stalks celery (optional)
6 chicken joints
3 tablespoons butter
1 tablespoon salad oil
6 slices smoked bacon

1 clove garlic, crushed
¼ cup all-purpose flour
1¼ cups cheap Burgundy
1¼ cups water or chicken
   stock
1 bay leaf
sprig of fresh thyme or ½
   teaspoon dried thyme
salt and pepper
1½ cups mushrooms
chopped parsley to garnish

Skin the onions and leave whole, and chop the celery if used. Remove the skin from the chicken joints. Melt two-thirds of the butter in a large pan with the oil. Cut the bacon into cubes or pieces and add to the pan, fry until golden brown, remove and drain. Fry the chicken joints on both sides then put them with the bacon in a 1·75-litre/3-pint (US 4-pint) ovenproof casserole.

Melt the remaining butter in a pan, add the crushed garlic and blend with the flour; cook until brown. Stir in the wine, water or stock and herbs. Bring to the boil and simmer until thick, stirring frequently. Add the onions and celery, season and pour over the chicken.

Cover and cook in a moderate oven (160°C, 325°F, Gas Mark 3) for 30 minutes. Stir in whole or sliced mushrooms, return to oven and cook for a further 10 minutes. Remove bay leaf and sprig of fresh thyme if used. Skim off any excess fat, adjust seasoning and serve. Garnish with chopped parsley.

Serves 6

Chicken in wine

Chicken Pilaff

Metric/Imperial	American
50 ml/2 fl oz salad oil	$\frac{1}{4}$ cup salad oil
4 chicken joints	4 chicken joints
1 onion	1 onion
2 sticks celery	2 stalks celery
1 green or red pepper	1 green or red pepper
225 g/8 oz long-grain rice	1 cup long-grain rice
750 ml/1$\frac{1}{4}$ pints water	3 cups water
227-g/8-oz can tomatoes	8-oz can tomatoes
1 chicken stock cube	1 chicken bouillon cube
1 clove garlic, crushed	1 clove garlic, crushed
$\frac{3}{4}$ teaspoon curry powder	$\frac{3}{4}$ teaspoon curry powder
$\frac{1}{4}$ teaspoon dried mixed herbs	$\frac{1}{4}$ teaspoon dried mixed herbs
$\frac{1}{4}$ teaspoon chilli powder	$\frac{1}{4}$ teaspoon chili powder
50 g/2 oz mushrooms	$\frac{1}{2}$ cup mushrooms
100 g/4 oz frozen peas	$\frac{3}{4}$ cup frozen peas
salt and pepper	salt and pepper

Heat two-thirds of the oil in a pan and fry the chicken quickly until golden brown on both sides, then reduce the heat, cover and continue to cook until joints are tender, about 20 minutes. Remove from pan and leave to drain on kitchen paper.

Chop the onion and celery, remove seeds from the pepper and slice. Fry in fat remaining in the pan for a few minutes until soft. Add the rice and fry for a further few minutes. Add water, tomatoes, stock cube, garlic, curry powder, mixed herbs and chilli powder.

Bring the mixture to boiling point, stir with a fork, then cover and simmer for about 25 minutes, or until all the liquid has been absorbed and the rice cooked.

Slice the mushrooms and fry in the rest of the oil for a few minutes in a small pan. When the rice mixture is ready, stir in the mushrooms, chicken and peas. Reheat the mixture, stirring frequently, adding salt and pepper to season well.

Note Leftover cooked chicken may also be used for this recipe. It should be removed from the bone, added at the end and reheated with the rice mixture.

Variation Cut the cooked chicken into bite-size pieces. To vary rice omit pepper, curry powder, mixed herbs, chilli powder, tomatoes and peas, and add 50 g/2 oz (us $\frac{1}{2}$ cup) peanuts and 50 g/2 oz (us $\frac{1}{3}$ cup) raisins to the cooked rice. Garnish with strips of cucumber and orange peel.

Serves 4

Chicken pilaff

Chilli beef pancakes

Savoury Pancakes

Metric/Imperial
Batter
100 g/4 oz plain flour
1 large egg
25 ml/1 fl oz salad oil
300 ml/½ pint milk
Filling
40 g/1½ oz butter
1 onion, sliced
20 g/¾ oz flour

300 ml/½ pint milk
½ teaspoon grated lemon rind
1 teaspoon salt
pepper
225 g/8 oz cooked chicken
50 ml/2 fl oz single cream
2 tablespoons grated cheese

American
Batter
1 cup all-purpose flour
1 large egg
2 tablespoons salad oil
1¼ cups milk
Filling
3 tablespoons butter
1 onion, sliced
3 tablespoons all-purpose
   flour
1¼ cups milk
½ teaspoon grated lemon rind
1 teaspoon salt
pepper
1 cup cooked chicken
¼ cup light cream
3 tablespoons grated cheese

Prepare batter: put the flour into a bowl, make a well in the centre, and drop in the egg, oil and half the milk. Beat to a thick batter for 2 minutes then stir in the remaining milk. Meanwhile prepare the filling.

Melt the butter in a saucepan, add the sliced onion and cook to a pale golden brown. Remove from the heat and stir in the flour, then pour on the milk and blend well before returning to the heat. Bring to the boil stirring well, add the lemon rind and season. Cover and leave to cool.

Make 12 pancakes 15 cm/6 inches in diameter or eight 18 cm/7 inches in diameter. To fry pancakes heat a 15-cm/6-inch or 18-cm/7-inch omelette pan with a few drops of oil in it. When hot hold the pan in one hand and pour in about one large

tablespoon of batter, revolving the pan to coat the base evenly. Allow to cook for approximately 1 minute. Turn over, using a palette knife, to brown the other side. Tip out on to a clean tea towel. Use remaining batter to make the rest of the pancakes. Stack pancakes as they are made and keep in the folded towel.

Add the chicken and cream to the filling. Divide the mixture between the pancakes placing a spoonful in the centre of each. Fold each pancake almost in half over the filling, then fold rounded edge down in two places to form a triangle. Place pancake, folded side down, in a shallow ovenproof dish. Complete other pancakes, placing them overlapping in the dish. Sprinkle with cheese. Bake just before serving for 20–25 minutes in a moderately hot oven (190°C, 375°F, Gas Mark 5).

To freeze Complete entire dish but do not bake. Thaw and bake before serving.
Note Pancakes may be made well in advance and kept in the refrigerator for 2–3 days, or frozen. More oil is not needed for frying each pancake as batter contains sufficient oil. Have a special frying pan for pancakes and omelettes only, and never use for bacon. Do not wash or scour but wipe out with a damp cloth if necessary, then dry well. This will prevent sticking.

Variation
Chilli Beef Pancakes Use 225 g/8 oz (us 1 cup) minced beef instead of the chicken and fry with the onion. Add ½ teaspoon chilli powder and 1 tablespoon tomato purée and omit the cream. Use beef stock instead of milk and simmer for 30–40 minutes. Allow to cool. Divide the filling between the pancakes and roll up. Serve with grilled bacon rolls, slices of fried mushroom and sprigs of parsley to garnish.

Serves 4

Chicken and mushroom pie

Chicken and Mushroom Pie

Metric/Imperial	American
225 g/8 oz cooked chicken	1 cup cooked chicken
225 g/8 oz cooked boiled bacon	1 cup cooked ham
25 g/1 oz butter	2 tablespoons butter
50 g/2 oz mushrooms, sliced	½ cup mushrooms, sliced
25 g/1 oz flour	¼ cup all-purpose flour
150 ml/¼ pint water	⅔ cup water·
½ chicken stock cube	½ chicken bouillon cube
150 ml/¼ pint milk	⅔ cup milk
2 tablespoons cooked peas	3 tablespoons cooked peas
Pastry	**Pie dough**
225 g/8 oz plain flour	2 cups all-purpose flour
¼ teaspoon salt	¼ teaspoon salt
50 g/2 oz butter	¼ cup butter
50 g/2 oz lard	¼ cup shortening
50 ml/2 fl oz water	¼ cup water
milk	milk

Cut the chicken and bacon into chunks of about 1·5 cm/¾ inch. Melt the butter in a pan, add the sliced mushrooms and cook gently for 2 minutes. Stir in the flour and cook for another minute. Slowly blend in the water, stock cube and milk, stirring until smooth. Bring the sauce to boiling point and stir until it thickens. Turn into a bowl, add the peas, chicken and bacon and leave to cool.

Make the shortcrust pastry: sift the flour and salt into a bowl. Rub the butter and lard into the flour until well blended. Gradually add sufficient of the water to form a dough. Divide in two. Roll each piece into a 23-cm/9-inch circle. Place one of these in a 20-cm/8-inch ovenproof pie plate and spread the chicken mixture in the centre. Moisten edge of the pastry with water, place the second circle on top of the first and gently press the edges of both circles to seal. Trim edges and decorate with a fork and a plait made from pastry trimmings.

Brush the pie with milk, make two slits in the top and bake in a hot oven (220°C, 425°F, Gas Mark 7) for 25 minutes, then reduce heat to moderately hot (190°C, 375°F, Gas Mark 5) and cook for a further 15 minutes.

Note If a pie plate is not available use a shallow oval oven-proof dish. Omit peas if wished.

Serves 4

Pigeon Casserole with Chestnuts

Metric/Imperial	American
350 g/12 oz chestnuts	¾ lb chestnuts
50 ml/2 fl oz salad oil	¼ cup salad oil
25 g/1 oz butter	2 tablespoons butter
3 plump pigeons, each split in half	3 plump pigeons, each split in half
25 g/1 oz flour	¼ cup all-purpose flour
300 ml/½ pint Beaujolais	1¼ cups Beaujolais or other red wine
300 ml/½ pint chicken stock	1¼ cups chicken stock
225 g/8 oz onions	½ lb onions
thinly peeled rind and juice of 1 orange	thinly peeled rind and juice of 1 orange
1 teaspoon redcurrant jelly	1 teaspoon red currant jelly
½ teaspoon salt	½ teaspoon salt
bouquet garni	bouquet garni
black pepper	black pepper
sprigs of parsley to garnish	sprigs of parsley to garnish

Simmer the chestnuts in boiling water for about 2 minutes. Drain, make a slit in each with a sharp knife and remove the outer skin. Simmer for 20 minutes in water, then drain.

Heat two-thirds of the oil in a pan, add the butter then the pigeons and fry until browned, turning once. Transfer the birds to a 2·25-litre/4-pint (US 5-pint) casserole. Add the remaining oil to the pan with the chestnuts. Fry until evenly browned then drain on kitchen paper.

Add the flour to the pan and cook gently until browned. Stir in the wine and stock, bring to the boil and pour into the casserole. Peel the onions and cut in wedges, and add to the casserole with the orange rind and juice, redcurrant jelly, salt, bouquet garni and black pepper. Cover and cook in a moderate oven (160°C, 325°F, Gas Mark 3) for about 1½–2 hours or until tender. Add the chestnuts about 45 minutes before the end of cooking time. Remove bouquet garni and orange rind. Check seasoning and garnish the casserole with sprigs of parsley before serving.

Serves 6

Gougère Hongroise

Metric/Imperial	American
Choux paste	**Choux paste**
115 g/4 oz butter	½ cup butter
300 ml/½ pint water	1¼ cups water
145 g/5 oz plain flour	1¼ cups all-purpose flour
4 eggs	4 eggs
½ teaspoon salt	½ teaspoon salt
pepper	pepper
1 teaspoon French mustard	1 teaspoon French mustard
75 g/3 oz cheese, diced	¾ cup diced cheese
Filling	**Filling**
2 onions	2 onions
40 g/1½ oz butter	3 tablespoons butter
2 teaspoons paprika	2 teaspoons paprika
15 g/½ oz flour	2 tablespoons all-purpose flour
300 ml/½ pint chicken stock	1¼ cups chicken stock
100 g/4 oz button mushrooms	1 cup button mushrooms
1 teaspoon salt	1 teaspoon salt
pepper	pepper
½ teaspoon yeast extract	½ teaspoon yeast extract
170-g/6-oz can pimento	6-oz can pimiento
225 g/8 oz cooked chicken	1 cup cooked chicken
1 tablespoon grated cheese	1 tablespoon grated cheese

Gougère hongroise

Grease sides of a 1·75-litre/3-pint (US 4-pint) shallow ovenproof dish.

Ingredients for choux paste must be accurately measured: place the butter and water in a pan, bring slowly to the boil and remove from the heat. Toss in the flour quickly and stir vigorously with a wooden spoon to a smooth thick paste which clings to the spoon. Leave to cool.

Meanwhile prepare filling: slice the onions and fry in butter until soft and transparent. Add the paprika and flour and cook gently for 1 minute. Pour on the stock and add the quartered mushrooms, salt, pepper and yeast extract. Bring to the boil and simmer for 5 minutes then set on one side to cool.

To complete choux paste whisk the eggs. Gradually beat into the cooled paste one spoonful at a time. This may be done with an electric mixer or in the pan with a wooden spoon. When all the egg is added the mixture should be almost able to hold its shape. If beaten sufficiently it will be stiffer than a sauce. Finally beat in the seasoning, mustard and cheese. Spoon round edge of the greased dish to form an even border.

Cut the pimento into strips and the chicken into fingers. Add to the paprika sauce. Spoon into centre of the dish and sprinkle with cheese. Bake in a moderately hot oven (200°C, 400°F, Gas Mark 6) for 35–40 minutes and serve straight from the oven with the choux paste well risen and golden round the edge.

To freeze Complete the dish without baking. Freeze in dish. Cover. Thaw at room temperature for 8 hours and bake.
Note If paprika sauce is cold before adding chicken and pimento, the dish may be assembled 24 hours in advance. Always serve immediately after baking for best results.

Variation Omit paprika and pimento from the filling and substitute four rashers lean bacon, cut into strips and added with the chicken to the sauce.

Serves 6

85

Celebration Gammon

Metric/Imperial	American
1·75-kg/4-lb gammon joint	4-lb ham steak or ham butt
450 ml/¾ pint apple juice	2 cups apple juice
1 onion	1 onion
freshly ground black pepper	freshly ground black pepper
2 tablespoons honey	3 tablespoons honey
3 Cox's apples	3 eating apples
50 g/2 oz demerara sugar	¼ cup light brown sugar
25 g/1 oz butter	2 tablespoons butter
2 tablespoons salad oil	3 tablespoons salad oil
12 Spanish stuffed green olives	12 Spanish stuffed green olives

Soak the gammon for 12 hours in cold water, then drain. Place in a pan, pour over the apple juice, slice the onion and add with the black pepper. Cover and simmer for 20 minutes per 0·5 kg/ 1 lb plus 20 minutes over. Remove gammon from pan and leave to cool slightly. Remove skin and score fat diagonally in diamond shapes. Put in a shallow ovenproof dish. Brush with honey and bake in a hot oven (220°C, 425°F, Gas Mark 7) for about 15 minutes until a rich golden brown.

Core the apples and cut into rings, leaving the skin on. Toss in the sugar. Heat the butter and oil together in a pan and fry the apple rings, turning once, until they are a golden syrupy brown. Place the gammon on a dish surrounded with apple rings. Put the olives on cocktail sticks and place all over the top of the gammon inside each diamond shape.

Serves 8–10

Celebration gammon

Venetian Liver

Metric/Imperial	American
0·5 kg/1 lb lamb's liver	1 lb lamb's liver
2 tablespoons salad oil	3 tablespoons salad oil
3 onions	3 onions
25 g/1 oz flour	¼ cup all-purpose flour
300 ml/½ pint water	1¼ cups water
1 stock cube	1 bouillon cube
1 clove garlic	1 clove garlic
1 teaspoon salt	1 teaspoon salt
pepper	pepper
2 teaspoons sage (optional)	2 teaspoons sage (optional)

Trim the liver of coarse tubes. Heat the oil in a frying pan and fry the liver quickly for 1 minute on each side. Slice the onions, push liver to one side and add onions to the pan. Cover and cook gently for 5 minutes until the onions begin to soften. Uncover pan and continue cooking. When the onions begin to turn brown stir in the flour. Pour in the water, crumble in the stock cube, crush garlic and add with salt and pepper. Bring to the boil and simmer for 10 minutes. Stir in the sage and serve.

This dish freezes well.

Variation For a creamier sauce reduce the water to 150 ml/ ¼ pint (US ⅔ cup) and add an equal amount of milk.

Serves 4

Venetian liver

Cidered glazed gammon

Cidered Glazed Gammon

Metric/Imperial
1·75-kg/4-lb piece boned and rolled gammon
1 litre/1¾ pints dry cider
Topping
100 g/4 oz demerara sugar
1 tablespoon dry mustard
melted butter
Spiced peaches
425-g/15-oz can peach halves
25 g/1 oz demerara sugar

¼ teaspoon ground cinnamon
2 tablespoons peach syrup
4 tablespoons cider vinegar
few cocktail cherries and watercress to garnish

American
4-lb rolled ham roast

4¼ cups dry cider
Topping
½ cup light brown sugar
1 tablespoon dry mustard
melted butter
Spiced peaches
15-oz can peach halves

2 tablespoons light brown sugar
¼ teaspoon ground cinnamon
3 tablespoons peach syrup
⅓ cup cider vinegar
few cocktail cherries and watercress to garnish

Before cooking, soak the bacon joint in cold water overnight. Next day, drain and put in a large pan. Add the cider and enough fresh cold water to cover. Bring to the boil, cover and simmer, allowing 20 minutes per 0·5 kg/1 lb. When cooked remove from pan, cool slightly and peel off skin.

Mix together the sugar and mustard, pat over the fat surface of the gammon and score diagonally in diamond shapes. Put the joint in a meat tin and cover the lean parts of the meat with foil. Brown in a hot oven (220°C, 425°F, Gas Mark 7) for about 15 minutes. Brush with a little melted butter during browning to give a rich golden colour.

Drain the peaches, reserving the syrup. In a large shallow pan dissolve the sugar with the cinnamon, peach syrup and vinegar. Add the peach halves, cut sides downwards; cover and poach gently for 15 minutes. Secure peaches with a cocktail stick over the bacon joint and spear with a halved cocktail cherry. Place remainder on the serving dish and garnish with watercress. Serve hot or cold.

Note Take care to simmer bacon joints slowly. Rapid boiling causes shrinkage and toughens the meat fibres.

Serves 8–10

Rabbit Bonne Femme

Metric/Imperial	American
1 rabbit, jointed	1 rabbit, jointed
100-g/4-oz piece bacon or gammon	¼ lb side of bacon or ham
1 tablespoon vinegar	1 tablespoon vinegar
40 g/1½ oz butter or bacon dripping	3 tablespoons butter or bacon drippings
100 g/4 oz button mushrooms	1 cup button mushrooms
6–8 small onions, peeled	6–8 small onions, peeled
25 g/1 oz flour	¼ cup all-purpose flour
450 ml/¾ pint stock	2 cups stock
1 teaspoon salt	1 teaspoon salt
pepper	pepper
0·5 kg/1 lb small or new potatoes	1 lb small potatoes

Soak the rabbit and bacon overnight in cold water with the vinegar. Dry the rabbit and bacon with kitchen paper or a cloth. Cut the bacon into fingers, removing any rind. Melt the butter or dripping in a saucepan and brown the rabbit and bacon quickly in this. Lift out and set aside.

Cook the whole mushrooms and onions in the pan for 3 minutes. Toss to brown evenly. Sprinkle the flour into the pan and when well mixed remove pan from heat and gradually add the stock, stirring well to make a smooth thin sauce. Season with salt and pepper and return meat and any meat juices to pan. Cover and simmer gently for 40 minutes. Add the peeled or scraped potatoes to the pan, cover and continue cooking until potatoes are tender, about 15–25 minutes.

To freeze Cook completely for 1 hour omitting potatoes. When thawed, reheat adding boiled or drained canned new potatoes; simmer gently for 5 minutes and serve.
Note Fresh rabbits are best from October to February, but frozen rabbits are available all year round. Rabbit bought from a butcher can be jointed for you, but frozen rabbit from a large supermarket may be unjointed. To joint a frozen rabbit, first thaw. Then cut off back legs through joints. Cut two large pieces off the back cutting through flesh and snapping through the joints of the backbone. Cut the remaining back with forelegs attached into two using heavy kitchen scissors and cutting just to one side of the backbone.

Serves 4

Sweetbreads Vichy

Metric/Imperial	American
0·75 kg/1½ lb sweetbreads	1½ lb sweetbreads
225 g/8 oz carrots	½ lb carrots
1 onion	1 onion
20 g/¾ oz butter	3 tablespoons butter
50 ml/2 fl oz sherry	¼ cup sherry
450 ml/¾ pint stock	2 cups stock
1 teaspoon salt	1 teaspoon salt
pepper	pepper
2 teaspoons cornflour	2 teaspoons cornstarch
4 tablespoons double cream	⅓ cup whipping cream

Soak the sweetbreads in cold water for 1 hour. Place in a pan of clean water, bring to the boil and drain. Rinse in cold water. Pull off any outer skin or membranes with fingers. Cut the carrots into 6-cm/2½-inch lengths, slice lengthwise and cut slices into matchsticks. Slice the onion.

Melt the butter in a saucepan and fry the onion until golden. Add the carrots and sherry and simmer for 1 minute. Pour on the stock, return sweetbreads to pan, and season. Cover and simmer for 20 minutes. Blend the cornflour with a little of the cooking liquor and pour into the pan, stirring well to thicken sauce evenly. Bring to the boil and simmer for 1 minute; stir in the cream and heat through before serving.

To freeze Freeze before thickening sauce with cornflour and cream. Thaw and reheat, finishing sauce just before serving.
Note Sweetbreads are one of the most easily digested meats. For a lighter meal, replace the cream with milk.

Serves 4

Lambs' Tongues Seville

Metric/Imperial	American
1 onion	1 onion
1 carrot	1 carrot
1 tablespoon salad oil	1 tablespoon salad oil
25 g/1 oz flour	¼ cup all-purpose flour
450 ml/¾ pint beef stock	2 cups beef stock
2 teaspoons redcurrant jelly	2 teaspoons red currant jelly
salt and pepper	salt and pepper
pinch rosemary	pinch rosemary
175 g/6 oz green grapes	1¼ cups white grapes
50 g/2 oz split almonds	½ cup slivered almonds
450-g/1-lb can lambs' tongues	1-lb can lambs' tongues
Potato purée	**Mashed potato**
0·75 kg/1½ lb potatoes	1½ lb potatoes
4 tablespoons milk	⅓ cup milk
25 g/1 oz butter	2 tablespoons butter
salt and pepper	salt and pepper
½ teaspoon grated orange rind	½ teaspoon grated orange rind

Finely dice the onion and carrot, place in a saucepan with the oil and cook until slightly shrivelled but not brown. Add the flour and cook to a rich brown. Pour on the stock and add the redcurrant jelly, seasoning and rosemary. Simmer slowly for 20 minutes. Meanwhile peel the grapes if the skins are tough and remove pips if any. Keep in a covered container. Soak the almonds in warm water and cut each into three sticks. Boil the potatoes.

Strain the sauce; do not sieve. Slice the lambs' tongues in half. Add to sauce with their jelly and simmer gently for 10 minutes. Drain and mash the potatoes with milk and butter, season and flavour with orange rind. Arrange potato purée down the centre of the serving dish in a long mound. Lift out lambs' tongues and arrange along this mound. Add the grapes and almonds to the sauce, bring to the boil and spoon over the lambs' tongues just before serving.

To freeze Freeze strained sauce without the addition of meat, grapes and almonds. Thaw and reheat adding the lambs' tongues.
Note Fresh lambs' tongues may be used but must first be cooked, skinned and freed of bone. Almonds lose their crispness if in the sauce for more than 1 minute.

Serves 4

Sherried kidneys

Sherried Kidneys

Metric/Imperial	**American**
12 lambs' kidneys	12 lambs' kidneys
1 large onion	1 large onion
50 g/2 oz butter	1/4 cup butter
50 g/2 oz mushrooms	1/2 cup mushrooms
20 g/3/4 oz flour	3 tablespoons all-purpose flour
1 clove garlic	1 clove garlic
225 ml/8 fl oz water	1 cup water
1 beef stock cube	1 beef bouillon cube
175 ml/6 fl oz dry sherry	3/4 cup dry sherry
1 bay leaf	1 bay leaf
salt and pepper	salt and pepper
1 tablespoon chopped parsley and grilled bacon rolls to garnish	1 tablespoon chopped parsley and grilled bacon rolls to garnish

Remove fat and skin from kidneys, then cut in half lengthwise and remove the cores. Finely chop the onion. Melt half the butter in a pan and fry the onion slowly until pale brown and soft. Add the halved kidneys and mushrooms and cook for about 2 minutes on each side until the kidneys are firm and just turning brown. Remove from pan and keep hot.

Melt the remaining butter in the pan and blend in the flour. Peel the clove of garlic and add with the water, stock cube and sherry, blending until smooth. Add the bay leaf and season to taste. Bring to the boil, stirring, and simmer until the sauce has thickened.

Return the onion, kidneys and mushrooms to the pan, cover and simmer for 5 minutes or until the kidneys are just cooked. Remove bay leaf and garlic clove. Turn into a serving dish and sprinkle with parsley. Garnish with grilled bacon rolls and serve with a good red wine.

Serves 4

Tripe and Cow-heel

Metric/Imperial
1 kg/2 lb tripe
1 cow-heel
600 ml/1 pint milk
1 teaspoon salt
1 bay leaf
0·5 kg/1 lb onions
225 g/8 oz carrots
Sauce
50 g/2 oz butter
25 g/1 oz flour
1 clove garlic, crushed
2 teaspoons chopped parsley
  (optional)
1 teaspoon vinegar
2 teaspoons Worcestershire
  sauce
pepper

American
2 lb tripe
1 cow-heel
2½ cups milk
1 teaspoon salt
1 bay leaf
1 lb onions
½ lb carrots
Sauce
¼ cup butter
¼ cup all-purpose flour
1 clove garlic, crushed
2 teaspoons chopped parsley
  (optional)
1 teaspoon vinegar
2 teaspoons Worcestershire
  sauce
pepper

Cut tripe and cow-heel into 3·5-cm/1½-inch squares, discarding cow-heel bone. Place in a large pan, cover with cold water and bring to the boil. Simmer for 5 minutes and drain. Add the milk to the pan with salt and bay leaf, simmer gently for 1¼ hours, then add the quartered onions and thickly sliced carrots. Continue cooking for 45 minutes.

To make the sauce: melt the butter in a pan, stir in the flour and remove from heat. Carefully blend in the liquid from the tripe. Bring to the boil and simmer for 2 minutes. Remove bay leaf and add tripe, cow-heel, vegetables, garlic and parsley to the sauce. Stir in the vinegar, Worcestershire sauce and pepper.

This dish freezes well.

Note Use thick seam tripe if available. Cow-heel should be purchased already prepared. Stock can be substituted for the milk.

Serves 4–6

Tripe and cow-heel

Roasts

When roasting a joint it is important to consider the cut of meat. The cheaper cuts of roasting meat should certainly be roasted slowly. If the meat is frozen, to get the best results thaw it slowly in the refrigerator before cooking. For the weekend joint this often takes about 24 hours.

Before roasting weigh the meat, including any stuffing of course, then calculate the cooking time from the chart below. If covered with foil for part of the cooking time remember either to increase the oven temperature or to cook for a little longer.

Stand the joint on a trivet or rack in the roasting tin. Put one tablespoon of fat or fresh dripping in the meat tin. Brush the joint over with oil or rub with a butter paper. Sprinkle with salt and pepper and baste the meat with fat from time to time during cooking.

Roasting Times

Beef

Oven roast (200°C, 400°F, Gas Mark 6)
For smaller joints: 15 minutes per 0·5 kg/1 lb plus 15 minutes.
For thicker joints: 20 minutes per 0·5 kg/1 lb plus 20 minutes.
For larger boned joints: 25 minutes per 0·5 kg/1 lb plus 25 minutes.
Slow roast (160°C, 325°F, Gas Mark 3)
For smaller joints: 30 minutes per 0·5 kg/1 lb plus 20 minutes.
For thicker joints: 35 minutes per 0·5 kg/1 lb plus 25 minutes.
For larger boned joints: 40 minutes per 0·5 kg/1 lb plus 30 minutes.

Serve with Yorkshire pudding (see page 96), made mustard, Horseradish cream sauce (see page 97) and Thin gravy (see page 96).

Veal

Oven roast (200°C, 400°F, Gas Mark 6)
For joints with bone: 25 minutes per 0·5 kg/1 lb plus 25 minutes.
For boned joints: 30 minutes per 0·5 kg/1 lb plus 30 minutes.
Slow roast (160°C, 325°F, Gas Mark 3)
For joints with bone: 50 minutes per 0·5 kg/1 lb plus 50 minutes.

Veal is best covered while roasting. Remove cover for the last 30 minutes so that the meat can brown.
Serve with Gravy (see page 96), Parsley and thyme stuffing (see page 97), roast potatoes or rice and mushrooms.

above Roast top rump of beef

below Roast veal

Roast chicken with chestnut stuffing

opposite Roast lamb

Pork

Oven roast (220°C, 425°F, Gas Mark 7 for 20 minutes to crisp crackling; 200°C, 400°F, Gas Mark 6 for remaining cooking time)
For joints with bone: 30 minutes per 0·5 kg/1 lb plus 30 minutes.
For boned joints: 35 minutes per 0·5 kg/1 lb plus 35 minutes.
Slow roast Not suitable.

To prepare Have your butcher score the fat deeply. For really crisp crackling rub the scored fat with dry mustard, brush liberally with oil or fat and sprinkle with salt.
Serve with Apple sauce (see page 97), Sage and onion stuffing (see page 97) and Thick gravy (see page 96).

Lamb

Oven roast (200°C, 400°F, Gas Mark 6)
For small or thin joints, e.g. shoulder: 20 minutes per 0·5 kg/1 lb plus 20 minutes.
For thicker joints: 25 minutes per 0·5 kg/1 lb plus 25 minutes.
For boned larger joints: 30 minutes per 0·5 kg/1 lb plus 30 minutes.
Slow roast (160°C, 325°F, Gas Mark 3)
For small or thin joints: 30 minutes per 0·5 kg/1 lb plus 30 minutes.
For thicker joints: 35 minutes per 0·5 kg/1 lb plus 35 minutes.
For boned larger joints: 45 minutes per 0·5 kg/1 lb plus 45 minutes.

Serve with Mint sauce (see page 96) or redcurrant jelly, Parsley and thyme stuffing (see page 97), Thin gravy (see page 96) and potatoes.

Chicken

Oven roast (200°C, 400°F, Gas Mark 6) for 15 minutes per 0·5 kg/ 1 lb.
Slow roast (160°C, 325°F, Gas Mark 3) for 20–22 minutes per 0·5 kg/1 lb.
Baste occasionally.

To prepare It is essential to allow the chicken to thaw completely if it has been frozen. Fill the centre cavity with stuffing or put in a sprig of herbs and a large knob of butter and cover the breast with bacon rashers.
Serve with bacon rolls, small chipolata sausages, chestnut or Parsley and thyme stuffing (see page 97), bread sauce, Thin gravy (see page 96) and watercress.

Duck

Oven roast (200°C, 400°F, Gas Mark 6) for 15 minutes per 0·5 kg/ 1 lb.
Slow roast Not suitable.

To prepare Stuff the duck with Sage and onion stuffing (see page 97) at the tail end. A duckling does not need stuffing. Prick the duck all over with a sharp pronged fork, rub with butter paper and sprinkle with salt and pepper.
Serve with watercress, peas, Apple sauce (see page 97), Thin gravy (see page 96), roast potatoes and Orange salad (see page 97).

Goose

Oven roast (200°C, 400°F, Gas Mark 6) for 15 minutes per 0·5 kg/ 1 lb plus 15 minutes.
Slow roast (180°C, 350°F, Gas Mark 4) for 25–30 minutes per 0·5 kg/1 lb.
Baste frequently. Cover with buttered greaseproof paper until the last 30 minutes.

To prepare Stuff with Sage and onion stuffing (see page 97) or .veal forecemeat stuffing. Sprinkle the goose with salt and spread with a little fat.
Serve with Giblet gravy (see page 96) and Apple (see page 97), gooseberry or cranberry sauce.

Turkey

Oven roast (180°C, 350°F, Gas Mark 4)
For birds 6·75 kg/15 lb and under: 15 minutes per 0·5 kg/1 lb plus 15 minutes.
For birds 6·75 kg/15 lb or over: 12 minutes per 0·5 kg/1 lb plus 12 minutes.
Cover loosely with foil for the first part of the cooking time; for the last 30–40 minutes remove foil to allow browning.

Serve with Thin gravy (see page 96), chipolata sausages, bacon rolls, chestnut or Parsley and thyme stuffing (see page 97), cranberry sauce, bread sauce and watercress.

Grouse

Grouse are in season from August to December.

Oven roast (200°C, 400°F, Gas Mark 6 for 15–45 minutes according to age).

To prepare Hang as for pheasants. Very young birds may be eaten after 2 days. One bird will serve 1–2 persons.
   Pluck, draw and truss the bird. Put a knob of butter, seasoned with salt and pepper, inside the bird and place it on a slice of toast in a meat tin. Put a rasher of bacon over the breast.
   Remove the bacon about 10 minutes before the end of cooking time. Dredge the breast with flour and return the bird to the oven to brown. Serve it on the toast on which it has been cooked.
Serve with Thin gravy (see page 96), bread sauce, fried breadcrumbs, watercress, potato crisps or straw potatoes.

Guinea Fowl

Oven roast (200°C, 400°F, Gas Mark 6) for 15 minutes per 0·5 kg/l lb.
Slow roast (160°C, 325°F, Gas Mark 3) for 20–22 minutes per 0·5 kg/l lb.
Baste occasionally.

To prepare Hang for about 4 days as for pheasants. Guinea fowl are usually served unstuffed. Put a rasher of bacon over the breast to keep the flesh from drying out. A fowl will serve 3–4 persons while a chick will serve only two persons.
Serve with bacon rolls, small chipolata sausages, Thin gravy (see page 96) and watercress.

Roast goose with cranberry sauce

Pheasant

Pheasants are in season from October to February.

Oven roast (220°C, 425°F, Gas Mark 7 for 10 minutes, then reduce to 200°C, 400°F, Gas Mark 6)
For a young bird: 30–40 minutes in all.
For a larger bird: 40–60 minutes.
Baste frequently.

To prepare After being shot the bird should hang in a cool airy larder for about 1 week, depending on the weather and how high you like the pheasant to be. Pluck and draw it before cooking.

Place a piece of butter inside the bird and season the inside with salt, pepper and lemon juice. Truss the bird, cover the breast with bacon rashers and place it on a trivet inside a meat tin. About 10 minutes before the end of cooking time remove the rashers from the breast, dredge with flour and return the bird to the oven.

Serve with watercress, game chips, chipolata sausages, bread sauce, Thin gravy (see below), cranberry sauce, redcurrant jelly, green salad, Orange salad (see opposite) or stuffed oranges.

Roast pheasants

Classic Accompaniments to Roasts

Yorkshire Pudding

Metric/Imperial	American
100 g/4 oz plain flour	1 cup all-purpose flour
¼ teaspoon salt	¼ teaspoon salt
1 egg	1 egg
300 ml/½ pint milk and water, mixed	1¼ cups milk and water, mixed

Sift the flour and salt into a bowl. Make a well in the centre of the flour and blend in the egg with a little of the milk and water, using a small wire whisk to make a smooth paste. Blend in enough of the remaining milk and water to make a batter the consistency of double or heavy pouring cream. Beat well.

Put a little fat or dripping from the roast into the bottom of a shallow Yorkshire pudding tin or 12-hole deep patty tin. Put the tin into a hot oven (220°C, 425°F, Gas Mark 7) to melt the fat. Remove from the oven and pour in the batter. Cook a large pudding for about 30 minutes or small puddings for about 15 minutes until well risen and golden brown. Serve at once.

Serves 4–6

Gravy

Remove the roast meat from the meat tin when it is cooked, then carefully pour away any fat so that only the sediment from the meat remains in the tin.

Thin gravy
Put about 300 ml/½ pint (US 1¼ cups) of stock preferably (for birds use the giblet stock) or water used in cooking the vegetables into the meat tin and bring to boiling point. Simmer until it has reduced by half, scraping the sediment from the bottom of the tin as the stock is simmering. Add plenty of salt and pepper and a few drops of gravy browning if required.

Thick gravy
Leave 1 tablespoon of fat in the meat tin and blend in 1–2 tablespoons flour depending on how thick you like the finished gravy to be. Cook this roux over a low heat, stirring constantly and scraping the sediment from the bottom of the tin until the roux is light brown.

Blend in about 300 ml/½ pint (US 1¼ cups) of stock or liquid from the cooked vegetables, bring to boiling point and simmer for 2–3 minutes. Add gravy browning to give a good colour and plenty of salt and pepper. Strain the gravy into a gravy boat and serve at once.

Makes approx. 300 ml/½ pint (US 1¼ cups)

Mint Sauce

Metric/Imperial	American
4–5 sprigs of mint	4–5 sprigs of mint
2 teaspoons castor sugar	2 teaspoons sugar
1 tablespoon boiling water	1 tablespoon boiling water
1–2 tablespoons vinegar	1½–2 tablespoons vinegar

Wash and dry the mint well, then strip the leaves from the stems and chop finely. Put the sugar in a sauce boat with the boiling water and stir until the sugar has dissolved. Add the chopped mint and vinegar to taste. Add more sugar if liked.

Makes approx. 100 ml/4 fl oz (US ½ cup)

Horseradish Cream Sauce

Metric/Imperial	American
fresh horseradish root	fresh root horseradish
4 tablespoons double cream or ½ small can condensed milk	⅓ cup whipping cream or ½ small can condensed milk
salt and pepper	salt and pepper
1 tablespoon lemon juice or vinegar	1 tablespoon lemon juice or vinegar
castor sugar	sugar

Wash and scrape the horseradish and grate 1 tablespoon very fine flakes (or use grated horseradish from a jar). Lightly whip the cream and add to the grated horseradish, stir in the seasoning and lastly the lemon juice or vinegar. Blend thoroughly and, if cream is used, add a little sugar. Chill before serving.

Note A prepared horseradish cream may be used instead.

Makes approx. 150 ml/¼ pint (US ⅔ cup)

Apple Sauce

Metric/Imperial	American
0·5 kg/1 lb cooking apples	1 lb baking apples
50 ml/2 fl oz water	¼ cup water
juice of ½ lemon	juice of ½ lemon
25 g/1 oz butter	2 tablespoons butter
sugar to taste	sugar to taste

Peel, core and slice the apples into a pan with the water and lemon juice. Cover the pan and cook the apples until soft, then remove the lid and beat the apples with a wooden spoon until they are smooth. Add the butter, then sugar as liked.

Pour the sauce into a sauce boat and serve cold. If it is being served with goose, duck or pork the sauce should be tart.

Note If you are in a hurry use canned apple purée or sauce.

Makes approx. 450 ml/¾ pint (US 2 cups)

Orange Salad

Metric/Imperial	American
3 large oranges	3 large oranges
½ teaspoon made mustard	½ teaspoon prepared mustard
1 teaspoon castor sugar	1 teaspoon sugar
pinch pepper	pinch pepper
½ teaspoon salt	½ teaspoon salt
50 ml/2 fl oz salad oil	¼ cup salad oil
1 tablespoon white wine or cider vinegar	1 tablespoon white wine or cider vinegar
1 tablespoon orange juice	1 tablespoon orange juice

Peel one orange very thinly, removing just the outside zest. Shred this finely and simmer in a little water for 3–4 minutes, until tender, then drain.

With a small sharp knife remove the peel and outside white pith from all the oranges. Slice each in very thin slices on a plate so as to catch any juice. Arrange the slices in a shallow glass dish and scatter with the tender, finely shredded orange peel.

Make a dressing by mixing the mustard, sugar, pepper and salt together and slowly working in the oil, then the vinegar and orange juice saved from the oranges. Spoon the dressing over the orange slices and leave to marinate in a cool place for 1 hour before serving.

Note Serve with duck or pheasant.

Serves 6

Sage and Onion Stuffing

Metric/Imperial	American
2 large onions	2 large onions
15–25 g/½–1 oz butter	1–2 tablespoons butter
100 g/4 oz fresh white breadcrumbs	2 cups fresh white bread crumbs
2 teaspoons sage	2 teaspoons sage
1 teaspoon salt	1 teaspoon salt
½ teaspoon freshly ground black pepper	½ teaspoon freshly ground black pepper

Peel the onions, put into a pan of cold water, bring to boiling point and simmer for 20 minutes, until tender. Drain well and chop, then add the remaining ingredients and mix well.

Note Use for stuffing goose, duck or pork.

Makes approx. 225 g/8 oz (US 3 cups)

Parsley and Thyme Stuffing

Metric/Imperial	American
50 g/2 oz suet, shredded	¼ cup chopped suet
100 g/4 oz fresh white breadcrumbs	2 cups fresh white bread crumbs
2 tablespoons chopped parsley	3 tablespoons chopped parsley
½ teaspoon dried mixed herbs	½ teaspoon dried mixed herbs
finely grated rind of 1 lemon	finely grated rind of 1 lemon
salt and pepper	salt and pepper
1 egg, beaten	1 egg, beaten

Mix together the suet and breadcrumbs in a bowl. Add the parsley, herbs and lemon rind. Season the mixture well with salt and pepper and add enough beaten egg to bind it together.

Note Use for stuffing veal, lamb, chicken or turkey, and also for savoury forcemeat balls.

Makes approx. 225 g/8 oz (US 2 cups)

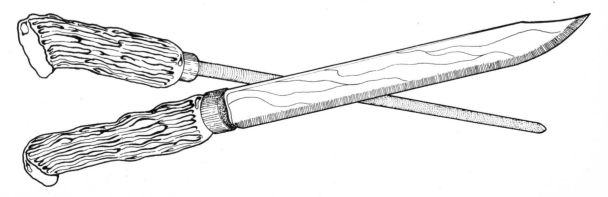

Roast Lamb with Oranges and Herbs

Roast lamb with apricot cups

Metric/Imperial	American
1·75-kg/4-lb boned shoulder of lamb	4-lb boneless lamb shoulder
1 medium onion	1 medium onion
25 g/1 oz butter	2 tablespoons butter
75 g/3 oz fresh white breadcrumbs	1½ cups fresh white bread crumbs
2 tablespoons chopped fresh mixed herbs	3 tablespoons chopped fresh mixed herbs
2 oranges	2 oranges
1 egg, beaten	1 egg, beaten
salt and pepper	salt and pepper
40 g/1½ oz dripping	3 tablespoons drippings
25 g/1 oz flour	¼ cup all-purpose flour
300 ml/½ pint stock	1¼ cups stock
1 rounded tablespoon redcurrant jelly	2 tablespoons red currant jelly

Spread out the boned lamb into an oblong and trim off any excess fat. Peel and finely chop the onion. Melt the butter in a small pan, add the onion and cook until soft but not browned, stir in the white breadcrumbs and herbs, and remove from the heat.

Grate the rind from one orange and squeeze the juice from both. Add the rind to the stuffing mixture with the beaten egg and just sufficient orange juice to bind, reserving the rest. Season to taste. Spread the stuffing over the meat, roll up and tie securely.

Heat the dripping in a meat tin in a moderate oven (180°C, 350°F, Gas Mark 4), put in the meat, and roast until cooked, about 2 hours, basting as required.

Remove the meat and place on a warm serving dish. Strain off all but 2 (US 3) tablespoons of the dripping, stir in the flour and cook for 1–2 minutes. Add the stock, reserved orange juice and redcurrant jelly and bring to the boil, stirring. Adjust seasoning, pour into a gravy boat and serve with the lamb.

Variation

Roast Lamb with Apricot Cups Drain a 425-g/15-oz can of apricot halves and reserve the syrup. Omit the oranges from the recipe and substitute three chopped apricot halves for the orange rind in the stuffing; use 2 tablespoons (US 3 tablespoons) lemon juice to bind.

Fill all but three of the remaining apricot halves with some of the stuffing rolled up into balls and bake round the lamb for the last 45 minutes of cooking time, brushing well with the fat from the meat. Brush the joint with some of the reserved apricot syrup when basting.

When making the gravy, substitute the remaining apricot syrup for the orange juice. Garnish the meat with the last three apricot halves.

Serves 6–8

98

Roast Saddle of Lamb

Metric/Imperial	American
saddle of lamb	saddle of lamb (see description below)
50 g/2 oz dripping	¼ cup drippings
2 sprigs of rosemary	2 sprigs of rosemary
salt and pepper	salt and pepper
Gravy	**Gravy**
2 tablespoons meat fat	3 tablespoons meat fat
25 g/1 oz flour	¼ cup all-purpose flour
300 ml/½ pint stock	1¼ cups stock
1 teaspoon redcurrant jelly	1 teaspoon red currant jelly
salt and pepper	salt and pepper
2 tablespoons sherry	3 tablespoons sherry

This cut is the two loins together from ribs to tail. Ask the butcher to cut the weight of meat you would like for your guests. For six take a saddle of spring lamb weighing 2–3 kg/4½–7 lb or a half full saddle of young mutton, which can weigh up to 4·5 kg/10 lb. The kidneys are sometimes sent attached to the saddle and may be roasted and served with the joint, a slice being served with each portion, or they may be removed and used for another dish.

Roast the joint in a large meat tin in a moderately hot oven (190°C, 375°F, Gas Mark 5), allowing 25 minutes per 0·5 kg/ 1 lb plus 25 minutes. Before putting it in the oven spread it with dripping, tuck the two sprigs of rosemary under the joint to give added flavour, and sprinkle with salt and pepper. Start roasting the joint with a piece of foil or greaseproof paper over it. Remove after 30 minutes; this prevents excessive browning. Serve with gravy and Mint sauce (see page 96) on a bed of vegetables, with rice handed separately.

To make the gravy: strain off all but 2 (US 3) tablespoons of the fat from the meat tin. To this add the flour and cook over direct heat in the meat tin for a few minutes until the flour is golden brown, stirring all the time with a wooden spoon. Remove from the heat and slowly add the stock; return to the heat, bring to the boil and allow to thicken, stirring all the time. Add the redcurrant jelly and seasoning with the sherry.

Note This is an expensive joint but well worth having for a special occasion.

Serves 6

Roast Lamb Lyonnaise

Metric/Imperial	American
0·75 kg/1½ lb potatoes	1½ lb potatoes
225 g/8 oz onions	½ lb onions
50 g/2 oz dripping	¼ cup drippings
1·5 kg/3 lb leg of lamb	3 lb leg of lamb
salt and pepper	salt and pepper
1–2 cloves garlic	1–2 cloves garlic

Peel the potatoes and cut into 1-cm/½-inch thick slices. Peel and slice the onions. Arrange the onions in a heavy ovenproof dish and put the potatoes, overlapping slightly, on top.

Spread the dripping over the lamb and season with salt and pepper. Cut the garlic into small pieces and insert into the fat of the lamb. Place the joint on top of the potatoes.

Roast in a moderate oven (180°C, 350°F, Gas Mark 4), allowing 30 minutes per 0·5 kg/1 lb plus 30 minutes. Baste occasionally. Remove the joint and place on a serving dish. Surround with the potatoes and onions.

Note If preparing this dish well in advance keep potato slices covered with cold water until the joint is about to go into the ovenproof dish which will keep the potato slices from browning too quickly.

Serves 6

Stuffed shoulder of lamb

Stuffed Shoulder of Lamb

Metric/Imperial	American
Stuffing	**Stuffing**
75 g/3 oz long-grain rice	⅓ cup long-grain rice
15 g/½ oz butter	1 tablespoon butter
1 onion, chopped	1 onion, chopped
1 clove garlic, crushed	1 clove garlic, crushed
75 g/3 oz lamb's liver, chopped	3 oz lamb's liver, chopped
1 tablespoon chopped parsley	1 tablespoon chopped parsley
1 teaspoon rosemary	1 teaspoon rosemary
50 g/2 oz raisins	⅓ cup raisins
1 small egg	1 small egg
2 tablespoons chutney	3 tablespoons chutney
½ teaspoon salt	½ teaspoon salt
pepper	pepper
1·5 kg/3 lb boned shoulder of lamb	3 lb boneless lamb shoulder
25 g/1 oz dripping	2 tablespoons drippings

Boil the rice for 12 minutes or until just tender; drain.

Melt the butter in a pan, add the onion and garlic and cook gently until golden, then stir in the liver and cook quickly for 1 minute. Turn into a bowl and add the rice and all the remaining stuffing ingredients. Stir to combine them well. When cold stuff into the lamb, close openings with skewers to hold the stuffing in place, and tie securely.

Lay the shoulder flat in a roasting tin with the dripping and roast in a moderately hot oven (200°C, 400°F, Gas Mark 6) for 1½ hours. Serve with a variety of vegetables and a gravy made from the juices from the roasting tin.

To freeze Freeze stuffing only. Use thawed stuffing to stuff meat just before cooking.
Note If the "pocket" in the lamb seems too small when the shoulder bone is removed, enlarge the inside using a small sharp knife so that the stuffing will not creep out during roasting.

Variation An alternative stuffing can be made from the chopped lamb's liver fried with 75 g/3 oz (US 5 slices) chopped bacon and 100 g/4 oz (US 1 cup) chopped mushrooms.

Serves 6

Remove the lamb and place on a warm serving dish. Strain off all but 2 (US 3) tablespoons of fat from the roasting tin. Stir in the flour and cook for 2–3 minutes to brown. Add the apricot syrup to the stock and if necessary make up to 450 ml/¾ pint (US 2 cups) with more stock; add to the pan and bring to the boil, stirring, then simmer for 3–4 minutes. Season to taste. A little gravy browning may be added if necessary. Serve with the stuffed breasts of lamb.

Note Only a very little dripping is needed when roasting this joint as it is fatty and makes its own dripping.

Variation Substitute 225 g/8 oz (US 1 cup) sausagemeat for half the breadcrumbs in the stuffing, and omit the egg. Garnish with tomatoes hollowed out and filled with peas, and sautéed mushroom caps.

Serves 6

Crown Roast of Lamb

Metric/Imperial	American
1 kg/2 lb potatoes	2 lb potatoes
225 g/8 oz onions	½ lb onions
1 teaspoon salt	1 teaspoon salt
crown roast of lamb prepared by the butcher	crown roast of lamb prepared by the butcher
salt and pepper	salt and pepper
40 g/1½ oz butter	3 tablespoons butter
baked tomatoes, peas, artichoke hearts and chopped parsley to garnish	baked tomatoes, peas, artichoke hearts and chopped parsley to garnish

Grease a meat tin and butter a generous 1-litre/2-pint (US 2½-pint) straight sided ovenproof dish. Peel the potatoes and onions and slice thinly. Put them into a pan, cover with cold water, add 1 teaspoon salt and bring to boiling point. Boil for 1 minute then drain in a colander.

Put the crown roast in the greased tin. Layer the potato and onion slices inside the crown, starting and finishing with a layer of potato. Season each layer with salt and pepper. Press down the filling to get as much as possible in, as it will shrink slightly during cooking. Dot with some of the butter. Continue to layer the remaining potato and onion in the buttered oven-proof dish.

Cover the top of each cutlet bone with foil to prevent burning during cooking. Roast the crown in the centre of a moderately hot oven (190°C, 375°F, Gas Mark 5) for 2 hours with the dish of potatoes and onions on the shelf below. Add a little more butter to the top of the potatoes during cooking if necessary.

To serve, carefully put the crown on to a serving dish and garnish with baked tomatoes, peas, artichoke hearts and parsley round the meat. When carving, remove the string with a sharp knife and then slice down between each bone, giving two chops to each person with a spoonful of the potato and onion mixture from the centre. Hand the dish of potatoes and onions separately.

Serve with Mint sauce (see page 96) and Thin gravy (see page 96).

Note The crown looks particularly special if cutlet frills are put on the tops of the bones after removing the foil. To bake tomatoes, make two cuts crosswise in the rounded end of the tomatoes, place them on a buttered dish and put in the oven below the lamb for the last 10 minutes of cooking time.

Variation Substitute 225 g/8 oz (US 1 cup) rice, boiled in salted water, to fill the centre of the crown roast after baking: place carefully on a bed of rice and fill with the remaining rice, sprinkled with parsley.

Serves 6–7

opposite Crown roast of lamb

Baked lamb with apricots and mint

Baked Lamb with Apricots and Mint

Metric/Imperial	American
3 breasts of lamb	3 pieces breast of lamb
1 large onion	1 large onion
40 g/1½ oz butter	3 tablespoons butter
100 g/4 oz fresh brown breadcrumbs	2 cups fresh brown bread crumbs
1 tablespoon chopped fresh mint	1 tablespoon chopped fresh mint
227-g/8-oz can apricots	8-oz can apricots
1 egg	1 egg
salt and pepper	salt and pepper
15 g/½ oz dripping	1 tablespoon drippings
25 g/1 oz flour	¼ cup all-purpose flour
300 ml/½ pint stock	1¼ cups stock

Skin and bone the breasts of lamb or ask the butcher to do this for you. Trim them to an even size if necessary.

Peel and finely chop the onion, melt the butter in a pan and add the onion, cover and cook gently until soft but not brown, about 5–10 minutes. Remove the pan from the heat and stir in the breadcrumbs and mint. Drain the apricots, reserve the syrup and roughly chop the fruit. Beat the egg, add to the stuffing mixture with the chopped fruit and season to taste.

Divide the stuffing in half and place one half on one of the breasts of lamb, cover with another breast and spread with the remaining stuffing. Cover with the last breast of lamb, skin side uppermost, and tie securely. Place in a roasting tin with the dripping and roast in a moderate oven (180°C, 350°F, Gas Mark 4) for about 1¼–1½ hours, allowing 30 minutes per 0·5 kg/1 lb.

Traditional pot roast

Roast Fillet of Beef with Mustard Cream Sauce

Metric/Imperial	**American**
0·75 kg/1½ lb beef fillet	1½ lb rump or sirloin steak
1 clove garlic	1 clove garlic
salt and pepper	salt and pepper
50 g/2 oz butter	½ cup butter
1 tablespoon salad oil	1 tablespoon salad oil
100 ml/4 fl oz stock	½ cup stock
2 rounded teaspoons Dijon mustard	2 rounded teaspoons Dijon mustard
50 ml/2 fl oz brandy	¼ cup brandy
150 ml/¼ pint double cream	⅔ cup whipping cream

Ask your butcher to cut the piece of meat from the thick end of the fillet and ask for a thin piece of fat the size of the fillet. Trim away any sinews and skin from the meat. Crush the clove of garlic and rub over the fillet, season well, cover with the piece of fat and tie in place.

Put the fillet in a roasting tin with the butter and oil and roast in a moderately hot oven (200°C, 400°F, Gas Mark 6), allowing about 15 minutes per 0·5 kg/1 lb, until cooked to your liking. Remove the meat and place on a serving dish, remove the string and fat and keep warm.

Strain off the fat from the pan, add the stock and boil rapidly for 2 minutes, until slightly reduced. Add the mustard and remove from the heat, stir in the brandy and cream and pour over the beef. Serve at once.

Serves 4

Traditional Pot Roast

Metric/Imperial	American
2 onions	2 onions
2 carrots	2 carrots
1–2 parsnips	1–2 parsnips
3 outside sticks celery	3 outside stalks celery
1 kg/2 lb topside of beef	2 lb beef round
flour to coat	all-purpose flour to coat
25 g/1 oz dripping	2 tablespoons drippings
salt and pepper	salt and pepper
bay leaf	bay leaf
150 ml/¼ pint stock	⅔ cup stock
15 g/½ oz cornflour	2 tablespoons cornstarch
2 tablespoons cold water	3 tablespoons cold water

Peel and quarter or slice onions and peel and slice carrots. Peel the parsnips and cut into 1-cm/½-inch pieces, wash and slice the celery.

Wipe the meat and roll in flour. Melt the dripping in a large pan and fry the meat until brown on all sides. Lift out of the pan and put aside. Add all the vegetables to the pan and fry for 2–3 minutes to brown. Season well, add bay leaf and place the meat back on top of the vegetables. Add just sufficient stock to cover the vegetables. Cover and simmer gently, allowing 30 minutes per 0·5 kg/1 lb plus 30 minutes. Extra stock may be added if necessary.

Remove the meat and place on a serving dish, strain the vegetables and spoon round. Make the cooking liquor up to 450 ml/¾ pint (US 2 cups) if necessary and return to the pan. Blend the cornflour with the cold water and stir in a little of the hot stock, blend well and return to the pan. Bring to the boil, stirring all the time. Adjust seasoning, pour into a sauce boat and serve with the pot roast and vegetables.

Note If liked, add more vegetables such as three quartered tomatoes and 75 g/3 oz (US ¾ cup) chopped mushrooms, and also 50 g/2 oz (US 3 slices) chopped streaky bacon.

Serves 6

Roast Chicken with Corn and Pepper Stuffing

Metric/Imperial	American
50 g/2 oz long-grain rice	¼ cup long-grain rice
1 large onion	1 large onion
25 g/1 oz butter	¼ cup butter
½ green pepper	½ green pepper
50 g/2 oz sweetcorn kernels	⅓ cup corn kernels
½ beaten egg	½ beaten egg
salt and pepper	salt and pepper
1·5-kg/3½-lb roasting chicken	3½-lb roasting chicken

Cook the rice in boiling salted water until tender, about 12 minutes, rinse well and drain. Peel and finely chop the onion. Melt the butter in a small saucepan, add the onion and cook for 5–10 minutes until soft but not brown.

Finely chop the pepper and place in a small pan, just cover with cold water and bring to the boil; drain immediately. Add to the onion with the rice, sweetcorn, egg and seasoning and mix well. Stuff the mixture into the neck end of the chicken, tuck the flap of skin down and secure.

Roast in a moderate oven (180°C, 350°F, Gas Mark 4) for 1¼ hours or until tender, basting well.

Serves 4–6

Hereford Roast Chicken

Metric/Imperial	American
1·75-kg/4-lb roasting chicken	4-lb roasting chicken
50 g/2 oz butter	½ cup butter
350 g/12 oz onions	¾ lb onions
175 g/6 oz streaky bacon	9 slices bacon
40 g/1½ oz flour	⅓ cup all-purpose flour
450 ml/¾ pint water	2 cups water
1 chicken stock cube	1 chicken bouillon cube
gravy browning	gravy browning
2–3 tablespoons sherry (optional)	3–4 tablespoons sherry (optional)
salt and pepper	salt and pepper

Place the chicken in a roasting tin, cover the breast with butter and roast in a moderate oven (180°C, 350°F, Gas Mark 4) for 1 hour, basting well.

Drain off the juices from the tin and reserve. Take 2 (US 3) tablespoons of the fat and place in a large frying pan. Peel and roughly chop the onions, remove the rind and bone from the bacon and cut in small pieces; fry in the fat with the onions for 5 minutes. Stir in the flour and cook for 1 minute. Add the water and stock cube and bring to the boil, stirring. Add a little gravy browning, sherry if liked and seasoning if necessary. Pour the gravy and chicken juices round the chicken in the roasting tin and return to the oven for a further 30 minutes or until the chicken is tender. The juices from the chicken will mix in with the gravy. Place the chicken on a serving dish and spoon the gravy over.

Serves 6

French Roast Chicken

Metric/Imperial	American
1·5-kg/3½-lb roasting chicken with giblets	3½-lb roasting chicken with giblets
40 g/1½ oz butter	3 tablespoons butter
small bunch fresh mixed herbs	small bunch fresh mixed herbs
300 ml/½ pint chicken stock or 300 ml/½ pint water and 1 stock cube	1¼ cups chicken stock or 1¼ cups water and 1 bouillon cube
25 g/1 oz cornflour	¼ cup cornstarch
1 tablespoon cold water	1 tablespoon cold water

Wipe the chicken inside and out and place two-thirds of the butter and the bunch of herbs inside.

Put the chicken in a roasting tin and cover the breast with the remaining butter, and place a piece of greaseproof paper on top. Pour the stock round the chicken and add the giblets.

Put in a moderate oven (180°C, 350°F, Gas Mark 4) and cook for about 30 minutes, remove the paper and turn the chicken to allow it to brown on its side. Cook for a further 45 minutes, turning every 15 minutes until done.

Remove the chicken and place on a warm serving dish. Blend the cornflour with the cold water and stir into the stock in the roasting tin. Bring to the boil, stirring, and simmer for 2 minutes. A little gravy browning may be added if necessary. Strain into a sauce boat and serve with the chicken.

Serves 4–5

Duck à l'Orange

Metric/Imperial	American
1 duck	1 duck
butter	butter
salt and pepper	salt and pepper
Orange sauce	**Orange sauce**
2 tablespoons duck fat	3 tablespoons duck fat
25 g/1 oz flour	¼ cup all-purpose flour
50 ml/2 fl oz port	¼ cup port
300 ml/½ pint giblet stock	1¼ cups giblet stock
salt and pepper	salt and pepper
2 large oranges	2 large oranges
1 tablespoon redcurrant jelly	1 tablespoon red currant jelly

Prick the duck all over with a sharp pronged fork, rub with butter paper and sprinkle the breast with salt and pepper. Put into a large meat tin and roast in a moderately hot oven (200°C, 400°F, Gas Mark 6), basting occasionally. Allow 15 minutes per 0·5 kg/1 lb.

When the duck is cooked remove it from the meat tin and keep hot on a serving dish.

Measure the fat into a small saucepan and add the flour; cook gently until it is pale golden brown. Remove the pan from the heat and slowly add the port and stock, stirring well. Add seasoning, return to the heat and allow to thicken. Bring to the boil and reduce the sauce by one-third.

Thinly peel the orange rinds, reserving a few slices for decoration, shred the peel finely and simmer in water for 3 minutes until tender. Drain, then add to the sauce with the juice of the oranges, the redcurrant jelly and the juices from the roasting tin, being careful to add none of the fat. The juices should amount to about 3 tablespoons (US ¼ cup).

Allow the redcurrant jelly to dissolve, adjust seasoning and add a little gravy browning if liked. Serve in a sauce boat with the duck, garnished with the orange slices.

Serves 4–6

Roast Pork Fillet

Metric/Imperial	American
0·5-kg/1-lb piece pork fillet	1-lb piece pork tenderloin
1 onion	1 onion
0·5 kg/1 lb pork sausagemeat	1 lb pork sausagemeat
1 tablespoon chopped fresh herbs	1 tablespoon chopped fresh herbs
salt and pepper	salt and pepper
100 g/4 oz streaky bacon	6 slices bacon
15 g/½ oz flour	2 tablespoons all-purpose flour
300 ml/½ pint stock	1¼ cups stock

Trim the pork. Chop the onion very finely and place in a bowl with the sausagemeat, herbs and seasoning; mix well. Turn on to a floured surface and pat out the sausagemeat to a rectangle about 33 × 18 cm/13 × 7 inches. Place the pork fillet in the centre and wrap the sausagemeat around to cover the fillet; seal the edges.

Place in a roasting tin. Remove the rind and bone from the bacon, cut each rasher in half and lay over the roll. Roast in a moderately hot oven (190°C, 375°F, Gas Mark 5) for 50–60 minutes. Remove and place on a serving dish.

Drain off all but 1 tablespoon of the fat from the roasting tin. Stir in the flour and cook for 2 minutes. Add the stock and bring to the boil, stirring, and simmer for 2 minutes more. Season to taste and add a little gravy browning if necessary. Pour into a gravy boat and serve with the pork fillet.

Note Pork fillet cooked in this way may be left to become cold and served sliced with salad.

Serves 6

Leida's Pork with Fruit

Metric/Imperial	American
100 g/4 oz dried prunes	⅔ cup dried prunes
100 g/4 oz dried apricots	⅔ cup dried apricots
½ teaspoon mixed spice	½ teaspoon mixed spice
grated rind and juice of 1 orange	grated rind and juice of 1 orange
300 ml/½ pint dry white wine	1¼ cups dry white wine
25 g/1 oz butter	2 tablespoons butter
1 tablespoon salad oil	1 tablespoon salad oil
1·75-kg/4-lb piece spare rib of pork without the skin	4-lb piece boned pork ribs without the skin
25 g/1 oz soft brown sugar	2 tablespoons soft brown sugar
300 ml/½ pint stock	1¼ cups stock
2 large cooking apples	2 large baking apples
15 g/½ oz cornflour	2 tablespoons cornstarch
1 tablespoon water	1 tablespoon water

Place the prunes, apricots, spice, orange rind and juice in a bowl. Add the wine, cover and leave to stand overnight.

Melt the butter and oil in a large frying pan, add the pork and fry, turning frequently, until it is lightly browned all over. Remove from the pan and place in a large ovenproof casserole. Pour over the soaked fruit and sprinkle over the sugar, pressing it into the fat. Add the stock, cover the casserole and cook in a moderate oven (180°C, 350°F, Gas Mark 4) for 1½–1¾ hours or until the pork is tender, basting occasionally.

Remove from the oven; skim off and discard any fat. Peel, core and slice the apples, add to the casserole, and return to the oven for 10–15 minutes until the apples are tender but not mushy.

Lift the meat on to a serving dish. Blend the cornflour with the water, stir into the sauce and cook for 1–2 minutes or until thickened. Serve the meat cut in slices with a little sauce spooned over and hand the remainder separately.

Serves 8

Bistro Pâté (to use up roast pork)

Metric/Imperial	American
350 g/12 oz fatty leftover cooked pork	¾ lb fatty leftover cooked pork
225 g/8 oz chicken livers	½ lb chicken livers
1 small onion	1 small onion
1–2 cloves garlic	1–2 cloves garlic
4 tablespoons brandy	⅓ cup brandy
1 teaspoon salt	1 teaspoon salt
freshly ground black pepper	freshly ground black pepper

Coarsely chop or mince the pork, chicken livers and onion and place in a large bowl. Crush the garlic and add with the brandy and seasoning, mix thoroughly and turn into a 0·5-kg/1-lb loaf tin or terrine. Cover with a piece of foil or lid and stand in a meat tin with about 2·5 cm/1 inch of hot water in the bottom. Cook in the centre of a moderate oven (180°C, 350°F, Gas Mark 4) for 1½ hours. Remove from the oven and leave to become quite cold.

Turn out and serve as a first course with French bread or toast and butter, or as a main course with salad.

Serves 6

Roast stuffed pork

Roast Stuffed Veal

Metric/Imperial
Stuffing
rind and juice of 1 small
  lemon
100 g/4 oz calves' or pig's
  liver
1 small onion
15 g/½ oz butter
0·5 kg/1 lb pork sausagemeat
100 g/4 oz fresh white
  breadcrumbs
1 egg
1 teaspoon rosemary
1½ tablespoons chopped
  parsley
1 teaspoon salt
pinch pepper

1·75-kg/4-lb piece boned
  shoulder of veal
salt and pepper
lard

American
Stuffing
rind and juice of 1 small
  lemon
¼ lb calves' or pork liver

1 small onion
1 tablespoon butter
1 lb pork sausagemeat
2 cups fresh white
  bread crumbs
1 egg
1 teaspoon rosemary
2 tablespoons chopped
  parsley
1 teaspoon salt
pinch pepper

4-lb boneless shoulder of veal

salt and pepper
shortening

To make the stuffing: grate the lemon rind and reserve the juice. Finely chop or mince the liver, peel and finely chop the onion. Melt the butter in a small pan and sauté the liver and onion for 2–3 minutes. Thoroughly mix the sausagemeat, breadcrumbs, lemon rind and egg and combine with the chopped liver and onion mixture; add the herbs and seasoning.

Lay the meat out on a board, splitting where necessary to flatten to an oblong shape. Spread with the stuffing, leaving 5 cm/2 inches clear down one side to allow for spreading and rolling up the joint. Roll tightly, securing with skewers, and tie neatly with string at 1·5-cm/¾-inch intervals. Place on a square of foil in a meat tin, pour over the reserved lemon juice, season and spread with lard. Lightly seal the foil. Cook in a moderately hot oven (200°C, 400°F, Gas Mark 6) allowing 30 minutes per 0·5 kg/1 lb plus 30 minutes.

Remove the foil for the last 20 minutes to brown and crisp the top.

Note Serve with redcurrant jelly if liked, and for a really delicious gravy add 50 ml/2 fl oz (US ¼ cup) port or red wine to the stock left in the tin.

The liver, sausage and parsley stuffing makes the joint more interesting if you are having it cold the next day.

Variation
Roast Stuffed Pork This stuffing is equally delicious with a boned loin of pork. Bake uncovered in a hot oven (220°C, 425°F, Gas Mark 7) for the first 20 minutes to crisp the crackling, then reduce the heat to moderately hot (200°C, 400°F, Gas Mark 6), allowing a total cooking time of 35 minutes per 0·5 kg/1 lb plus 35 minutes. Garnish with rosemary.

Serves 6

Monday Curry

(to use up roast meat)

Metric/Imperial
25 g/1 oz butter
1 large onion
2 sticks celery
1 tablespoon curry powder
25 g/1 oz flour
450 ml/¾ pint stock or gravy
  from the joint
1 tablespoon tomato purée
1 rounded tablespoon mango
  chutney
350 g/12 oz leftover cooked
  lamb, pork or beef
salt

American
2 tablespoons butter
1 large onion
2 stalks celery
1 tablespoon curry powder
¼ cup all-purpose flour
2 cups stock or gravy from the
  joint
1 tablespoon tomato paste
1 rounded tablespoon mango
  chutney
1½ cups leftover cooked lamb,
  pork or beef
salt

Melt the butter in a pan, peel and chop the onion and slice the celery, add to the butter and cook gently for about 10 minutes or until the onion is soft. Stir in the curry powder and cook for 2–3 minutes, add the flour and mix well.

Stir in the stock or gravy and bring to the boil, stirring; add the tomato purée and chutney, cover and simmer for about 30 minutes. Add the cooked meat cut in neat pieces, salt to taste and simmer for a further 10 minutes. Serve with plain boiled rice and side dishes (see page 163).

Serves 4

Preserves

Wash bottling jars in hot soapy water and rinse in clear hot water. Do not dry but leave upside down to drain. Place clean screw-tops and new kilner lids into a bowl. Pour over a kettle of boiling water to scald. Drain off water and leave.

After the jars are filled and the tops screwed down, the jars will cool and a vacuum form inside. The kilner lid 'pops' and becomes concave instead of domed upwards in the centre. This shows the jars are correctly sealed and may be labelled and stored for at least 1 year without the fruit deteriorating. Any jars which have not become concave should not be stored but used within 1 week.

Manufacturers advise new kilner lids to be used each time, and packets of replacements are available. It is possible to re-use lids if they are pressed to dome upwards again, but there is a much greater risk of jars not sealing properly, because the rubber on the lid may have perished or come unstuck. Jars can be used repeatedly unless cracked or chipped and screw-tops may also be used again if kept dry and free of rust inside.

To open jars unscrew the tops. It may be necessary to dip them in hot water first. To remove lid twist a coin between the edge of the lid and the ridge of the jar.

Tests for the set of jam
1. The pan and contents should weigh the recommended yield of jam, plus weight of pan.
2. The jam should have reached 105°C/220°F on a cooking thermometer.
3. Two teaspoonfuls of jam cooled on a saucer should have a wrinkled skin if a finger is drawn through.

Preserving and bottling

Bottled Black Cherries with Orange

Metric/Imperial	American
4·5–5·5 kg/10–12 lb black cherries	10–12 quarts Bing cherries
rind of 2 oranges	rind of 2 oranges
2·25 litres/4 pints water	5 pints water
0·75 kg/1½ lb granulated sugar	3 cups granulated sugar

Wash the cherries and discard any bad ones.

Remove stalks and stone the cherries using a cherry stoner, reserving any juice that runs from the fruit. If a cherry stoner is not available use the slightly cupped tip of a swivel potato peeler to lift out the stones. It is not essential to stone cherries before bottling but it is helpful when you come to use them. Pack cherries into jars quite tightly to within 2 cm/¾ inch of the tops of the jars.

Remove rind from oranges with a potato peeler so that no pith is removed. Place orange rind, water and sugar in a pan with any juice from the cherries. Bring very slowly to the boil, stirring to help the sugar dissolve and gain maximum flavour from the orange rind. When boiling, quickly fill jars to within 1 cm/½ inch of the top. Add extra boiling water if there is insufficient syrup. Place lids on jars. Rest screw-tops in place but DO NOT SCREW DOWN as contents will expand in processing.

Stand jars in a large roasting tin containing 2·5 cm/1 inch of hot water on a low shelf in the oven and cook in a cool oven (150°C, 300°F, Gas Mark 2) until bubbles rise through the syrup, about 1¼–1¾ hours.

Remove jars carefully from the oven, one at a time, and immediately screw down tops very tightly. Wipe jars with a warm damp cloth to remove any syrup on the outsides of the jars. Leave to cool.

Yields 6 kg/12 lb (US 10 quarts)

Bottled Gooseberries with Elderflowers

Metric/Imperial	American
4–5 kg/9–11 lb gooseberries	5–7 quarts gooseberries
3 handfuls elderflowers	3 handfuls elder flowers
2·25 litres/4 pints boiling water	5 pints boiling water
0·75 kg/1¾ lb granulated sugar	3½ cups granulated sugar

Wash the gooseberries. Top and tail them using a knife so that a very little of the gooseberry skin is taken off. This saves pricking them to prevent shrivelling.

Pack the fruit tightly into jars. If there is a wide variety in size of fruit, grade by packing smallest and largest fruits in separate bottles.

Place the elderflowers in a pan. Pour on the measured boiling water. Cover pan and leave to infuse for 15 minutes. Strain off liquid and discard flowers. Bring flavoured water and sugar to the boil. Top up jars of gooseberries to within 1 cm/½ inch of the tops of the jars. Place lids on jars. Rest screw-tops in place but DO NOT SCREW DOWN yet. Stand jars in a roasting tin containing 2·5 cm/1 inch hot water and cook in a cool oven (150°C, 300°F, Gas Mark 2) until bubbles rise in the jars, the gooseberries have changed from green to greeny-yellow and the fruit has shrunk slightly and risen 5 mm–1 cm/¼–½ inch from bottoms of jars, about 1½–2 hours.

Screw lids down tightly as jars are removed from the oven.

Note Gooseberries bottled in this way with flavoured syrup can be opened and served immediately.

The elderflowers are from elder trees and bushes, which grow in hedgerows. The scented, cream-coloured clusters (umbels) are in flower when the first gooseberries are in season.

Gooseberries required for use in pies when they will have further cooking should not be given such a long processing. Cook for 1 hour only in the oven and label accordingly.

Yields 6 kg/12 lb (US 5 quarts)

Apricot Jam

Metric/Imperial	American
1 kg/2 lb dried apricots	5 cups dried apricots
scant 3 litres/5 pints boiling water	6 pints boiling water
2 tablespoons lemon juice	3 tablespoons lemon juice
2·75 kg/6 lb granulated sugar	12 cups granulated sugar

Choose very dark dried apricots, and not the pale, soft, sweet variety. Place the apricots in a large bowl and pour on the boiling water and lemon juice. Leave to soak for 48 hours. The fruit should be quite pulpy – if not, place in a covered pan or pressure cooker and stew until really soft. Add the sugar and stir well until dissolved, then bring to the boil and boil fast, uncovered, until it will set when tested, about 1–2 hours. Pour into warm, dry jars and cover.

Note Do not attempt to make this jam with pale dried apricots as the result is syrupy and disappointing. Stewing time will vary, depending on the variety of apricots used.

Yields 4·5 kg/10 lb (US 4 quarts)

Bramble Jelly

Metric/Imperial	American
1·5 kg/3 lb blackberries	3 quarts blackberries
1·5 kg/3 lb cooking apples	3 lb baking apples
generous 1 litre/2 pints water	2½ pints water
1·75–2·75 kg/4–6 lb granulated sugar	8–12 cups granulated sugar

Wash the blackberries and apples. Chop the apples roughly, discarding any bad parts but leaving in the core and peel. Place the fruit in a pan and almost cover with water. Cover pan with a lid and simmer slowly until soft and pulpy, about 40 minutes. Mash well with a potato masher to ensure that fruit is really soft. Strain through a jelly bag for at least 2 hours or overnight.

Measure quantity of juice and for each 600 ml/1 pint (US 2½ cups) allow 0·5 kg/1 lb (US 2 cups) sugar. Bring juice to the boil in the pan before adding the sugar, then stir well to make sure it is dissolved. Boil fast and remove any scum which forms with a slotted spoon. Boil until setting point is reached, 10–20 minutes. Pot and cover quickly.

Note A jelly bag may be made or improvised from close woven flannel, cotton or wool. It should be scalded with boiling water just before use. The piece of cloth may be laid in a large bowl, the fruit poured in and the corners gathered up and tied. A long spoon or stick threaded through the top of the bag can be supported on the rungs of an upturned stool with the bowl set underneath while straining.

Yields 3–4·5 kg/7–10 lb (US 2½–4 quarts)

Crab Apple Jelly

Metric/Imperial	American
2·75 kg/6 lb crab apples	6 lb crabapples
2·5 litres/4½ pints water	5½ pints water
1 heaped teaspoon cloves	1 rounded teaspoon cloves
4 tablespoons lemon juice	⅓ cup lemon juice
granulated sugar	granulated sugar

Lemon curd

Wash the crab apples and remove all stalks and leaves. Put in a large pan with the water, cloves and lemon juice and bring to the boil; simmer for 20–30 minutes or until the crab apples are soft. Remove from the heat, mash well and leave to stand for 20 minutes. Pour into two jelly bags and leave to strain overnight.

Measure the juice into a large pan, bring to the boil and add 0·5 kg/1 lb (US 2 cups) sugar for each 600 ml/1 pint (US 2½ cups) of juice. Allow the sugar to dissolve and then boil rapidly for about 10 minutes or until setting point is reached.

Remove pan from the heat and skim. Pour at once into clean warm jars and cover with waxed paper circles. Leave to cool, and then seal.

Yields 4–4·5 kg/9–10 lb (US 7–7½ quarts)

Lemon Curd

Metric/Imperial
3 lemons
225 g/8 oz castor sugar
100 g/4 oz butter
3 large eggs

American
3 lemons
1 cup granulated sugar
½ cup butter
3 large eggs

Very finely grate the lemon rind to remove as much of the yellow skin as possible but not the inner white pith, which is bitter. Put the rind, the juice from the lemons, the sugar and butter into a pan. Heat gently to dissolve sugar and melt butter until the sides of the pan are just too hot to touch but the juice is not boiling.

Whisk the eggs in a bowl. Pour in the lemon mixture. Stir well and return to the pan. Place the pan in a roasting tin containing hot water and return to the heat. Allow the water to simmer. Stir the lemon curd well round the sides and corners so that it thickens but does not boil, for about 10 minutes. When the lemon curd has the consistency of a thick coating sauce, pour into jars. Cover with waxed paper and a screw-top or snap-on lid. When cold store in refrigerator or a cool larder.

To freeze Freeze in waxed containers.
Note Keep jars in refrigerator once opened. Lemon curd is not like a true jam and will not keep more than 1–2 months.

Yields 0·75 kg/1½ lb (US 1 pint)

Seville and Satsuma Marmalade

Metric/Imperial	American
0·75 kg/1½ lb Seville oranges	1½ lb Seville oranges
1 kg/2 lb satsumas	2 lb tangerines
juice of 2 lemons	juice of 2 lemons
scant 1·5 litres/2½ pints water	3 pints water
2·75 kg/6 lb granulated sugar	12 cups granulated sugar

Pressure cook the washed, whole unpeeled fruit with lemon juice and water for 40 minutes, or place in a pan with a tight-fitting lid and simmer for 2–2½ hours until the fruit skins are really soft. There should be 600–900 ml/1–1½ pints (US 2½–4 cups) liquid in the pan. The fruit should pierce easily with a fork and disintegrate if pinched firmly. Allow fruit to cool, then cut into quarters. Take out all the pips and add these to the liquid in the pan. Simmer for 15 minutes.

Meanwhile finely shred the fruit with a stainless steel knife. Put into a bowl and strain on the juice from the pips. Discard pips and return fruit peel, pulp and juices to pan. Add the sugar, stir well to dissolve and then bring to the boil. Remove any scum which rises to the top with a slotted spoon. Boil rapidly, stirring occasionally, for about 20 minutes until the marmalade will set if tested.

Leave marmalade to cool in pan for 3 minutes so that the peel does not rise to the top of the jar when potted. Ladle into clean, warm, dry jars. Cover with waxed paper, wax side down, and leave until cold. Finally cover pots with cellophane covers and screw-tops or snap-on plastic lids.

To freeze Marmalade keeps well so is not normally frozen but as Seville oranges are in season for such a short time, freeze these in bags. When making marmalade with frozen oranges use a slightly generous weight of fruit for best results. Do not thaw fruit – cook from frozen.

Note Satsumas and tangerines do not contain much acid or pectin to make a well set marmalade, but can be combined with Seville oranges or lemons with good results. Check the recommended quantity of liquid for the cooked fruit. Reduce by boiling fast before adding sugar, or add water if more than 150 ml/¼ pint (US ⅔ cup) below recommended level. Cooking with sugar for too long spoils the flavour and texture. Jelly bags can be used to strain out the peel for Seville and satsuma jelly.

Yields 4·5 kg/10 lb (US 4 quarts)

Mint Sauce Concentrate

Metric/Imperial	American
150 ml/¼ pint malt vinegar	⅔ cup malt vinegar
150 g/5 oz granulated sugar	⅔ cup granulated sugar
1 kg/2 lb mint, finely chopped	4 cups finely chopped mint

Bring the vinegar and sugar slowly to the boil. Simmer for 2 minutes. Stir the mint into the pan of vinegar and just bring to the boil stirring all the time.

Turn into screw-top jars with a gap of not less than 1 cm/½ inch below the rims. Wipe the tops of the jars and screw down tightly. Stand jars in cold water to cool quickly. Store up to 1 year until required.

Note Pick mint in June or July before flowering, and you will have a second crop in early autumn. Mint sauce should not come into contact with a metal lid because it includes vinegar. To use as mint sauce: add extra water, lemon juice or vinegar to 1–2 tablespoons of concentrate for the desired consistency. Serve with roast lamb. Or use the concentrated sauce to flavour new potatoes, carrots or peas.

Yields 0·75 kg/1½ lb (US 3 cups)

Apple and Rhubarb Chutney

Metric/Imperial	American
1·5 kg/3½ lb cooking apples	3½ lb baking apples
900 ml/1½ pints vinegar	2 pints vinegar
0·5 kg/1 lb rhubarb	1 lb rhubarb
225 g/8 oz stoned dates	1¼ cups pitted dates
25 g/1 oz pickling spice	¼ cup pickling spice
1 tablespoon ground ginger	1 tablespoon ground ginger
1 teaspoon mixed spice	1 teaspoon mixed spice
2 tablespoons salt	3 tablespoons salt
1 kg/2 lb soft dark brown sugar	4 cups soft dark brown sugar

Wash and chop the apples, put in a pan with the vinegar, cover and simmer for 20 minutes until soft and pulpy. Rub through a sieve to separate pips and peel from apple pulp. Return apple purée to the pan, add chopped rhubarb and dates and simmer for 10 minutes.

Meanwhile grind the pickling spice in a pepper mill or electric grinder, or place in a thick polythene bag and crush with a hammer. Add the ground spice with all remaining ingredients to the pan and simmer for 20 minutes. Pot and cover while very hot with a plastic or screw-top (not cellophane).

Note If windfall apples and late summer rhubarb are used this can be a very cheap chutney to make. It has a very good flavour even if not matured before use. Sieving apples after cooking saves peeling time and gives a nuttier flavour.

Yields 4 kg/9 lb (US 7 quarts)

Marrow and Apple Chutney

Metric/Imperial	American
1 kg/2 lb prepared marrow	2 lb prepared summer squash
1 kg/2 lb prepared cooking apples	2 lb prepared baking apples
225 g/8 oz onions, sliced	½ lb onions, sliced
1–2 red peppers, chopped	1–2 red peppers, chopped
350 g/12 oz sultanas	2 cups seedless raisins
900 ml/1½ pints vinegar	2 pints vinegar
0·75 kg/1½ lb soft light brown sugar	3 cups soft light brown sugar
1 tablespoon ground ginger	1 tablespoon ground ginger
1 tablespoon cayenne pepper	1 tablespoon cayenne pepper
2 tablespoons salt	3 tablespoons salt

Peel, seed or core and dice the marrow and apples, then weigh. Place in a large pan with the sliced onions, chopped deseeded peppers, sultanas and vinegar. Bring to the boil and simmer for 30 minutes. Add the remaining ingredients, stirring in the sugar well, then simmer for a further 30 minutes.

Stir occasionally as the chutney is liable to stick after the sugar is added. Pour into jars and cover while very hot with a plastic or screw-top (not cellophane).

Note Choose mature, thick skinned marrow if possible as these contain less water. The flavour of the chutney improves on keeping, so store for 2 months before use if possible. Make sure the chutney does not come in contact with a metal lid. If plastic or lined metal lids are not available, do not fill the jars too full and protect the contents from the lids by lining with waxed paper.

Yields 3·5 kg/8 lb (US 6 quarts)

Three Fruit Marmalade

Metric/Imperial
1·75 kg/4 lb citrus fruit
   including:
   2 lemons
   2–3 grapefruit
   4–6 oranges
1·75 litres/3 pints water
3·5 kg/8 lb granulated sugar

American
4 lb citrus fruit
   including:
   2 lemons
   2–3 grapefruit
   4–6 oranges
4 pints water
16 cups granulated sugar

Wipe fruit and cut into quarters. Remove and reserve all pips. Place pips on a square of muslin or cotton and tie up to form a bag. Put in a large pan.

With a serrated knife cut out the flesh of all fruits, then cut up roughly and add to pan. Coarsely mince the peel or very finely shred with a knife (the latter is much more laborious). Add peel and water to the pan. Pressure cook for 40 minutes or bring to the boil in a tightly covered pan and simmer for 2 hours, or until peel is very tender when pinched. Remove bag of pips.

When peel is cooked the contents of the pan should weigh about 2·75 kg/6 lb. Add the sugar – you may need a larger pan at this stage. Bring to the boil and remove any scum with a slotted spoon. Simmer for about 20 minutes or until marmalade will set when tested. Pot and cover.

Note If peel is more coarsely cut it may need up to a further 20 minutes (if pressure cooked) or 1 hour (if boiled) to become tender. To help speed cooking of the peel, the prepared fruit and peel may be pre-soaked overnight in the water in a plastic, glass or china bowl (but not in a metal container).

Yields 6 kg/13 lb (US 10 quarts)

Three fruit marmalade

Christmas mincemeat

Christmas Mincemeat

Metric/Imperial
225 g/8 oz raisins
225 g/8 oz currants
225 g/8 oz sultanas
100 g/4 oz mixed peel
350 g /12 oz cooking apples
350 g/12 oz soft dark brown
  sugar
1 lemon
225 g/8 oz shredded suet
100 ml/4 fl oz brandy
pinch mixed spice

American
1½ cups raisins
1½ cups currants
1½ cups seedless raisins
¾ cup candied peel
¾ lb baking apples
1½ cups soft dark brown
  sugar
1 lemon
1½ cups chopped suet
½ cup brandy
pinch mixed spice

Wash the raisins, currants and sultanas unless pre-washed fruit is used. If using large raisins, chop them. Place all these fruits in a large bowl. Add the chopped or coarsely grated mixed peel.

Peel the apples and grate coarsely, mix with the other fruits and quickly mix in the sugar. Finely grate the lemon rind, and add with the suet, juice of the lemon, brandy and spice to the fruits. Stir very well. Leave to stand in a large bowl for 1 hour, stir again, then pack tightly into screw-top jars. Store for 1 month to 1 year before use.

Note For the best flavour choose large raisins, removing seeds if not already deseeded. Choose also whole caps of candied orange and lemon. These will need coarse grating before use. An extra grated apple per 0·5 kg/1 lb (US 2 cups) may be mixed in when making into mince pies to make a juicy filling, but it should not be added before storing or the mincemeat may ferment.

Allow approx. 0·5 kg/1 lb (US 2 cups) mincemeat and a 0·5-kg/1-lb quantity of pastry per 24 mince pies.

Yields 1·5 kg/3½ lb (US 4 quarts)

Apple and Mint Jelly

Metric/Imperial
1·5 kg/3 lb cooking apples
1 lemon
900 ml/1½ pints water
granulated sugar
1 bunch of mint
green colouring

American
3 lb baking apples
1 lemon
2 pints water
granulated sugar
1 bunch of mint
green food coloring

Wash the fruit and slice the apples and lemon including peel, core and pips. Place in a pan with the water, cover and simmer slowly for 30 minutes or until very soft and the apples are pulpy. Mash the fruit well with a potato masher. Tip into a jelly bag or cloth. Strain for at least 2 hours or overnight.

Measure the strained juice and for each 600 ml/1 pint (US 2½ cups) allow 0·5 kg/1 lb (US 2 cups) sugar. Place the sugar and the juice in the pan. Reserve two spoonfuls of the most tender mint leaves. Tie the remainder in a bunch and lower into the juice and sugar. Bring to the boil and boil fast until setting point is reached, 5–20 minutes.

Lift out the bunch of mint and discard. Colour the jelly lightly with a few drops of green colouring. Add reserved mint leaves, very finely chopped, and stir into jelly. Continue to stir jelly until it begins to thicken slightly and the mint no longer floats on the surface or sinks to the bottom. Pot quickly and cover with waxed paper only until cool. When cold cover with screw-top lids or cellophane covers.

Note Mint jelly should be potted in small jars (50–100-g/ 2–4-oz size) so that once opened it is quickly used, as it does not keep well afterwards.

Yields 1·5 kg/3 lb (US 2 quarts)

Home baking

The tempting smell of freshly baked bread, cakes or biscuits must surely be one of the most satisfying aromas in any kitchen. In this chapter are recipes for Victoria sandwich cake and Swiss rolls, gingerbread and Christmas cake, brandy snaps and chocolate brownies, as well as the ever popular white and wheatmeal breads, hot cross and Chelsea buns, lardy cake and doughnuts.

Baking is not difficult when the methods involved become part of a familiar process, and after trying out some of these delicious breads you can confidently go on to your own variations on scones, savoury teabreads or fruity shortbread.

When you serve a few of the baked goodies in this chapter, you can be assured that your family will be asking for more.

Victoria Sandwich

Metric/Imperial
100 g/4 oz butter
100 g/4 oz castor sugar
2 large eggs, lightly beaten
100 g/4 oz self-raising flour

American
½ cup butter
½ cup sugar
2 large eggs, lightly beaten
1 cup all-purpose flour sifted
    with 1 teaspoon baking
    powder

Filling and topping
2 tablespoons strawberry jam
50 ml/2 fl oz double cream
2–3 teaspoons icing
    sugar

Filling and topping
3 tablespoons strawberry jam
¼ cup whipping cream
2–3 teaspoons confectioners'
    sugar

Well grease two 15- or 18-cm/6- or 7-inch sandwich tins. Cream the butter and sugar until pale and creamy, then beat in the eggs. Sieve the flour and add 1 tablespoon with the last amount of egg to prevent it curdling. Fold in the rest of the flour with a metal spoon, then divide the mixture equally between the two tins.

Bake in a moderate oven (180°C, 350°F, Gas Mark 4) for 20 minutes. When the cake is cooked it should be pale golden in colour and shrinking away from the edge of the tin, and when lightly pressed with a finger should spring back into shape. Turn out to cool on a wire rack.

When completely cold, sandwich together with a layer of jam and a layer of cream and dust with icing sugar.

Note Leave the cake to cool in the tin for 5 minutes before turning out to allow shrinkage and therefore an easier removal from the tin.

Victoria sandwich

114

Chocolate Button Cake

Metric/Imperial	American
150 g/5 oz self-raising flour	1¼ cups all-purpose flour sifted with 1 rounded teaspoon baking powder
25 g/1 oz cocoa powder	¼ cup unsweetened cocoa
175 g/6 oz butter	¾ cup butter
175 g/6 oz castor sugar	¾ cup sugar
3 eggs, beaten	3 eggs, beaten
1–2 tablespoons milk	2–3 tablespoons milk
Buttercream	**Buttercream**
175 g/6 oz butter	¾ cup butter
175 g/6 oz icing sugar	1⅓ cups confectioners' sugar
50 g/2 oz chocolate powder	½ cup chocolate powder
25 g/1 oz chocolate buttons to decorate	3 tablespoons chocolate buttons to decorate

Line the base and sides of a 20-cm/8-inch cake tin with a double thickness of greaseproof paper and grease well. Sieve the flour and cocoa powder into a bowl and leave on one side. Cream the butter and sugar together until light and creamy. Gradually beat in the eggs adding 1 tablespoon of flour with the last addition. Fold in the flour and cocoa then stir in the milk. Turn into the prepared tin, smooth the top and bake in a moderate oven (180°C, 350°F, Gas Mark 4) for 50–60 minutes, until centre of cake springs back when pressed with a finger. Turn cake out on to a wire rack and leave to cool.

Beat the butter and icing sugar for the buttercream until light and fluffy. Beat in the chocolate powder.

When the cake is completely cold cut across into three. Sandwich layers together again with two-thirds of the buttercream. Spread top of cake with remaining buttercream and decorate with chocolate buttons.

Cherry Cake

Metric/Imperial	American
225 g/8 oz glacé cherries	1 cup candied cherries
75 g/3 oz self-raising flour	¾ cup all-purpose flour sifted with scant 1 teaspoon baking powder
75 g/3 oz plain flour	¾ cup all-purpose flour
pinch salt	pinch salt
175 g/6 oz butter	¾ cup butter
175 g/6 oz castor sugar	¾ cup sugar
finely grated rind of 1 lemon	finely grated rind of 1 lemon
3 eggs, beaten	3 eggs, beaten
75 g/3 oz ground almonds	¾ cup ground almonds
milk if necessary	milk if necessary

Grease an 18-cm/7-inch cake tin and line with greased greaseproof paper. Put the cherries in a sieve and rinse under running water. Drain well and dry very thoroughly on absorbent kitchen paper. Cut each cherry in half. Sieve the flours and salt together twice then toss the cherries in a little of the flour.

Cream the butter, sugar and lemon rind together until the mixture is pale and creamy. Add the eggs a little at a time, beating well after each addition and keeping the mixture stiff. Add 1 tablespoon of flour with the last amount of egg. Fold in the remaining flour, cherries and ground almonds, adding a little milk to make a fairly stiff dropping consistency; the stiff consistency will help the cherries remain suspended evenly in the cake while it is baking.

Turn the mixture into the prepared tin and bake in a moderate oven (180°C, 350°F, Gas Mark 4) until a skewer inserted in the centre of the cake comes out clean, about 1 hour 20 minutes.

Leave to cool in the tin for 5 minutes then turn out on to a wire rack to finish cooling; remove paper. When cold wrap in foil or store in an airtight tin.

Chocolate to decorate

Madeira Cake

Metric/Imperial	American
225 g/8 oz self-raising flour	2 cups all-purpose flour sifted with 2 teaspoons baking powder
¼ teaspoon salt	¼ teaspoon salt
100 g /4 oz butter	½ cup butter
150 g/5 oz castor sugar	⅔ cup sugar
2 eggs, beaten	2 eggs, beaten
few drops vanilla essence	few drops vanilla extract
approx. 50 ml/2 fl oz milk	approx. ¼ cup milk
3 slices citron peel	3 slices citron peel

Sift together the flour and salt and set aside. Cream the butter and sugar until soft and light. Gradually beat in the blended eggs and essence, adding a little flour with the last few additions. Using a metal spoon, fold in the remaining flour and enough milk to mix to a soft consistency.

Spoon the mixture into a greased and lined 15-cm/6-inch round deep cake tin. Bake in the centre of a moderate oven (180°C, 350°F, Gas Mark 4) for 50 minutes, then place the slices of peel gently on the top of the cake where the crack appears. Return to the oven for 10 minutes. When baked the cake should feel firm to the touch and a warmed skewer, pushed into the centre, should come out clean.

Allow the baked cake to cool for 5 minutes in the tin before cooling on a wire rack.

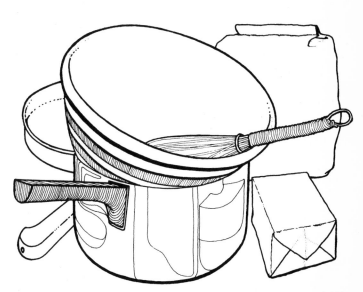

Orange Almond Cake

Coffee almond cake

Metric/Imperial	American
100 g/4 oz butter	$\frac{1}{2}$ cup butter
100 g/4 oz castor sugar	$\frac{1}{2}$ cup sugar
grated rind of 1 orange	grated rind of 1 orange
2 eggs, beaten	2 eggs, beaten
100 g/4 oz self-raising flour	1 cup all-purpose flour sifted with 1 teaspoon baking powder
approx. 1 tablespoon milk	approx. 1 tablespoon milk
75 g/3 oz almonds	$\frac{1}{2}$ cup almonds
Icing	Frosting
150 g/5 oz butter	$\frac{2}{3}$ cup butter
275 g/10 oz icing sugar	$2\frac{1}{2}$ cups confectioners' sugar
1 tablespoon orange juice	1 tablespoon orange juice

Grease two 18-cm/7-inch sandwich tins and line bases with circles of greased greaseproof paper. Cream the butter, sugar and orange rind until the mixture is pale and creamy. Beat in the eggs a little at a time; add 1 tablespoon of the flour with the last amount of egg to prevent curdling. Fold in the rest of the flour and enough milk to make a soft dropping consistency. Divide between the tins and bake in a moderate oven (180°C, 350°F, Gas Mark 4) for 15–20 minutes, until the cakes spring back when lightly pressed with a finger. Turn out and cool on a wire rack.

Blanch, sliver and lightly toast the almonds; take care not to do this too quickly otherwise the edges will overbrown and taste bitter. Gently brown under a medium grill, turning frequently.

Cream the butter for the icing until it is soft. Sieve the icing sugar and beat in with the orange juice. Sandwich cakes together with one-third of the buttercream icing. Spread remaining icing and scatter almonds over top and sides of the cake.

Variation

Coffee Almond Cake   For an equally delicious dessert cake, substitute 1 tablespoon coffee essence (US strong black coffee) for the grated orange rind in the cake mixture and another tablespoon for the orange juice in the icing.

Glacé Pineapple Ring

Metric/Imperial	American
225 g/8 oz self-raising flour	2 cups all-purpose flour sifted with 2 teaspoons baking powder
175 g/6 oz butter	$\frac{3}{4}$ cup butter
175 g/6 oz castor sugar	$\frac{3}{4}$ cup sugar
3 eggs, beaten	3 eggs, beaten
75 g/3 oz glacé cherries	$\frac{1}{3}$ cup candied cherries
25 g/1 oz glacé pineapple	2 tablespoons candied pineapple
50 ml/2 fl oz milk	$\frac{1}{4}$ cup milk
50–75 g/2–3 oz icing sugar for icing	$\frac{1}{2}$–$\frac{3}{4}$ cup confectioners' sugar for frosting

Well grease and flour a 21-cm/8$\frac{1}{2}$-inch ring mould. Sieve the flour into a bowl. In another bowl cream together the butter and sugar until pale and creamy. Beat the eggs and add a little at a time, beating well after each addition. Add 1 tablespoon of flour with the last amount of egg.

Quarter the cherries and chop the pineapple, reserving some for the topping, and fold into the mixture with the rest of the flour and the milk.

Turn into the prepared mould and bake in a moderate oven (180°C, 350°F, Gas Mark 4) for 50–60 minutes or until golden brown and shrinking away from the edges. Turn ring out and cool on a wire rack.

Mix the sieved icing sugar with enough warm water to make a thin glacé icing. Spread a layer on top of the ring and arrange the reserved pineapple and cherry pieces on top, then trickle the remaining icing down the sides and over the fruit. Leave to set.

Note   If glacé pineapple is not available use chopped almonds and raisins with the cherries in the mixture. Decorate with chopped almonds.

Peter's Chocolate Cake

Metric/Imperial	American
Cake	**Cake**
2 tablespoons milk	3 tablespoons milk
50 g/2 oz plain chocolate	2 squares semi-sweet chocolate
225 g/8 oz self-raising flour	2 cups all-purpose flour sifted with 2 teaspoons baking powder
1 tablespoon cocoa powder	1 tablespoon unsweetened cocoa
$\frac{1}{4}$ teaspoon salt	$\frac{1}{4}$ teaspoon salt
175 g/6 oz butter	$\frac{3}{4}$ cup butter
175 g/6 oz castor sugar	$\frac{3}{4}$ cup sugar
3 eggs	3 eggs
Filling	**Filling**
1 tablespoon hot water	1 tablespoon hot water
1 tablespoon cocoa powder	1 tablespoon unsweetened cocoa
50 g/2 oz butter	$\frac{1}{4}$ cup butter
75 g/3 oz icing sugar	$\frac{3}{4}$ cup confectioners' sugar
Icing	**Frosting**
50 ml/2 fl oz boiling water	$\frac{1}{4}$ cup boiling water
2 tablespoons cocoa powder	3 tablespoons unsweetened cocoa
$\frac{1}{2}$ teaspoon corn oil	$\frac{1}{2}$ teaspoon corn oil
225–250 g/8–9 oz icing sugar	$1\frac{3}{4}$–2 cups confectioners' sugar
8 walnuts	8 walnuts

Prepare two 20-cm/8-inch sandwich cake tins, the bases lined with discs of greaseproof paper. Oil the paper and sides of tins and dust out with flour.

Bring the milk to the boil in a small pan, remove from the heat, drop in the chocolate broken into small pieces, cover pan and leave without stirring for chocolate to melt. Shake occasionally. Sieve the flour, cocoa and salt together.

Cream the butter and gradually beat in the sugar until mixture is light. Whisk the eggs and beat into the butter mixture 1 tablespoon at a time keeping the mixture really stiff. Beat in 1 tablespoon of sieved flour if it begins to curdle, then continue adding egg. Fold cooled chocolate in with a metal spoon. Tip in the flour and cocoa and just fold in sufficiently to mix; do not overstir.

Divide the mixture between the tins, spreading it out a little (it is not necessary to flatten completely as mixture levels in cooking). Bake in a moderate oven (180°C, 350°F, Gas Mark 4) for 35 minutes until cake is springy in the centre when lightly pressed. Remove from the oven and leave in the tin for 1–2 minutes before turning out on to a wire rack to cool.

To make filling: stir the hot water into the cocoa to make a smooth paste. Beat the butter in a small bowl. Gradually beat in the icing sugar and lastly the cooled cocoa paste. Use all the filling to sandwich the cold cakes together, placing tops of cakes to the centre with flat base of cake on top to give a neat finish when iced.

To make icing: set the cake on a wire rack when completely ready to ice. Place rack on a clean table or board. Pour the water into a basin, stir in the cocoa and oil, and beat in the icing sugar a spoonful at a time. While warm pour over top of cake. Spread once over top of cake using a palette knife to remove surplus icing. Allow icing to trickle down sides; spread evenly round with knife, lifting up any icing that has dripped under rack. Dust walnuts lightly with icing sugar and press round top edge of cake before icing sets.

To freeze Leave walnuts unfrosted, open freeze finished cake and then pack in an airtight box to protect. Leave at room temperature to thaw, during which time any mottling on icing should disappear and condensation should dry off.

Note Do not move cake until icing is really set or it may crack. Lift on to a plate by slipping flat baking tray or fish slice underneath.

Coffee Ginger Cake

Metric/Imperial	American
4 eggs, beaten	4 eggs, beaten
75 g/3 oz castor sugar	6 tablespoons sugar
75 g/3 oz plain flour	$\frac{3}{4}$ cup all-purpose flour
Buttercream filling	**Buttercream filling**
350 g/12 oz icing sugar	$2\frac{2}{3}$ cups confectioners' sugar
1 tablespoon coffee essence	1 tablespoon strong black coffee
2 tablespoons rum	3 tablespoons rum
175 g/6 oz butter	$\frac{3}{4}$ cup butter
50 g/2 oz crystallised ginger	$\frac{1}{4}$ cup candied ginger
Icing	**Frosting**
175 g/6 oz icing sugar	$1\frac{1}{3}$ cups confectioners' sugar
1 tablespoon coffee essence	1 tablespoon strong black coffee
50 g/2 oz almonds	$\frac{1}{3}$ cup almonds

Grease two 19-cm/$7\frac{1}{2}$-inch straight sided sandwich tins and line bases with circles of greased greaseproof paper. Put the eggs and sugar in a bowl placed over a pan of hot water. Whisk until mixture is pale and mousse-like. Remove from the heat and carefully fold in the sieved flour. Divide the mixture between the tins and bake for 20–25 minutes in a moderately hot oven (190°C, 375°F, Gas Mark 5) until the centre of each sponge springs back when lightly pressed. Turn out and cool on a wire rack. Cut each cake into two layers.

Make the buttercream filling: sieve the icing sugar and stir in the coffee essence and rum. Cream the butter until it is soft, then gradually add the icing sugar mixture, beating well. Chop the ginger, mix with the filling and use to sandwich the cakes together. Thinly spread the sides.

Make a thick glacé icing with the sieved icing sugar, coffee essence and a little water. Use to cover top of cake. Blanch, chop and lightly toast almonds; press against sides of cake.

Marmalade Gingerbread

Metric/Imperial	American
175 g/6 oz self-raising flour	$1\frac{1}{2}$ cups all-purpose flour sifted with $1\frac{1}{2}$ teaspoons baking powder
1 teaspoon bicarbonate of soda	1 teaspoon baking soda
4 teaspoons ground ginger	4 teaspoons ground ginger
2 teaspoons mixed spice	2 teaspoons mixed spice
$\frac{1}{2}$ teaspoon salt	$\frac{1}{2}$ teaspoon salt
175 g/6 oz wholemeal flour	$1\frac{1}{4}$ cups wholewheat flour
350 g/12 oz golden syrup	1 cup corn syrup
175 g/6 oz butter	$\frac{3}{4}$ cup butter
100 g/4 oz soft brown sugar	$\frac{1}{2}$ cup soft brown sugar
3 tablespoons marmalade	4 tablespoons marmalade
2 eggs, beaten	2 eggs, beaten
200 ml/7 fl oz milk	$\frac{3}{4}$ cup milk

Grease and line a small roasting tin about 23 × 30 cm/9 × 12 inches with greased greaseproof paper. Sift together all dry ingredients except wholemeal flour and sugar, to ensure the bicarbonate of soda and spices are thoroughly mixed. Add wholemeal flour to dry ingredients.

Next melt the syrup and butter in a pan with the sugar and marmalade and heat gently until granules have dissolved. Leave to cool, then whisk eggs in the milk and pour into the cooled syrupy mixture and stir. Pour liquid on to dry ingredients and beat to a smooth thick batter.

Turn into prepared tin and bake in a moderate oven (160°C, 325°F, Gas Mark 3) until cooked when tested with a skewer, about $1\frac{1}{2}$ hours. Turn out of tin when hand hot.

Note The cake is best stored with its greaseproof paper on for 1 week or more before use. Gingerbreads become more moist and sticky as they age. Keep in a tin in a fairly cool place, but not in the refrigerator.

Swiss roll

Swiss Roll

Metric/Imperial	American
3 large eggs	3 large eggs
75 g/3 oz castor sugar, warmed	6 tablespoons sugar, warmed
75 g/3 oz self-raising flour	¾ cup all-purpose flour sifted with scant teaspoon baking powder

Filling	**Filling**
castor sugar	sugar
4 tablespoons raspberry jam, warmed	⅓ cup raspberry jam, warmed

Grease and line a shallow 23 × 30-cm/9 × 12-inch Swiss roll tin with greased greaseproof paper. Leave eggs at room temperature then whisk with the sugar until the mixture is light and creamy and leaves a trail when the whisk is lifted out. Sieve the flour and fold in using a metal spoon.

Turn into the prepared tin and smooth level with a palette knife. Bake in a hot oven (220°C, 425°F, Gas Mark 7) for 7–10 minutes until sponge begins to shrink from edges of the tin and is pale golden.

Turn out on to a sheet of greaseproof paper dredged with castor sugar. Trim edges of sponge, spread with warmed jam and roll up tightly. Dredge with castor sugar and cool on a wire rack.

Note For a smaller Swiss roll baked in an 18 × 28-cm/ 7 × 11-inch tin use two-thirds the amount of ingredients. Heat the jam until it is just easy to spread; if it is too hot it will soak into the sponge.

Family Fruit Cake

Metric/Imperial	American
150 g/5 oz plain flour	1¼ cups all-purpose flour
150 g/5 oz self-raising flour	1¼ cups all-purpose flour sifted with 1 rounded teaspoon baking powder
225 g/8 oz butter	1 cup butter
225 g/8 oz soft brown sugar	1 cup soft brown sugar
grated rind of 1 orange	grated rind of 1 orange
5 eggs, beaten	5 eggs, beaten
0·5 kg/1 lb mixed dried fruit	3 cups mixed dried fruit
100 g/4 oz finely chopped mixed peel	⅔ cup finely chopped candied peel
100 g/4 oz glacé cherries, quartered	½ cup quartered candied cherries
1 tablespoon black treacle	1 tablespoon dark corn syrup

Grease and line a 20-cm/8-inch square cake tin with greased greaseproof paper. Sieve the flours together.

Cream together the butter, sugar and orange rind until the mixture is pale and creamy. Add the eggs a little at a time, beating well after each addition. Fold in the flour alternately with the dried fruit, peel and quartered cherries. Blend in the treacle. Turn the mixture into the prepared tin and bake in a cool oven (150°C, 300°F, Gas Mark 2) for 2½ hours or until a skewer inserted in the centre comes out clean.

Remove cake from the oven and leave to cool in the tin for 10 minutes. Turn out on to a wire rack to finish cooling then remove paper.

Note This cake makes far better eating when it has been well cooled, then stored and matured in a cake tin or wrapped in foil for at least 1 week.

Easter Cake

Metric/Imperial	American
350 g/12 oz plain flour	3 cups all-purpose flour
½ teaspoon salt	½ teaspoon salt
¾ teaspoon each mixed spice and ground cinnamon	¾ teaspoon each mixed spice and ground cinnamon
75 g/3 oz each glacé cherries and mixed peel	⅓ cup each candied cherries and candied peel
250 g/9 oz butter	1 cup plus 2 tablespoons butter
250 g/9 oz soft brown sugar	1 cup plus 2 tablespoons soft brown sugar
grated rind of 1 lemon	grated rind of 1 lemon
5 large eggs, lightly beaten	5 large eggs, lightly beaten
175 g/6 oz seeded raisins	1 cup seeded raisins
100 g/4 oz each sultanas and currants	¾ cup each seedless raisins and currants
50 g/2 oz blanched, chopped almonds	½ cup blanched, chopped almonds
approx. 4 tablespoons milk	approx. ⅓ cup milk
Almond paste	**Almond paste**
150 g/5 oz ground almonds	1¼ cups ground almonds
150 g/5 oz castor sugar	⅔ cup sugar
juice of ¼ lemon	juice of ¼ lemon
beaten egg	beaten egg
apricot jam for topping	apricot jam for topping
coloured hard-boiled eggs to decorate	dyed hard-cooked eggs to decorate

Grease and line a 23-cm/9-inch cake tin. Sieve the flour, salt and spices. Halve the cherries and chop the peel. Cream the butter and sugar until pale and creamy then add the lemon rind. Gradually beat in the eggs, adding a small amount of flour towards the end to prevent curdling. Fold in the remaining flour, fruit, almonds and enough milk to make a soft dropping consistency. Spoon half the mixture into the tin and spread evenly.

Make the almond paste: combine the ground almonds with the castor sugar and lemon juice and sufficient beaten egg to make a stiff paste.

Roll one half of the paste to a 23-cm/9-inch circle on greaseproof paper. Lift paste on top of the mixture in the tin. Wrap remainder of paste in foil. Spoon the remaining cake mixture into the tin and hollow out the centre slightly. Bake in a moderate oven (180°C, 350°F, Gas Mark 4) for 30 minutes then reduce heat to 160°C (325°F, Gas Mark 3) and continue cooking for a further 2¼ hours. Cool in tin for 15 minutes. Turn out on to a wire rack and remove paper.

Brush centre and edge of the top of the cake with apricot jam. Roll the remaining almond paste into strips and plait; place round the edge of the cake and in the centre. Decorate with coloured eggs.

Gingerbread

Metric/Imperial	American
225 g/8 oz plain flour	2 cups all-purpose flour
1 teaspoon mixed spice	1 teaspoon mixed spice
2 teaspoons ground ginger	2 teaspoons ground ginger
75 g/3 oz sultanas	½ cup seedless raisins
75 g/3 oz soft dark brown sugar	6 tablespoons soft dark brown sugar
150 ml/¼ pint milk	⅔ cup milk
100 g/4 oz lard	½ cup shortening
100 g/4 oz golden syrup	⅓ cup light corn syrup
100 g/4 oz black treacle	⅓ cup dark corn syrup
1 teaspoon bicarbonate of soda	1 teaspoon baking soda
1 egg, beaten	1 egg, beaten

Line a 1-kg/2-lb loaf tin with greaseproof paper and grease. Sieve the flour and spices into a bowl and add the sultanas and sugar. Warm the milk in a small pan and place in a jug. Place the lard, syrup and treacle in the same pan and heat until the lard has melted. Add the bicarbonate of soda to the milk and stir until dissolved. Pour the lard mixture into the centre of the flour mixture, with the milk and beaten egg. Beat thoroughly.

Pour into the tin and bake for 1½–1¾ hours in the centre of a moderate oven (180°C, 350°F, Gas Mark 4). When cooked the gingerbread will spring back to the touch and have stopped bubbling. Leave in the tin to cool, then remove paper and store in an airtight tin. Cut into slices to serve.

Note To vary the gingerbread use equal quantities of white and wholemeal flour or add 100 g/4 oz (us ⅔ cup) dried figs or chopped dates instead of the sultanas. If you don't like the taste of treacle, substitute twice the given amount of golden syrup. The gingerbread can be decorated with an icing made up from 150 g/5 oz icing (us 1 cup confectioners') sugar mixed with water to give a soft consistency. Spoon over the top of the cake and allow to run down the sides.

Gingerbread

above Dundee cake

opposite Traditional iced Christmas cake

Dundee Cake

Metric/Imperial	American
225 g/8 oz plain flour	2 cups all-purpose flour
1 teaspoon baking powder	1 teaspoon baking powder
175 g/6 oz butter	$\frac{3}{4}$ cup butter
100 g/4 oz castor sugar	$\frac{1}{2}$ cup sugar
1 tablespoon clear honey	1 tablespoon clear honey
3 large eggs, beaten	3 large eggs, beaten
50 ml/2 fl oz milk	$\frac{1}{4}$ cup milk
175 g/6 oz currants	1 cup currants
100 g/4 oz dates, chopped	$\frac{1}{2}$ cup chopped dates
175 g/6 oz seeded raisins, chopped	1 cup chopped seeded raisins
25 g/1 oz glacé cherries, quartered	2 tablespoons quartered candied cherries
50 g/2 oz chopped mixed peel	$\frac{1}{3}$ cup chopped candied peel
finely grated rind of 1 lemon	finely grated rind of 1 lemon
50 g/2 oz almonds	$\frac{1}{2}$ cup almonds

Grease and line an 18-cm/7-inch round cake tin with greased greaseproof paper. Sift together the flour and baking powder.

Cream the butter, sugar and honey until pale and creamy. Add the eggs a little at a time, beating well after each addition. Lightly fold in the flour, milk, all the fruit and the lemon rind.

Turn the mixture into the tin. Blanch and split the almonds and arrange over the top of the cake.

Bake in a moderate oven (180°C, 350°F, Gas Mark 4) for 30 minutes, then reduce the heat to 160°C (325°F, Gas Mark 3) and continue cooking for a further 1–1½ hours, covering the top of the cake with greaseproof paper if necessary to prevent it overbrowning. Cool in tin for 10 minutes before turning out.

Note If the blanched almonds break when you try to split them, leave them soaking in hot water for 30 minutes or so to allow them to soften first.

Traditional Christmas Cake

Metric/Imperial	American
50 g/2 oz mixed peel	$\frac{1}{3}$ cup candied peel
75 g/3 oz glacé cherries	$\frac{1}{3}$ cup candied cherries
50 g/2 oz almonds	$\frac{1}{2}$ cup almonds
4 eggs	4 eggs
250 g/9 oz plain flour	2$\frac{1}{4}$ cups all-purpose flour
$\frac{1}{4}$ teaspoon salt	$\frac{1}{4}$ teaspoon salt
1 teaspoon mixed spice	1 teaspoon mixed spice
225 g/8 oz butter	1 cup butter
225 g/8 oz soft brown sugar	1 cup soft brown sugar
1½ tablespoons black treacle	2 tablespoons dark corn syrup
350 g/12 oz seeded raisins	2 cups seeded raisins
350 g/12 oz sultanas	2 cups seedless raisins
350 g/12 oz currants	2 cups currants
2 tablespoons brandy	3 tablespoons brandy

Line the base and sides of a 20-cm/8-inch round cake tin with a double layer of greased greaseproof paper, then tie a double band of brown paper, 2·5 cm/1 inch wider than the depth of the tin, around the outside.

Chop the peel, quarter the cherries, blanch and chop the almonds. Lightly beat the eggs. Sieve the flour into a large bowl with the salt and spice. Cream the butter and sugar together until pale and creamy. Beat in the eggs a little at a time. Stir in the treacle, then the flour, dried fruit, peel, cherries and almonds. Turn into the prepared tin and bake in a cool oven (150°C, 300°F, Gas Mark 2) for 3 hours, then reduce the heat to very cool (120°C, 250°F, Gas Mark $\frac{1}{2}$) and bake for 1 further hour, or until a skewer inserted in the centre comes out clean.

Leave cake to cool for 10 minutes, then turn it out on to a wire rack; remove paper. When almost cold turn it upside down, pierce with a skewer and spoon brandy over. When completely cold wrap in greaseproof paper and foil, or store in an airtight tin.

Note Make the cake at least 1 month before Christmas as this gives it time to mature. Before serving, spoon a little more brandy over the top of the cake and spread with almond paste and royal icing.

Christmas Cake Icing

Metric/Imperial	American
Almond paste	**Almond paste**
175 g/6 oz ground almonds	1½ cups ground almonds
175 g/6 oz castor sugar	$\frac{3}{4}$ cup sugar
175 g/6 oz sieved icing sugar	1$\frac{1}{3}$ cups sifted confectioners' sugar
3 egg yolks	3 egg yolks
few drops almond essence	few drops almond extract
3 tablespoons apricot jam, sieved	$\frac{1}{4}$ cup apricot jam, sifted
Royal icing	**Royal frosting**
4 egg whites	4 egg whites
1 kg/2 lb sieved icing sugar	6½ cups sifted confectioners' sugar
4 teaspoons lemon juice	4 teaspoons lemon juice
2 teaspoons glycerine	2 teaspoons glycerine

Mix the ground almonds and sugars in a bowl, then blend in the egg yolks and almond essence to make a soft paste. Knead until smooth and divide into three equal portions. Roll one piece on a sugared board to a 20-cm/8-inch circle. Roll remaining two-thirds to a strip the same depth as the cake, and long enough to go all the way round the outside edge. Brush sides of cake with apricot jam. Place the long strip of paste round sides and press firmly to join. Place circle of paste on top of cake. Allow to dry for at least 3 days before icing.

For royal icing: whisk the egg whites until they become frothy. Add the sugar, 1 tablespoon at a time, and beat well after each addition. Finally beat in the lemon juice and glycerine. To prevent icing hardening, cover bowl with a damp cloth.

Spread icing thickly over top and sides of cake and draw it up in peaks with the handle of a teaspoon, or smooth it over with a palette knife and a metal ruler. Pipe a border of icing round the edges. Leave for 1 day to set then place decorations.

Barm brack

Barm Brack

Metric/Imperial
450 ml/¾ pint cold tea
200 g/7 oz soft brown sugar

350 g/12 oz mixed dried fruit
275 g/10 oz self-raising flour

1 egg

American
2 cups cold tea
¾ cup plus 2 tablespoons soft
   brown sugar
2 cups mixed dried fruit
2½ cups all-purpose flour
   sifted with 2½ teaspoons
   baking powder
1 egg

Put the tea, sugar and dried fruit in a bowl, cover and leave to soak overnight. (Tea that has been left over during the day can be saved and used.) Well grease a 20-cm/8-inch round cake tin or 1-kg/2-lb loaf tin.

Mix the soaked fruit and sugar with its liquid into the flour. Beat the egg and add to make a smooth mixture. Turn into the tin and bake in a moderate oven (180°C, 350°F, Gas Mark 4) for 1¾ hours. Cool on a wire rack.

Serve sliced with butter.

Cheese and Celery Loaf

Metric/Imperial
0·5 kg/1 lb self-raising flour

2 teaspoons salt
40 g/1½ oz butter
3 large sticks celery
1 clove garlic or few
   dehydrated garlic flakes
175 g/6 oz mature Cheddar
   cheese
1 egg
300 ml/½ pint less 2 tablespoons milk

American
4 cups all-purpose flour sifted
   with 4 teaspoons baking
   powder
2 teaspoons salt
3 tablespoons butter
3 large stalks celery
1 clove garlic or few
   dehydrated garlic flakes
6 oz mature Cheddar cheese

1 egg
1¼ cups less 3 tablespoons
   milk

Grease a 1-kg/2-lb loaf tin. Sift the flour and salt into a bowl and rub in the butter until the mixture resembles fine breadcrumbs.

Wash and chop the celery finely. Crush the garlic (if a clove is used) and grate the cheese coarsely. Add the celery, garlic and cheese to the flour. Beat the egg and milk together, add gradually to the dry ingredients and mix to form a soft dough. Knead lightly and quickly on a floured surface, then shape into an oblong. Place in the loaf tin and bake in a hot oven (220°C, 425°F, Gas Mark 7) until well risen and golden brown, about 55 minutes.

Turn out and cool on a wire rack. Serve fresh with butter.

Cheese Scones

Metric/Imperial
225 g/8 oz self-raising flour

¼ teaspoon salt
½ teaspoon dry mustard
25 g/1 oz butter
100 g/4 oz Cheddar cheese,
   finely grated
150 ml/¼ pint milk

American
2 cups all-purpose flour sifted
   with 2 teaspoons baking
   powder
¼ teaspoon salt
½ teaspoon dry mustard
2 tablespoons butter
1 cup finely grated Cheddar
   cheese
⅔ cup milk

Sift together the flour, salt and mustard. Rub in the butter until the mixture resembles fine breadcrumbs. Add most of the cheese to the flour mixture; bind together with the milk to form a soft dough.

Roll out on a floured surface to 1-cm/½-inch thickness and cut into 15 rounds with a 3·5-cm/1½-inch plain cutter. Place on a greased baking tray, brush with milk and sprinkle the remaining grated cheese on top.

Bake in a hot oven (220°C, 425°F, Gas Mark 7) for about 12 minutes, then cool on a wire rack. Serve with butter.

Makes 15

Glazed Fruit Bread

Metric/Imperial
350 g/12 oz self-raising flour

½ teaspoon salt
50 g/2 oz castor sugar
50 g/2 oz walnuts
50 g/2 oz dates
2 rounded tablespoons malt
   extract
50 g/2 oz butter
150 ml/¼ pint milk
2 eggs, beaten
Glaze and topping
3 tablespoons apricot jam
glacé or dried apricots
glacé cherries
4 dates
25 g/1 oz walnuts
50 g/2 oz icing sugar

American
3 cups all-purpose flour sifted
   with 3 teaspoons baking
   powder
½ teaspoon salt
¼ cup sugar
½ cup walnuts
¼ cup dates
3 rounded tablespoons
   molasses
¼ cup butter
⅔ cup milk
2 eggs, beaten
Glaze and topping
¼ cup apricot jam
candied or dried apricots
candied cherries
4 dates
¼ cup walnuts
½ cup confectioners' sugar

Well grease a 1-kg/2-lb loaf tin. Sift the flour and salt into a bowl and add the sugar. Chop the walnuts and stone and chop the dates, and add to the flour. Gently heat the malt and butter until the butter has melted. Pour into the centre of the flour mixture with the blended milk and eggs. Mix to a smooth soft dough. Turn the dough into the tin and bake for 1 hour in a moderate oven (160°C, 325°F, Gas Mark 3).

To make the glaze: heat the jam slowly with a little water and spread over top of the loaf. Place glacé or dried apricots down centre of loaf with a cherry in the centre of each. Stone and halve the dates and arrange along either side with the walnuts. Mix the icing sugar with 1 tablespoon water and trickle over the top to give a criss-cross effect.

Note For a quicker finish, brush the top of the loaf with warmed honey or golden syrup and scatter with chopped walnuts.

Apple Scone

Metric/Imperial	American
1 medium cooking apple	1 medium baking apple
225 g/8 oz self-raising flour	2 cups all-purpose flour sifted with 2 teaspoons baking powder
½ teaspoon salt	½ teaspoon salt
1 teaspoon baking powder	1 teaspoon baking powder
50 g/2 oz butter	¼ cup butter
50 g/2 oz castor sugar	¼ cup sugar
125 ml/scant ¼ pint milk	scant ⅔ cup milk
Glaze	**Glaze**
milk	milk
25 g/1 oz demerara sugar	2 tablespoons light brown sugar

Peel, core and finely chop the apple. Sift together the flour, salt and baking powder. Rub in the butter, then add the castor sugar and chopped apple. Mix to a soft dough with the milk.

Roll out on a floured surface to 5 mm/¼ inch thick and 20 cm/ 8 inches round. Mark into eight wedges. Place on a greased baking tray, brush with milk and sprinkle with demerara sugar. Bake for 20–25 minutes in a moderately hot oven (200°C, 400°F, Gas Mark 6).

Serve warm with butter.

Honey Loaf

Metric/Imperial	American
50 g/2 oz mixed peel	⅓ cup candied peel
350 g/12 oz self-raising flour	3 cups all-purpose flour sifted with 3 teaspoons baking powder
1 teaspoon salt	1 teaspoon salt
1 tablespoon mixed spice	1 tablespoon mixed spice
100 g/4 oz soft brown sugar	½ cup soft brown sugar
175 g/6 oz clear honey	½ cup clear honey
150 ml/¼ pint milk	⅔ cup milk
25 g/1 oz lump sugar	1 oz lump sugar

Line and grease a 1-kg/2-lb loaf tin. Chop the peel finely. Sift together the flour, salt, spice and stir in the peel and brown sugar. Add the honey and milk and blend together until a smooth, stiff dough is formed.

Place in loaf tin. Lightly crush the lump sugar and sprinkle over the top of the loaf. Bake in a moderate oven (180°C, 350°F, Gas Mark 4) for 1¼ hours.

Turn out and cool on a wire rack. A little more sugar can be sprinkled on top of the loaf if liked; serve sliced and spread with butter.

Devonshire Scones

Metric/Imperial	American
0·5 kg/1 lb self-raising flour	4 cups all-purpose flour sifted with 4 teaspoons baking powder
1 teaspoon salt	1 teaspoon salt
100 g/4 oz butter	½ cup butter
50 g/2 oz castor sugar	¼ cup sugar
300 ml/½ pint milk	1¼ cups milk
beaten egg to glaze	beaten egg to glaze

Sift the flour and salt into a bowl. Rub in the butter until the mixture resembles fine breadcrumbs. Add the sugar and mix to a soft dough with the milk.

Turn on to a lightly floured surface, knead quickly, then roll out to 1-cm/½-inch thickness. Cut into 20 rounds with a 6-cm/2½-inch cutter.

Devonshire scones

Place scones on greased baking trays and brush tops with beaten egg or milk. Bake in a hot oven (230°C, 450°F, Gas Mark 8) for 8–10 minutes and leave to cool on a wire rack.

When cold, split and serve with strawberry or raspberry jam and whipped cream.

Note To save time and effort make up 1·5 kg/3 lb of the rubbed-in scone mixture using 1·5 kg/3 lb (US 12 cups) flour and 350 g/ 12 oz (US 1½ cups) butter. Store in polythene bags for up to 3 months in a refrigerator. To use, simply weigh out the required quantity.

Makes 20

Savoury Butter Scones

Metric/Imperial	American
350 g/12 oz plain flour	3 cups all-purpose flour
1 tablespoon baking powder	1 tablespoon baking powder
1 teaspoon salt	1 teaspoon salt
175 g/6 oz butter	$\frac{3}{4}$ cup butter
1 onion	1 onion
2 cloves garlic	2 cloves garlic
75 g/3 oz Cheddar cheese, grated	$\frac{3}{4}$ cup grated Cheddar cheese
2 tablespoons chopped parsley or snipped chives	3 tablespoons chopped parsley or snipped chives
300 ml/$\frac{1}{2}$ pint milk	$1\frac{1}{4}$ cups milk

Sieve the dry ingredients into a bowl and rub in 50 g/2 oz (US $\frac{1}{4}$ cup) of the butter. Finely chop the onion and garlic. Add with the grated cheese and parsley or chives to the flour. Using a palette knife mix the milk in to make a soft but not sticky dough.

Pat out in a greased 20 × 30-cm/8 × 12-inch square dish or roasting tin. Bake in a moderately hot oven (200°C, 400°F, Gas Mark 6) for 35 minutes or until firm and golden. Remove from the oven and pour over the remaining butter, melted.

Cut into fingers 2·5 × 7·5 cm/1 × 3 inches and serve hot.

To freeze This dish freezes well, but should be reheated and served warm.

Note Scones must be baked as soon as liquid is added to the dry ingredients, otherwise the baking powder will become inactive. Baking powder should be bought in small quantities and used up quickly.

Makes 32

Drop Scones

Metric/Imperial	American
225 g/8 oz plain flour	2 cups all-purpose flour
1 teaspoon cream of tartar	1 teaspoon cream of tartar
$\frac{1}{2}$ teaspoon bicarbonate of soda	$\frac{1}{2}$ teaspoon baking soda
50 g/2 oz castor sugar	$\frac{1}{4}$ cup sugar
2 eggs	2 eggs
300 ml/$\frac{1}{2}$ pint milk	$1\frac{1}{4}$ cups milk
lard for greasing	shortening for greasing

Sieve the flour, cream of tartar and bicarbonate of soda into a bowl. Stir in the sugar. Beat the eggs, add with the milk and mix together to a fairly thick batter with a wooden spoon.

Have ready a moderately hot griddle or heavy frying pan over a moderate heat and grease lightly with lard. Drop 5 (US 6) tablespoons of the mixture on to the griddle or frying pan and cook over a moderate heat for 3–4 minutes until bubbles appear on the surface. Turn over with a palette knife and cook the other side until brown.

Remove from the heat, place on half of a clean tea towel, and cover with the other half to keep warm and moist. Cook the remaining batter in the same way.

Serve hot or cold with butter.

Makes 36

Flapjacks

Metric/Imperial	American
100 g/4 oz margarine	$\frac{1}{2}$ cup margarine
100 g/4 oz demerara sugar	$\frac{1}{2}$ cup light brown sugar
1 tablespoon golden syrup	1 tablespoon corn syrup
150 g/5 oz rolled oats	$1\frac{1}{2}$ cups rolled oats

Grease an 18-cm/7-inch square shallow tin. Melt margarine in a pan, add the sugar and syrup and when blended stir in the oats. Mix thoroughly. Press the mixture into the tin and bake in a moderate oven (160°C, 325°F, Gas Mark 3) until pale golden brown, about 25 minutes.

Leave to cool for 10 minutes and then mark into 12 bars. Leave in the tin until quite cold. Store in an airtight tin.

Makes 12

New Zealand Biscuits

Metric/Imperial	American
1 rounded tablespoon golden syrup	1 rounded tablespoon corn syrup
150 g/5 oz butter	$\frac{2}{3}$ cup butter
100 g/4 oz castor sugar	$\frac{1}{2}$ cup sugar
75 g/3 oz rolled oats	1 cup rolled oats
50 g/2 oz desiccated coconut	$\frac{2}{3}$ cup shredded coconut
100 g/4 oz plain flour	1 cup all-purpose flour
2 teaspoons bicarbonate of soda	2 teaspoons baking soda

Grease two baking trays. Put the syrup, butter and sugar into a pan and melt over a low heat. Remove the pan from the heat and stir in the oats, coconut and flour. Dissolve the bicarbonate of soda in a bowl with 1 tablespoon hot water. Add to the other ingredients and leave to cool for a few minutes.

Divide into 30 portions, roll into balls and place on the baking trays, leaving plenty of space between each. Bake in a moderate oven (160°C, 325°F, Gas Mark 3) for about 20 minutes or until the biscuits have browned evenly. Remove from the oven and leave on the baking trays to harden. Cool on a wire rack.

Note These biscuits are fun for the children to make. If mother does the weighing out first they are easy to finish.

Makes 30

Florentines

Metric/Imperial	American
50 g/2 oz almonds	$\frac{1}{3}$ cup almonds
15 g/$\frac{1}{2}$ oz mixed peel	$1\frac{1}{2}$ tablespoons candied peel
15 g/$\frac{1}{2}$ oz glacé cherries	1 tablespoon candied cherries
15 g/$\frac{1}{2}$ oz sultanas	$1\frac{1}{2}$ tablespoons seedless raisins
50 g/2 oz butter	$\frac{1}{4}$ cup butter
50 g/2 oz castor sugar	$\frac{1}{4}$ cup sugar
1 tablespoon single cream	1 tablespoon light cream
75 g/3 oz plain chocolate	3 squares semi-sweet chocolate

Place the almonds in a bowl, cover with boiling water and leave to stand for a few minutes; remove the skins and chop very finely. Chop the peel, cherries and sultanas.

Melt the butter in a pan, add the sugar, stir until dissolved and then boil rapidly for 1 minute. Add the nuts, peel, cherries and sultanas to the pan with the cream and mix well.

Line baking trays with silicone (non-stick) paper. Put teaspoonfuls of mixture on the baking trays, allowing plenty of room for them to spread. Bake in a moderate oven (180°C, 350°F, Gas Mark 4) until a pale golden brown, about 8–10 minutes. Remove from the oven and press the florentines into shape with a palette knife. Allow to cool slightly before lifting on to a wire rack to cool.

Melt the chocolate in a small bowl over a pan of hot water and spread over the backs of the florentines with a knife, mark with a fork and leave to set.

Makes approx. 16

Brandy Snaps

Metric/Imperial	American
50 g/2 oz butter	$\frac{1}{4}$ cup butter
50 g/2 oz castor sugar	$\frac{1}{4}$ cup sugar
2 tablespoons golden syrup	3 tablespoons corn syrup
50 g/2 oz plain flour	$\frac{1}{2}$ cup all-purpose flour
$\frac{1}{2}$ teaspoon ground ginger	$\frac{1}{2}$ teaspoon ground ginger
1 teaspoon lemon juice or brandy	1 teaspoon lemon juice or brandy
150 ml/$\frac{1}{4}$ pint double cream	$\frac{2}{3}$ cup whipping cream
2 tablespoons top of milk	3 tablespoons rich milk

Line baking trays with non-stick silicone paper and butter the handles of wooden spoons.

Melt the butter with the sugar in a small pan and stir in the syrup. When smooth, remove from the heat and stir in the flour and ginger, add the lemon juice or brandy and leave to cool for 2 minutes. Drop the mixture in teaspoonfuls on to the baking trays allowing plenty of room to spread and bake for 7–8 minutes in a moderate oven (180°C, 350°F, Gas Mark 4) until bubbly and golden brown. Remove the biscuits from the oven, leave for about 30 seconds and then quickly roll each brandy snap around the handle of a wooden spoon. Leave to set, then twist gently to remove and cool on a wire rack.

Just before serving whisk the cream with the milk until thick and pipe or spoon into the ends of the brandy snaps. Unfilled brandy snaps will keep for 1 week in an airtight tin.

Makes 16

Chocolate Crispies

Metric/Imperial	American
50 g/2 oz butter	$\frac{1}{4}$ cup butter
2 tablespoons drinking chocolate	3 tablespoons drinking chocolate
1 rounded tablespoon golden syrup	1 rounded tablespoon corn syrup
65 g/2$\frac{1}{2}$ oz rice krispies	2$\frac{1}{2}$ cups rice krispies

Melt the butter in a pan, then stir in the chocolate and golden syrup and blend well. Toss in the rice krispies and stir well so that they become evenly coated with the chocolate mixture. While still warm, using two spoons, neatly spoon into piles on an oiled tray or spoon into paper cases. Leave to harden at room temperature for 30 minutes and then keep in an airtight tin.

These are not suitable for freezing as the rice krispies easily become soggy.

Note Use only very fresh rice krispies; if slightly soft crispen in a warm oven, then cool before use. Make and use on the same day for best results.

Makes 12–15

Brandy snaps

Rock Cakes

Metric/Imperial	American
225 g/8 oz plain flour	2 cups all-purpose flour
$\frac{1}{2}$ teaspoon salt	$\frac{1}{2}$ teaspoon salt
2 teaspoons baking powder	2 teaspoons baking powder
65 g/2$\frac{1}{2}$ oz butter	5 tablespoons butter
65 g/2$\frac{1}{2}$ oz castor sugar	5 tablespoons sugar
100 g/4 oz dried fruit	$\frac{2}{3}$ cup dried fruit
$\frac{1}{4}$ teaspoon grated nutmeg	$\frac{1}{4}$ teaspoon grated nutmeg
1 egg	1 egg
2 tablespoons milk	3 tablespoons milk

Sieve the flour, salt and baking powder together. Rub the butter into the flour until the mixture resembles fine breadcrumbs. Stir in the sugar, fruit and nutmeg.

Beat the egg with the milk and add to the flour mixture. Mix well with a fork; the mixture should be stiff but not too sticky and should leave the sides of the bowl clean.

Divide the mixture into 12 and place on a greased baking tray; rough up with a fork. Bake for 15–20 minutes in a moderately hot oven (200°C, 400°F, Gas Mark 6) until a pale golden brown. Cool on a wire rack.

Note Rock cakes are not rich and are therefore best eaten on the day of baking. For a crunchy topping sprinkle with demerara sugar before baking.

Makes 12

Flapjacks

Chocolate brownies

Orange Shortbread

Metric/Imperial	American
100 g/4 oz plain flour	1 cup all-purpose flour
50 g/2 oz cornflour	½ cup cornstarch
100 g/4 oz butter	½ cup butter
50 g/2 oz castor sugar	¼ cup sugar
grated rind of 1 orange	grated rind of 1 orange

Sieve the flour and cornflour together. Cream the butter until it is soft then add the sugar and beat until the mixture is pale and creamy. Add the orange rind then work in the flour mixture 1 tablespoon at a time.

Lift the shortbread on to a large baking tray. Roll out to a 20-cm/8-inch circle. Pinch the edges and prick the shortbread well with a fork. Cut through into 12 sections with the back of a knife and sprinkle with castor sugar.

Leave to chill in the refrigerator for 15 minutes, then bake in a moderate oven (160°C, 325°F, Gas Mark 3) for 35 minutes until a pale golden brown. Cool on the baking tray for a few minutes, then lift on to a wire rack to finish cooling.

Makes 12

Chocolate Brownies

Metric/Imperial	American
100 g/4 oz self-raising flour	1 cup all-purpose flour sifted with 1 teaspoon baking powder
40 g/1½ oz cocoa powder	⅓ cup unsweetened cocoa
100 g/4 oz butter	½ cup butter
150 g/5 oz soft brown sugar	⅔ cup soft brown sugar
2 eggs	2 eggs
1 tablespoon milk	1 tablespoon milk
Chocolate fudge icing	Chocolate fudge frosting
40 g/1½ oz butter	3 tablespoons butter
25 g/1 oz cocoa powder	¼ cup unsweetened cocoa
approx. 50 ml/2 fl oz milk	¼ cup milk
100 g/4 oz icing sugar	1 cup confectioners' sugar

Line the base of an 18-cm/7-inch by 3·5-cm/1½-inch deep square tin with a piece of greaseproof paper and grease.

Sift together the flour and cocoa. In another bowl beat the butter and sugar together until light and fluffy. Beat the eggs and add a little at a time, beating well after each addition. Fold the sifted ingredients into the butter mixture with the milk and mix well. Turn into the prepared tin and bake in a moderately hot oven (190°C, 375°F, Gas Mark 5) for 30 minutes or until the centre springs back when lightly pressed. Turn out on to a wire rack, remove paper and cool.

Melt the butter for the icing, add the cocoa, and cook over a low heat for 1 minute. Remove from the heat, stir in the milk and sifted icing sugar, and mix well to spreading consistency. Spread over the cake and leave to set. Cut into 16 squares.

To freeze This dish freezes well but is best frozen whole and cut into squares after thawing.
Note Cocoa gives a strong chocolate flavour. It is essential to cook it and to add sweetening. Chocolate powder is already sweetened and does not require cooking in recipes; the result is a less strong chocolate flavour.

Makes 16

Viennese Biscuits

Metric/Imperial	American
100 g/4 oz butter, warmed	½ cup butter, warmed
25 g/1 oz icing sugar	¼ cup confectioners' sugar
150 g/5 oz plain flour	1¼ cups all-purpose flour
Buttercream	Buttercream
50 g/2 oz butter	¼ cup butter
100 g/4 oz icing sugar	1 cup confectioners' sugar
25 g/1 oz cooking chocolate	1 square unsweetened cooking chocolate

Cream the butter and sieved icing sugar until very soft. Stir in the sieved flour and mix well. If the butter is not very soft the mixture will be too stiff to pipe and a few drops of milk may be added if necessary. Put the mixture into a piping bag fitted with a large star tube and pipe on to a greased baking tray in small circles, rosettes or fingers, making sure that there are an even number of each different shape.

Leave in the refrigerator or a cold place for at least 15 minutes to chill. Bake in a moderately hot oven (190°C, 375°F, Gas Mark 5) until they are just beginning to turn brown, about 10 minutes. Cool on a wire rack.

Cream together the butter and icing sugar for the filling. Melt the chocolate and mix well. When the biscuits are cold, sandwich together in pairs with the buttercream and dust the tops with sieved icing sugar.

Viennese biscuits

Strawberry Shortcakes

Metric/Imperial	American
225 g/8 oz self-raising flour	2 cups all-purpose flour sifted with 2 teaspoons baking powder
½ teaspoon salt	½ teaspoon salt
75 g/3 oz butter	⅓ cup butter
1 egg	1 egg
approx. 4 tablespoons milk	approx. ⅓ cup milk
25 g/1 oz castor sugar	2 tablespoons sugar
milk to glaze	milk to glaze
Filling	**Filling**
225 g/8 oz strawberries	2 cups strawberries
150 ml/¼ pint double cream	⅔ cup whipping cream
2 teaspoons icing sugar	2 teaspoons confectioners' sugar

Sift together the flour and salt and rub in the butter. Beat the egg with the milk. Add the sugar and mix to a soft dough with the egg and milk.

Turn on to a lightly floured surface, knead quickly until smooth, then roll out to 1-cm/½-inch thickness. Cut into six rounds with an 8·5-cm/3½-inch plain cutter. Place on a greased baking tray and brush the tops with milk.

Bake for 10–12 minutes in a hot oven (220°C, 425°F, Gas Mark 7). Leave to cool on a wire rack but, while still warm, split each shortcake in half by pulling carefully apart (do not cut with a knife).

Hull and slice the strawberries keeping six whole for decoration. Whip the cream and sweeten with sieved icing sugar. Sandwich the shortcakes together with cream and sliced strawberries. Dust with icing sugar and decorate the serving plate with whole strawberries.

Makes 6

Strawberry shortcakes

Strawberry Cream Tarts

Metric/Imperial	American
100 g/4 oz plain flour	1 cup all-purpose flour
¼ teaspoon salt	¼ teaspoon salt
65 g/2½ oz butter	5 tablespoons butter
15 g/½ oz castor sugar	1 tablespoon sugar
Filling	**Filling**
150 ml/¼ pint double cream	⅔ cup whipping cream
225 g/8 oz strawberries	2 cups strawberries
3 tablespoons redcurrant jelly to glaze	¼ cup red currant jelly to glaze

Sift the flour and salt into a bowl, add the butter and sugar and rub in until the mixture resembles fine breadcrumbs. Add sufficient cold water to make a firm dough. Roll out the pastry on a lightly floured surface. Cut into nine circles with 5-cm/2-inch fluted cutter and use to line patty tins. Prick and then chill for 15 minutes. Line each with greaseproof paper and baking beans or with foil and bake in a moderately hot oven (190°C, 375°F, Gas Mark 5) for 10 minutes. Remove paper and beans and bake for a further 5 minutes. Cool on a wire rack.

Whip the cream until it forms soft peaks and divide it between the pastry cases. Arrange the strawberries on top. Melt the redcurrant jelly over a low heat in a small pan. Heat gently, stirring occasionally, until smooth. Spoon glaze over tarts.

Makes 9

Almond Macaroons

Metric/Imperial	American
2 large egg whites	2 large egg whites
100 g/4 oz ground almonds	1 cup ground almonds
175 g/6 oz castor sugar	¾ cup sugar
25 g/1 oz ground rice	¾ cup ground rice
few drops almond essence	few drops almond extract
8 blanched almonds	8 blanched almonds

Line two large baking trays with rice paper or, if this is not available, with non-stick silicone or greaseproof paper. Put 1 teaspoon egg white into a small bowl and reserve for glazing.

Whisk the remaining egg white until it forms soft peaks. Fold in the ground almonds, sugar, ground rice and almond essence. Mix well. Put 16 heaped teaspoons of the mixture on to the rice paper and smooth them slightly with the back of a spoon. Put half a blanched almond in the centre of each macaroon. Brush the tops with the reserved egg white.

Bake in a cool oven (150°C, 300°F, Gas Mark 2) until the macaroons are pale golden, about 25–30 minutes. Allow to cool slightly before removing from the baking tray. Tear away excess rice paper from around the edge of the macaroons. If using non-stick silicone paper peel it away carefully. When they are quite cold store in an airtight tin.

Note When a trifle recipe (see page 152) calls for ratafias, try using crushed almond macaroons instead. They taste the same and are quicker to make.

Makes 16

Family Fudge

Metric/Imperial
170-g/6-oz can evaporated milk
75 g/3 oz butter
0·5 kg/1 lb granulated sugar
150 ml/¼ pint water
¼ teaspoon vanilla essence

American
6-oz can evaporated milk

⅓ cup butter
2 cups sugar
⅔ cup water
¼ teaspoon vanilla extract

Butter a shallow 18-cm/7-inch square tin.

Put the milk, butter, sugar and water into a heavy pan and heat slowly until the sugar has dissolved, without boiling. Then boil steadily, stirring constantly, to 114°C (237°F), or until a small amount of mixture forms a soft ball when dropped into a glass of water. (If the water becomes cloudy and the mixture dissolves the fudge is not ready.)

Remove from the heat and add the vanilla essence. Cool slightly then beat when the mixture thickens and begins to crystallise on the spoon.

Pour into the tin and leave to set. When firm cut into 36 squares; store in an airtight tin.

Note   Nuts, chopped mixed peel, sultanas or chopped glacé cherries can be added with the vanilla essence.

Makes 36 pieces

Family fudge

Meringues

Metric/Imperial
4 egg whites
225 g/8 oz castor sugar
Filling
150 ml/¼ pint double cream
1 tablespoon drinking chocolate

American
4 egg whites
1 cup sugar
Filling
⅔ cup whipping cream
1 tablespoon drinking chocolate

Oil three large baking trays thoroughly, or line with non-stick silicone paper.

Put the egg whites into a china or ovenglass mixing bowl. Whisk with a rotary whisk until they are very stiff. Continue to whisk, adding the sugar 1 teaspoon at a time and whisking well after each addition until all the sugar has been added. Using two wet dessertspoons, spoon the meringue on to the prepared baking trays, or pipe in rosettes using a large star tube.

Sprinkle with sugar and dry out in a very cool oven (110°C, 225°F, Gas Mark ¼) until crisp, about 1½–2 hours. Remove and leave to cool on a wire rack. Whip the cream and add the chocolate. Sandwich pairs of meringues together with filling. Store unfilled meringues in an airtight tin until required.

Note   Non-stick silicone paper or household vegetable parchment may be bought from good stationers in rolls. It is paper specially treated to make it non-stick for sugar confections such as meringues and brandy snaps.

Variation   Stud the double cream with slivered almonds and chopped glacé cherries for an attractive party dish.

Meringues

Peppermint Creams

Metric/Imperial	American
0·5 kg/1 lb icing sugar	3½ cups confectioners' sugar
1 egg white	1 egg white
2 tablespoons double cream	3 tablespoons whipping cream
few drops peppermint essence	few drops peppermint extract

Sift the sugar into a large bowl. Blend together the egg white, cream and peppermint essence. Pour into the sugar and work to a firm but soft paste.

Well sprinkle a table or large sheet of greaseproof paper with sifted icing sugar. Divide the paste into four portions and roll each piece out to a 5-mm/¼-inch thickness and stamp into rounds with a 2·5-cm/1-inch cutter or tiny glass.

Place on a fine wire rack and re-roll all the trimmings until the paste is used up. Leave to dry overnight and then store in an airtight container.

Note One side of the peppermint cream may be dipped in melted chocolate, in which case leave to dry on waxed paper before storing.

Makes approx. 0·5 kg/1 lb

White Bread

Metric/Imperial	American
1 teaspoon sugar	1 teaspoon sugar
450 ml/¾ pint warm water (43°C, 110°F)	2 cups warm water (110°F)
2 teaspoons dried yeast	2 teaspoons active dry yeast
15 g/½ oz lard, melted	1 tablespoon shortening, melted
0·75 kg/1½ lb plain flour	6 cups all-purpose flour
1 tablespoon salt	1 tablespoon salt

Prepare the yeast liquid by dissolving the sugar in the water and sprinkling the yeast on top. Leave until frothy, about 10 minutes. Add the lard to the yeast liquid then mix in the flour and salt. Work to a firm dough until the sides of the bowl are clean. Turn on to a lightly floured surface and knead thoroughly, about 10 minutes.

Place in a lightly greased polythene bag, loosely tied, and leave to rise until doubled in size. Remove polythene and turn out dough on to a lightly floured surface, flatten to knock out air bubbles, and knead to make dough firm. Grease two 0·5-kg/1-lb loaf tins. Divide dough in half, shape each piece into an oblong the same width as the tin and fold over in three. With the seam underneath, smooth over top, tuck in ends and place in tin. Place in greased polythene bags and leave until dough rises to the tops of the tins.

Remove from bags and bake in a hot oven (230°C, 450°F, Gas Mark 8) for 30–40 minutes, until well risen and they sound hollow when tapped on bases. Turn out and cool on a wire rack.

Makes 2

Rolls

Metric/Imperial	American
1 teaspoon sugar	1 teaspoon sugar
450 ml/¾ pint warm water (43°C, 110°F)	2 cups warm water (110°F)
2 teaspoons dried yeast	2 teaspoons active dry yeast
15 g/½ oz lard	1 tablespoon shortening
0·75 kg/1½ lb plain flour	6 cups all-purpose flour
1 tablespoon salt	1 tablespoon salt

Prepare the yeast liquid by dissolving the sugar in the water and sprinkling the yeast on top. Leave until frothy, about 10 minutes. Rub the lard into the flour and salt and mix in the yeast liquid. Work to a firm dough until the sides of the bowl are clean. Turn on to a lightly floured surface and knead thoroughly, about 10 minutes.

Place in a lightly greased polythene bag, loosely tied, and leave to rise until doubled in size. Remove the dough from the bag and divide into 18 equal pieces and shape as desired.

Dinner rolls On an unfloured surface, roll each piece of dough into a ball, pressing down hard at first with floured palm of hand then easing up.

Finger rolls Prepare as for dinner rolls then roll into a sausage shape about 10 cm/4 inches long.

Knot Shape as for dinner rolls then roll into a 20-cm/8-inch rope and tie into a simple knot.

Cloverleaf Divide each piece of dough into three and shape as for dinner rolls. Place together to form a clover leaf.

Place all the rolls on greased baking trays about 2·5 cm/1 inch apart. Put to rise in a greased polythene bag for approximately 30 minutes at room temperature. Remove bag and bake in a hot oven (230°C, 450°F, Gas Mark 8) until a pale golden brown, about 15–20 minutes. Cool on a wire rack.

Note Strong flour is best for yeast recipes as it absorbs liquid easily and kneads quickly into a firm dough. Some flours are labelled as strong. If not available, use a top quality plain flour.

Makes 18

Wheatmeal Bread

Metric/Imperial	American
450 ml/¾ pint warm water (43°C, 110°F)	2 cups warm water (110°F)
1 teaspoon sugar	1 teaspoon sugar
1 tablespoon dried yeast	1 tablespoon active dry yeast
350 g/12 oz strong plain flour	3 cups strong all-purpose flour
350 g/12 oz wholemeal flour	2¾ cups wholewheat flour
2 teaspoons sugar	2 teaspoons sugar
2–3 teaspoons salt	2–3 teaspoons salt
1 tablespoon salad oil	1 tablespoon salad oil
milk to glaze	milk to glaze
cracked wheat or oatmeal	cracked wheat or oatmeal

Mix the water and sugar together and stir in the dried yeast. Leave for about 10 minutes or until frothy. Put all the remaining dry ingredients in a large bowl. Pour on the yeast mixture and the oil, mix with a fork then knead until smooth and no longer sticky, about 10 minutes. Put into a lightly greased polythene bag, loosely tied, and leave until doubled in size; this will take about 1 hour at room temperature or overnight in the refrigerator.

Remove polythene, turn dough on to a lightly floured surface and flatten to knock out the air bubbles. Divide the dough in half. Shape one piece of dough into a round and place in a 13-cm/5-inch well greased and seasoned flower pot. Shape the second portion of dough and put on a baking tray or in a well greased 0·5-kg/1-lb loaf tin. Glaze with milk and sprinkle with cracked wheat or oatmeal. Place in a greased polythene bag. Put to rise in a warm place until doubled in size or the dough has reached the top of the pot or loaf tin.

Remove from polythene and bake in a hot oven (230°C, 450°F, Gas Mark 8) for 30–40 minutes until evenly browned and the loaves sound hollow when tapped on the bases. Cool on a wire rack.

To freeze Wheatmeal bread, like all bread, freezes well and is best left to thaw for about 4 hours at room temperature.
Note Do *not* use a plastic flower pot.

Makes 2

Baps

Metric/Imperial	American
1 teaspoon sugar	1 teaspoon sugar
300 ml/½ pint warm milk and water (43°C, 110°F)	1¼ cups warm milk and water (110°F)
2 teaspoons dried yeast	2 teaspoons active dry yeast
50 g/2 oz lard	¼ cup shortening
0·5 kg/1 lb plain flour	4 cups all-purpose flour
1 teaspoon salt	1 teaspoon salt

Prepare the yeast liquid by dissolving the sugar in the milk and water and sprinkling the yeast on top. Leave until frothy, about 10 minutes. Rub the lard into the flour and salt. Add the yeast liquid to the flour and work to a soft dough. Turn on to a lightly floured surface and knead until the dough is smooth, about 10 minutes. Leave to rise in a lightly greased polythene bag, loosely tied, until doubled in size.

Remove from the polythene bag, knock out air bubbles and knead to make a firm dough. Divide into ten equal pieces. Shape each into a ball and roll out to an oval about 1 cm/½ inch thick. Place on a floured baking tray and dredge tops with flour.

Cover with greased polythene and leave to rise at room temperature for approximately 30 minutes. Remove polythene and bake in a moderately hot oven (200°C, 400°F, Gas Mark 6) for 15–20 minutes. Cool on a wire rack.

Makes 10

Wheatmeal bread

Brioche

Metric/Imperial	American
½ teaspoon sugar	½ teaspoon sugar
1½ tablespoons warm water (43°C, 110°F)	2 tablespoons warm water (110°F)
2 teaspoons dried yeast	2 teaspoons active dry yeast
50 g/2 oz butter	¼ cup butter
2 eggs	2 eggs
225 g/8 oz plain flour	2 cups all-purpose flour
½ teaspoon salt	½ teaspoon salt
15 g/½ oz sugar	1 tablespoon sugar
beaten egg to glaze	beaten egg to glaze

Prepare the yeast liquid: dissolve the ½ teaspoon sugar in the water and sprinkle the yeast on top. Leave until frothy, about 10 minutes.

Melt the butter, allow to cool, and beat the eggs. Add the yeast liquid, eggs and butter to the flour, salt and remaining sugar. Work to a soft dough. Turn out on to a lightly floured surface and knead well for 5 minutes. Place dough in a lightly greased polythene bag and allow to rise in a cool place for 2–3 hours or in a refrigerator for up to 12 hours. A cool rising makes dough easier to shape.

Grease twelve 7·5-cm/3-inch brioche or deep bun tins. Turn out the risen dough on to a lightly floured surface, divide into quarters, and divide each quarter into three. With each piece use three-quarters to form a ball, place in tin and firmly press down each one in the centre. Form the remaining quarter of dough into a knob and place in the centre. Place tins on a baking tray inside a greased polythene bag and leave to rise in a warm place for about 1 hour, until light and puffy. Remove from polythene bag. Brush brioches with beaten egg or milk and water and bake in a moderately hot oven (200°C, 400°F, Gas Mark 6) for 15–20 minutes. Serve warm.

Note For something different, scoop out centres of brioches and fill with finely chopped fruit mixed with cream, fruit purée or a mousse mixture.

Makes 12

Hot Cross Buns

Metric/Imperial	American
Yeast liquid	**Yeast liquid**
1 tablespoon dried yeast	1 tablespoon active dry yeast
150 ml/¼ pint warm milk (43°C, 110°F)	⅔ cup warm milk (110°F)
150 ml/¼ pint less 3 tablespoons warm water	⅔ cup less ¼ cup warm water
1 teaspoon sugar	1 teaspoon sugar
100 g/4 oz plain flour	1 cup all-purpose flour
Dough	**Dough**
350 g/12 oz plain flour	3 cups all-purpose flour
1 teaspoon salt	1 teaspoon salt
½ teaspoon each mixed spice, ground cinnamon and grated nutmeg	½ teaspoon each mixed spice, ground cinnamon and grated nutmeg
50 g/2 oz sugar	¼ cup sugar
100 g/4 oz currants	⅔ cup currants
25–50 g/1–2 oz mixed peel	¼–⅓ cup candied peel
50 g/2 oz butter, melted	¼ cup butter, melted
1 egg, beaten	1 egg, beaten
Glaze	**Glaze**
2 tablespoons mixed water and milk	3 tablespoons mixed water and milk
40 g/1½ oz sugar	3 tablespoons sugar

Blend the yeast with the mixed milk and water, sugar and flour. Leave until frothy, about 20–30 minutes.

For the dough, sift together the flour, salt and spices. Add the sugar, currants and mixed peel. Stir the butter and egg into the yeast batter, add the flour and fruit mixture and mix well. Knead the dough on a floured surface for approximately 10 minutes.

Divide the dough into 12 pieces and shape into buns by using the palm of one hand, first pressing down hard and then easing up. Place on a floured baking tray spaced well apart. Put inside a greased polythene bag and leave to rise at room temperature for about 45 minutes. Remove from bag. Make a cross on each bun with a very sharp knife to just cut the surface of the dough. Bake in a hot oven (220°C, 425°F, Gas Mark 7) until golden brown, about 15–20 minutes. Leave to cool on a wire rack.

For the glaze: bring water and milk to the boil, stir in sugar and boil for 2 minutes. Brush hot buns twice.

Note For a more definitely shaped cross, place two strips of shortcrust pastry on the buns after glazing with milk and before baking. There is no need to glaze afterwards.

Makes 12

Brioche

Doughnuts

Metric/Imperial	American
Yeast liquid	**Yeast liquid**
2 teaspoons dried yeast	2 teaspoons active dry yeast
150 ml/¼ pint less 3 tablespoons warm milk (43°C, 110°F)	⅔ cup less ¼ cup warm milk (110°F)
½ teaspoon castor sugar	½ teaspoon sugar
50 g/2 oz plain flour	½ cup all-purpose flour
Dough	**Dough**
½ teaspoon salt	½ teaspoon salt
175 g/6 oz plain flour	1½ cups all-purpose flour
1 egg, beaten	1 egg, beaten
15 g/½ oz butter, melted	1 tablespoon butter, melted
Filling	**Filling**
2 tablespoons raspberry jam	3 tablespoons raspberry jam
hot fat for frying (187°C, 370°F)	hot fat for frying (370°F)
Coating	**Coating**
50 g/2 oz castor sugar	¼ cup sugar
½ teaspoon ground cinnamon	½ teaspoon ground cinnamon

Blend the yeast with the warm milk, sugar and flour. Leave until frothy, about 20–30 minutes.

For the dough, sift the salt and flour together, add to the yeast mixture with the egg and butter and mix well.

Knead the dough well on a lightly floured surface and divide into eight equal pieces. Form into eight rounds by rolling each piece of dough into a ball, pressing down hard at first with the floured palm of the hand then easing up. Cover with a greased polythene sheet and leave to rise for about 30 minutes at room temperature. Remove polythene. Make a hole in the middle of each round with the handle of a wooden spoon. Fill each with ½ teaspoon jam and pinch back into shape.

Deep fry in hot fat for 4 minutes. Drain on crumpled absorbent paper and roll while hot in mixed sugar and cinnamon to coat.

Makes 8

Harvest Loaf

Metric/Imperial	American
2 teaspoons dried yeast	2 teaspoons active dry yeast
300 ml/½ pint less 2 tablespoons warm water (43°C, 110°F)	1¼ cups less 3 tablespoons warm water (110°F)
1 teaspoon sugar	1 teaspoon sugar
15 g/½ oz lard	1 tablespoon shortening
0·5 kg/1 lb plain flour	4 cups all-purpose flour
2 teaspoons salt	2 teaspoons salt
beaten egg or milk and water to glaze	beaten egg or milk and water to glaze

Blend the yeast with the warm water and sugar and leave until frothy, about 10 minutes. Rub the lard into the flour and salt. Add the yeast liquid and mix to a firm dough until sides of bowl are clean. Turn on to a floured surface and knead for about 10 minutes until smooth. Leave to rise in a greased polythene bag, loosely tied, until doubled in size.

Remove from polythene bag, knock out air bubbles and knead dough well on a lightly floured surface. Divide into four pieces. Roll three pieces into strands 50 cm/20 inches long and join together at one end. Place on a greased baking tray, plait loosely together and tuck ends underneath. Brush with beaten egg or milk and water. Divide the remaining dough in half and roll each half into a strand. Join at one end and twist strands loosely. Lay along centre of plait, tucking ends underneath. Brush with beaten egg or milk and water.

Cover and leave to rise at room temperature for about 30 minutes. Bake for 30–40 minutes in a hot oven (230°C, 450°F, Gas Mark 8) until well risen and golden brown. Cool on a wire rack, and use as a centrepiece for a party buffet.

Malt Loaf

Metric/Imperial	American
1 teaspoon sugar	1 teaspoon sugar
150 ml/¼ pint plus 3 table-spoons warm water (43°C, 110°F)	⅔ cup plus ¼ cup warm water (110°F)
1 tablespoon dried yeast	1 tablespoon active dry yeast
0·5 kg/1 lb plain flour	4 cups all-purpose flour
1 teaspoon salt	1 teaspoon salt
3 tablespoons malt extract	4 tablespoons molasses
2 tablespoons black treacle	3 tablespoons dark corn syrup
25 g/1 oz margarine	2 tablespoons margarine
honey for glazing	honey for glazing

Prepare the yeast liquid by dissolving the sugar in the water and sprinkling the yeast on top. Leave until frothy, about 10 minutes. Sift the flour and salt together. Warm together the malt extract, treacle and margarine; cool. Add with the yeast liquid to the flour and work to a soft dough. Add a little extra flour if too soft. Turn on to a floured surface and knead well until smooth and elastic.

Divide the dough in half, flatten each piece and roll up as for a Swiss roll to fit two greased 0·5-kg/1-lb loaf tins. Put to rise in large lightly greased polythene bags until the dough rises to the tops of the tins and springs back when lightly pressed.

Remove from bags and bake the loaves in a moderately hot oven (200°C, 400°F, Gas Mark 6) for 40–45 minutes. Turn out and brush the tops of the hot loaves with a wet brush dipped in honey; cool on a wire rack.

Makes 2

Orange and Cinnamon Whirl

Metric/Imperial	American
Yeast liquid	**Yeast liquid**
1 teaspoon sugar	1 teaspoon sugar
150 ml/¼ pint warm water (43°C, 110°F)	⅔ cup warm water (110°F)
2 teaspoons dried yeast	2 teaspoons active dry yeast
Dough	**Dough**
0·5 kg/1 lb plain flour	4 cups all-purpose flour
2 teaspoons salt	2 teaspoons salt
40 g/1½ oz castor sugar	3 tablespoons sugar
2 eggs, beaten	2 eggs, beaten
grated rind and juice of 1 orange	grated rind and juice of 1 orange
Filling	**Filling**
4 tablespoons apricot jam	⅓ cup apricot jam
1 tablespoon ground cinnamon	1 tablespoon ground cinnamon
50 g/2 oz soft brown sugar	¼ cup soft brown sugar

Prepare the yeast liquid by dissolving the sugar in the water, sprinkling the yeast on top and leaving until frothy, about 10 minutes.

Mix together the flour, salt, sugar and beaten eggs, add the orange rind and juice and add to the yeast liquid. Work to a firm dough, adding 2–3 (US 3–4) tablespoons extra water if required. Turn out and knead well on a floured surface for about 10 minutes. Put to rise in a greased polythene bag, loosely tied, until doubled in size.

Turn out and knead the dough until firm. Roll into two 15 × 33-cm/6 × 13-inch rectangles. Spread each rectangle with apricot jam and sprinkle on the cinnamon and sugar. Roll up as for a Swiss roll. Place in two 0·5-kg/1-lb greased loaf tins. Put inside a greased polythene bag and leave to rise for about 30 minutes.

Remove bag and bake in a moderately hot oven (200°C, 400°F, Gas Mark 6) for 30–35 minutes. Turn out and cool on a wire rack. Serve sliced with butter and apricot jam.

Makes 2

Orange and cinnamon whirl

Chelsea Buns

Metric/Imperial	American
Yeast liquid	**Yeast liquid**
2 teaspoons dried yeast	2 teaspoons active dry yeast
150 ml/¼ pint less 3 table-spoons warm milk (43°C, 110°F)	⅔ cup less ¼ cup warm milk (110°F)
½ teaspoon sugar	½ teaspoon sugar
50 g/2 oz plain flour	½ cup all-purpose flour
Dough	**Dough**
175 g/6 oz plain flour	1½ cups all-purpose flour
½ teaspoon salt	½ teaspoon salt
1 egg, beaten	1 egg, beaten
15 g/½ oz butter, melted	1 tablespoon butter, melted
Filling	**Filling**
15 g/½ oz butter, melted	1 tablespoon butter, melted
50 g/2 oz soft brown sugar	¼ cup soft brown sugar
75 g/3 oz currants	½ cup currants
25 g/1 oz chopped mixed peel	3 tablespoons chopped candied peel
honey for glazing	honey for glazing

Blend the yeast with the warm milk, sugar and flour. Leave until frothy, about 20–30 minutes.

To make the dough, mix the flour and salt together, add to the yeast mixture with the egg and butter and mix well. Knead dough on a lightly floured surface for about 10 minutes. Put to rise in a large greased polythene bag, loosely tied, until doubled in size.

Remove from polythene, knead well on a lightly floured surface and roll to a rectangle approximately 23 × 30 cm/9 × 12 inches. Brush with the butter and sprinkle on the sugar, currants and peel. Roll up as for a Swiss roll and seal edge. Cut into nine slices. Place in a greased 18-cm/7-inch square tin, cut sides down. Leave to rise inside a greased polythene bag until the dough feels springy. Remove from polythene bag and bake in a moderately hot oven (190°C, 375°F, Gas Mark 5) for 30–35 minutes. Remove buns from tin, place on a wire rack and glaze hot buns with a wet brush dipped in honey.

Note Pick a rising time to fit in with the day's plans. *Quick rise* 45–60 minutes in a warm place. *Slower rise* 2 hours at average room temperature. *Overnight rise* Up to 12 hours in a cold larder or up to 24 hours in a refrigerator.

Makes 9

Welsh Currant Bread

Metric/Imperial	American
Yeast liquid	**Yeast liquid**
100 g/4 oz plain flour	1 cup all-purpose flour
1½ tablespoons dried yeast	2 tablespoons active dry yeast
1 teaspoon sugar	1 teaspoon sugar
300 ml/½ pint less 6 table-spoons warm water (43°C, 110°F)	¾ cup warm water (110°F)
Dough	**Dough**
75 g/3 oz margarine	⅓ cup margarine
350 g/12 oz plain flour	3 cups all-purpose flour
75 g/3 oz demerara sugar	6 tablespoons light brown sugar
1 teaspoon salt	1 teaspoon salt
1 teaspoon mixed spice	1 teaspoon mixed spice
0·75 kg/1½ lb mixed raisins, currants, sultanas and peel	4½ cups mixed raisins, currants, seedless raisins and candied peel
1 egg, beaten	1 egg, beaten
honey for glazing	honey for glazing

Put the flour into a large bowl. Add the yeast, sugar and water, mix well. Set aside until frothy, about 20 minutes.

To make the dough, rub margarine into the flour and mix in the sugar, salt, spice and fruit. Add the egg and flour mixture to the yeast liquid and mix well. Knead the dough thoroughly on a lightly floured surface. Place in a greased polythene bag, loosely tied, and allow to rise until doubled in size.

Turn out the dough and knock out air bubbles; knead well. Divide in half and shape to fit two greased 0·5-kg/1-lb loaf tins. Place each tin in a greased polythene bag and allow dough to rise to 2·5 cm/1 inch above tops of tins. Remove from poly-thene bags and bake in a moderate oven (180°C, 350°F, Gas Mark 4) for 50–60 minutes. Turn out, place on a wire rack and, while still hot, glaze with a wet brush dipped in honey.

Note To test if loaf is cooked, tap underneath with knuckles; it should sound hollow. The loaf will also shrink slightly from sides of tin.

Makes 2

Orange Raisin Ring

Metric/Imperial	American
Yeast liquid	**Yeast liquid**
2 teaspoons dried yeast	2 teaspoons active dry yeast
150 ml/¼ pint less 3 table-spoons warm milk (43°C, 110°F)	⅔ cup less ¼ cup warm milk (110°F)
½ teaspoon sugar	½ teaspoon sugar
50 g/2 oz plain flour	½ cup all-purpose flour
Dough	**Dough**
½ teaspoon salt	½ teaspoon salt
175 g/6 oz plain flour	1½ cups all-purpose flour
15 g/½ oz butter, melted	1 tablespoon butter, melted
1 egg, beaten	1 egg, beaten
Filling and decoration	**Filling and decoration**
15 g/½ oz butter, melted	1 tablespoon butter, melted
50 g/2 oz brown sugar	¼ cup brown sugar
50 g/2 oz raisins	⅓ cup raisins
grated rind of 1 orange	grated rind of 1 orange
50 g/2 oz icing sugar	½ cup confectioners' sugar
25 g/1 oz shredded almonds	¼ cup shredded almonds

Blend the yeast with the warm milk, sugar and flour. Leave until frothy, about 20–30 minutes.

For the dough, mix the salt with the flour, add to the yeast mixture with the butter and egg, and mix well. Knead dough on a floured surface for about 10 minutes.

Put to rise in a greased polythene bag, loosely tied, until doubled in size. Remove from polythene bag and roll dough into a rectangle 30 × 23 cm/12 × 9 inches. Brush with the butter, sprinkle the sugar, raisins and orange rind on top. Roll up as for a Swiss roll and seal edge. Bring ends of roll together to form a ring, seal ends and put on a greased baking tray. With scissors make 2·5-cm/1-inch slashes to within 1 cm/½ inch of the centre and separate by turning each piece gently sideways. Leave to rise inside a greased polythene bag for about 30 minutes. Remove from polythene and bake for 30–35 minutes in a moder-ate oven (180°C, 350°F, Gas Mark 4). Cool on a wire rack. Ice with water icing and decorate with shredded almonds.

Note To make water icing sieve the icing sugar twice. Beat in a tablespoonful of cold water at a time until mixture coats the back of a wooden spoon. Use this icing to cover cakes as well as bread.

Lardy cake

Lardy Cake

Metric/Imperial	American
1 teaspoon sugar	1 teaspoon sugar
300 ml/½ pint warm water (43°C, 110°F)	1¼ cups warm water (110°F)
2 teaspoons dried yeast	2 teaspoons active dry yeast
115 g/4½ oz lard	9 tablespoons shortening
0·5 kg/1 lb plain flour	4 cups all-purpose flour
2 teaspoons salt	2 teaspoons salt
Glaze	**Glaze**
oil	oil
100 g/4 oz castor sugar	½ cup sugar

Prepare the yeast liquid by dissolving the sugar in the water and sprinkling the yeast on top. Leave until frothy, about 10 minutes. Rub 15 g/½ oz (US 1 tablespoon) lard into the flour and salt and mix in the yeast liquid. Work to a firm dough until the sides of the bowl are clean. Turn out on to a lightly floured surface and knead thoroughly, about 10 minutes. Place in a greased polythene bag, loosely tied, and leave to rise until doubled in size.

Turn the dough on to a lightly floured surface and roll to a rectangle approximately 38 × 15 cm/15 × 6 inches and 5 mm/¼ inch thick. Dot one-third of the lard over the top two-thirds of the dough. Fold the uncovered one-third upwards and the top one-third over it. Seal edges, turn dough so that folded edge is on the left and repeat rolling once more.

Roll out the dough to fit a 20 × 25-cm/8 × 10-inch shallow baking tin and press down to fill corners. Place in a greased polythene bag and leave to rise until doubled in size. Remove from bag. Brush with oil and sprinkle with sugar. Criss-cross top by lightly scoring with a very sharp knife. Bake for 30 minutes in a hot oven (220°C, 425°F, Gas Mark 7). Turn out and cool on a wire rack.

Serve hot with jam as a pudding or cold as a cake for tea.

Hot and cold puddings

One of the most difficult problems in planning a dinner party is the choice of a sweet that will suitably complement and crown the rest of the meal. That problem should be made somewhat easier with the wealth of ideas in this chapter, ranging from a creamy pear flan to a refreshing melon sorbet.

And your family will find much of interest here as well. The children will love a treacle tart, caramel custards or home-made coffee ice cream. Easy-to-make recipes for using up what you already have in the pantry, like hot banana or bread and butter pudding, will also prove useful. Meringues and cheesecakes, cold soufflés and traditional trifle, all should be delicious answers to that ever-present question of what to serve after a super meal.

Tyrolean Shortbread

Metric/Imperial	American
175 g/6 oz plain flour	1½ cups all-purpose flour
100 g/4 oz butter	½ cup butter
50 g/2 oz castor sugar	¼ cup sugar
1 large cooking apple	1 large baking apple
4 teaspoons dark brown sugar	4 teaspoons dark brown sugar
¼ teaspoon ground cinnamon	¼ teaspoon ground cinnamon
15 g/½ oz flaked almonds	½ oz flaked almonds

Sift the flour into a bowl, add the butter cut in small pieces and the sugar. Rub in the butter until the mixture resembles fine breadcrumbs, then knead until it leaves the bowl clean. Turn on to a lightly floured surface and knead until smooth. Roll out to a 20-cm/8-inch round and place on a baking tray; flute the edges.

Peel, core and slice the apple and arrange on top of the shortbread, leaving a 1-cm/½-inch border around the edge.

Mix the sugar and cinnamon together, sprinkle over the apple slices, and scatter the almonds on top.

Bake in the centre of a moderate oven (160°C, 325°F, Gas Mark 3) until the shortbread is a pale golden brown and the apples tender, about 30 minutes. Leave to cool on the baking tray for 10 minutes, transfer to a dish and serve warm, cut in wedges with whipped cream or ice cream.

Note This pudding may be served cold, in which case mark into eight wedges while still warm.

Walnuts and almonds to decorate

Creamy Pear Flan

Metric/Imperial	American
175 g/6 oz rich shortcrust pastry (see page 136)	1½ cups rich basic pie dough (see page 136)
Filling	Filling
3 small peeled, cored and halved pears	3 small peeled, cored and halved pears
150 ml/¼ pint double cream	⅔ cup whipping cream
50 g/2 oz castor sugar	¼ cup sugar
1 teaspoon vanilla essence	1 teaspoon vanilla extract

Line a 20-cm/8-inch fluted flan tin with the pastry. Fill with a piece of crumpled foil or greaseproof paper and baking beans and bake in a moderately hot oven (190°C, 375°F, Gas Mark 5) for 10 minutes. Remove paper and bake for a further 5 minutes to dry base of flan. Remove from oven and leave to cool.

Arrange pears in the base of the flan. Blend the cream, sugar and vanilla essence and pour over pears. Return to the oven for about 40 minutes. Serve hot or cold.

Lemon Meringue Pie

Metric/Imperial
Rich shortcrust pastry
175 g/6 oz plain flour
100 g/4 oz butter
1 egg yolk
25 g/1 oz castor sugar
2 teaspoons water
Filling
2 large lemons
40 g/1½ oz cornflour
300 ml/½ pint water
2 egg yolks
75 g/3 oz castor sugar
Meringue topping
3 egg whites
150 g/5 oz castor sugar
orange wedges to garnish

American
Rich basic pie dough
1½ cups all-purpose flour
½ cup butter
1 egg yolk
2 tablespoons sugar
2 teaspoons water
Filling
2 large lemons
⅓ cup cornstarch
1¼ cups water
2 egg yolks
⅓ cup sugar
Meringue topping
3 egg whites
⅔ cup sugar
orange wedges to garnish

Make the shortcrust pastry in the usual way, adding the egg yolk and sugar to the dough (see page 38). Use to line a 20-cm/ 8-inch metal pie plate or fluted china flan dish. Prick base with a fork and leave in a cool place for 20 minutes. Fill with a piece of crumpled foil or greaseproof paper and baking beans. Bake in a moderately hot oven (200°C, 400°F, Gas Mark 6) for about 15 minutes. Remove paper and baking beans. Return to oven for 5–10 minutes.

Grate the rind and squeeze the juice from the lemons. Place in a bowl with cornflour, add 2 (US 3) tablespoons of the water and blend until smooth. Boil the remaining water and pour it on to the cornflour mixture. Return to pan, bring to the boil and simmer for 3 minutes until thick. Remove from the heat and add the egg yolks and sugar. Cool slightly then spoon into the flan case.

Whisk the egg whites until they form soft peaks. Add the sugar 1 teaspoon at a time, whisking well after each addition. Pipe or spoon meringue over lemon filling. Bake in a moderate oven (180°C, 350°F, Gas Mark 4) for about 15 minutes. Garnish with orange wedges.

Treacle tart

Treacle Tart

Metric/Imperial	American
100 g/4 oz plain flour	1 cup all-purpose flour
pinch salt	pinch salt
25 g/1 oz lard	2 tablespoons shortening
25 g/1 oz butter	2 tablespoons butter
water	water
Filling	**Filling**
6 tablespoons golden syrup	½ cup corn syrup
50 g/2 oz fresh white breadcrumbs	1 cup fresh white bread crumbs
juice and rind of 1 lemon	juice and rind of 1 lemon
25 g/1 oz demerara sugar	2 tablespoons light brown sugar
chopped glacé cherries to decorate	chopped candied cherries to decorate

Sieve the flour and salt into a bowl. Add fats cut in small pieces and rub them into the flour until mixture resembles fine bread-crumbs. Add sufficient water to mix to a firm dough. Roll out pastry thinly on a floured surface and use to line an 18-cm/7-inch ovenglass or fluted flan dish.

Mix together the syrup, breadcrumbs, lemon juice and rind. Spoon filling into flan. Sprinkle with demerara sugar. Bake in a moderately hot oven (200°C, 400°F, Gas Mark 6) for 25 minutes until pastry is pale golden. Decorate with chopped glacé cherries and serve with cream or evaporated milk.

Note To make sure that pastry browns underneath when using an ovenglass dish, place, while baking, on a metal baking tray that has been heated in the oven.

Bakewell Tart

Metric/Imperial	American
175 g/6 oz plain flour	1½ cups all-purpose flour
¼ teaspoon salt	¼ teaspoon salt
40 g/1½ oz butter	3 tablespoons butter
40 g/1½ oz lard	3 tablespoons shortening
water	water
milk	milk
Filling	**Filling**
100 g/4 oz butter	½ cup butter
100 g/4 oz castor sugar	½ cup sugar
1 egg	1 egg
25 g/1 oz ground almonds	¼ cup ground almonds
75 g/3 oz ground rice	½ cup ground rice
½ teaspoon almond essence	½ teaspoon almond extract
1½ tablespoons raspberry or strawberry jam	1½ tablespoons raspberry or strawberry jam

Sieve the flour and salt into a bowl. Cut fats in small pieces and rub into the flour until mixture resembles fine breadcrumbs. Mix to a firm dough with water. Roll pastry out thinly on a lightly floured surface and use to line a 20-cm/8-inch plain flan ring. Place on a baking tray; reserve trimmings and prick the base. Cool for 10 minutes.

Heat the butter for the filling until it has just melted but is not brown. Stir in the sugar and cook for 1 minute, then add the egg, ground almonds, rice and essence. Spread base of flan with jam and pour filling on top. Roll strips from the pastry trimmings and arrange in a lattice pattern on top of the tart, fixing with milk.

Bake in a moderately hot oven (200°C, 400°F, Gas Mark 6) for 30 minutes until well risen and golden brown. The filling should spring back into shape when lightly pressed with a finger. Remove flan ring and cool on a wire rack.

Caramel Custards

Metric/Imperial	American
Caramel	**Caramel**
75 g/3 oz granulated sugar	⅓ cup sugar
50 ml/2 fl oz water	¼ cup water
Custard	**Custard**
4 eggs	4 eggs
40 g/1½ oz castor sugar	3 tablespoons sugar
600 ml/1 pint milk	2½ cups milk
few drops vanilla essence	few drops vanilla extract

First make the caramel: place the sugar with the water in a heavy pan over a low heat and allow the sugar to dissolve without boiling. When it has dissolved bring syrup to boiling point and boil until it is a pale golden brown. Pour the caramel into dariole moulds and make sure the bases are evenly covered. When cool, butter the sides of the moulds.

Now make the custard: blend together the eggs and sugar. Warm the milk, then pour it on to the egg mixture, mix well and add a few drops of vanilla essence.

Strain the custard into the moulds and place the moulds in a meat tin half filled with hot water. Bake in a cool oven (150°C, 300°F, Gas Mark 2) until set or when a knife inserted in the centre comes out clean, about 45–60 minutes.

Remove from the oven and leave to become completely cold, at least 12 hours or preferably overnight in the refrigerator. Turn out carefully on to a flat serving dish.

Note Do not worry if the custard takes longer to cook than the time given – it will set eventually. Do not increase the oven temperature or the custard will boil.

Serves 4–6

Crème Brûlée

Metric/Imperial	American
Cream custard	**Cream custard**
4 egg yolks	4 egg yolks
50 g/2 oz castor sugar	¼ cup sugar
300 ml/½ pint double cream	1¼ cups whipping cream
300 ml/½ pint single cream	1¼ cups light cream
few drops vanilla essence	few drops vanilla extract
Caramel topping	**Caramel topping**
75 g/3 oz granulated sugar	6 tablespoons sugar
50 ml/2 fl oz water	¼ cup water

Blend together the egg yolks and sugar. Pour the creams on to the egg mixture and stir in a few drops of vanilla essence. Strain the custard into a 900-ml/1½-pint (US 2-pint) ovenproof serving dish and stand dish in a meat tin containing 2·5 cm/ 1 inch of hot water.

Bake the custard in a cool oven (150°C, 300°F, Gas Mark 2) for 45 minutes until just firm. Cool and leave in a cold place or the refrigerator overnight.

Next day make the caramel: put the sugar and water in a heavy pan and dissolve over a low heat, then boil rapidly until a pale caramel colour. Quickly pour three-quarters of the caramel over the top of the custard and pour the remainder on to a well oiled tray. When set, crush and arrange round edge of dish.

Note For a quicker topping simply sprinkle the custard with demerara sugar and place under a hot preheated grill until sugar melts. Leave to harden, then serve.

Serves 4

Norwegian Cream

Metric/Imperial	American
2 tablespoons apricot jam	3 tablespoons apricot jam
3 eggs	3 eggs
25 g/1 oz castor sugar	2 tablespoons sugar
450 ml/¾ pint hot milk	2 cups hot milk
few drops vanilla essence	few drops vanilla extract
Decoration	**Decoration**
1 tablespoon castor sugar	1 tablespoon sugar
4 tablespoons double cream, whipped	⅓ cup whipped cream
2 tablespoons grated chocolate	3 tablespoons grated chocolate

Spread jam at the bottom of a 15-cm/6-inch soufflé dish. Beat two eggs and one extra yolk with the sugar. Pour on the hot milk and stir in the vanilla. Strain this mixture into the prepared dish and cover with foil. Then stand dish in a meat tin containing 2·5 cm/1 inch of hot water. Cook for 45–55 minutes in a moderate oven (180°C, 350°F, Gas Mark 4) until firm to touch. Remove from hot water and leave to cool.

Whisk the remaining egg white until stiff, then whisk in the sugar and fold in the whipped cream. Sprinkle chocolate over the cold custard and pile cream on top.

Note To test that custard is cooked in centre insert a skewer which should come out damp but clean.

Serves 4

Oranges in Liqueur

Metric/Imperial	American
6 large seedless oranges	6 large seedless oranges
175 g/6 oz castor sugar	¾ cup sugar
2–3 tablespoons Cointreau, Grand Marnier or Curaçao	3–4 tablespoons Cointreau, Grand Marnier or Curaçao

Peel one orange thinly with a potato peeler. Cut peel into fine shreds. Put in a bowl and cover with boiling water. Leave for 10 minutes then drain and put on one side.

Cut peel and pith from all oranges. Cut oranges in thin slices. Arrange orange slices, overlapping, in a serving dish. Sprinkle with sugar and liqueur. Cover and leave in a cold place to chill overnight.

Just before serving, top with orange shreds and serve with whipped cream.

Note To prepare orange segments instead of slices, peel orange and remove pith. Then hold orange in one hand and with a sharp knife dissect out each segment, leaving the membrane and skin behind. This takes longer than slices but is well worth it.

Serves 6

Oranges in liqueur

Pineapple salad

Loganberry Mousse

Metric/Imperial	American
425-g/15-oz can loganberries	15-oz can loganberries
	1 package raspberry-flavoured gelatin
170-g/6-oz can evaporated milk	6-oz can evaporated milk
1 teaspoon lemon juice	1 teaspoon lemon juice
Decoration	**Decoration**
2 tablespoons double cream, whipped	3 tablespoons whipped cream
few fresh loganberries (optional)	few fresh loganberries (optional)

Strain juice from loganberries into a measuring jug and make up to 300 ml/½ pint (US 1¼ cups) with water. Put juice in a pan and bring to boiling point. Add the jelly in small pieces and stir until dissolved. Leave in a cool place until just beginning to set.

Sieve loganberries. Put evaporated milk and lemon juice in a bowl and whisk until it forms soft peaks. Fold loganberry purée and evaporated milk into the half set jelly. Mix well, then spoon into a serving dish.

Leave in a cool place. Just before serving decorate the mousse with whipped cream and, if desired, fresh loganberries.

Note   Chill evaporated milk before whisking for cold desserts. Not only do you get more volume, but it helps to set the jelly more rapidly.

Serves 4

Pineapple Salad

Metric/Imperial	American
2 small pineapples	2 small pineapples
1 apple	1 apple
3 pears	3 pears
225 g/8 oz green grapes	½ lb white grapes
castor sugar	sugar
1 tablespoon Grand Marnier or Cointreau	1 tablespoon Grand Marnier or Cointreau

Cut the pineapples in half lengthwise. Scoop out the flesh and remove the core. Cut the flesh into small pieces and place in a bowl.

Peel, core and slice the apple and pears and if desired seed the grapes. Add to the pineapple. Sprinkle with sugar to taste and add the liqueur. Leave the bowl covered in a cool place until the sugar has dissolved.

Just before serving pile the fruit back in the pineapple shells. Remaining fruit may be offered separately.

Serves 4

Loganberry mousse

Blackcurrant Fool

Metric/Imperial	American
0·5 kg/1 lb fresh or frozen blackcurrants	4 cups fresh or frozen black currants
150 ml/¼ pint water	⅔ cup water
150 g/5 oz castor sugar	⅔ cup sugar
150 ml/¼ pint double cream	⅔ cup whipping cream

Stew the blackcurrants slowly in a covered pan with the water for 20 minutes. Using a nylon sieve purée the fruit. (It may be puréed in a liquidiser first if you wish to make sieving quicker, but the fruit must be sieved as well to remove seeds.) Stir in the sugar while the purée is still hot, then leave to cool and chill.

To serve, pour into a serving dish then lightly whip the cream until beginning to thicken but not so firm that it will hold in peaks. Pour cream into blackcurrant purée stirring slowly so that the cream makes streaks but is not mixed in.

To freeze   Freeze sweetened purée only, then thaw and add cream.

Note   Do not stir in cream more than 1 hour before eating or the acid fruit will stiffen cream to a solid consistency. Over-stirring cream into purée results in an unattractive mauve pudding instead of dramatic dark and white streaks.

Serves 4–6

Quick orange mousse

Quick Lemon Mousse

Metric/Imperial	**American**
4 eggs	4 eggs
100 g/4 oz castor sugar	½ cup sugar
2 large lemons	2 large lemons
4 teaspoons powdered gelatine	4 teaspoons powdered gelatin
50 ml/2 fl oz water	¼ cup water

Separate the eggs, place the yolks in a bowl with the sugar and beat until creamy.

Grate the rind and squeeze the juice from the lemons and add to the egg mixture.

Put the gelatine in a small bowl or cup with the water and leave to stand for 3 minutes to become a sponge. Stand bowl in a pan of simmering water and allow the gelatine to dissolve.

Cool slightly and stir into lemon mixture. Leave for a few minutes until the mixture begins to set.

Whisk the egg whites until stiff and fold into the lemon mixture. Put in a generous 1-litre/2-pint (US 2½-pint) straight sided dish and chill for at least 2 hours.

To freeze Freeze until solid then wrap in foil and label. To serve remove foil and thaw overnight in the refrigerator or for 4 hours at room temperature.

Variation
Quick Orange Mousse Substitute two medium oranges for the lemons. Decorate with maraschino cherries and a swirl of whipped cream if liked.

Serves 6

Apricot Mousse

Metric/Imperial	American
0·5 kg/1 lb fresh apricots	1 lb fresh apricots
4 tablespoons cold water	⅓ cup cold water
thinly peeled rind and juice of ½ lemon	thinly peeled rind and juice of ½ lemon
150 g/5 oz castor sugar	⅔ cup sugar
4 teaspoons powdered gelatine	4 teaspoons powdered gelatin
3 large eggs	3 large eggs
1 tablespoon apricot or ordinary brandy	1 tablespoon apricot or ordinary brandy
150 ml/¼ pint double cream	⅔ cup whipping cream
150 ml/¼ pint single cream	⅔ cup light cream
few flaked almonds to decorate	few flaked almonds to decorate

Wash apricots. Put in a pan with 1 tablespoon of the water, lemon rind and one-third of the sugar. Cover and simmer until tender.

Discard lemon rind and apricot stones. Sieve apricots to make about 300 ml/½ pint (US 1¼ cups) purée. Dissolve the gelatine in the remaining water in a small bowl over a pan of simmering water.

Separate eggs and put yolks and remaining sugar with the lemon juice in a large bowl over a pan of hot water. Whisk until thick and pale, remove from the heat and blend in the apricot purée, dissolved gelatine and brandy. Leave in a cool place until just beginning to set.

Whisk both creams together until forming soft peaks. Whisk egg whites until stiff. Fold most of the cream and all of the egg whites into the apricot mixture, pour into six individual glasses or a generous 1-litre/2-pint (US 2½-pint) glass dish and leave in a cool place to set. Just before serving decorate with flaked almonds.

Serves 6

Otto's Pavlova

Metric/Imperial	American
icing sugar	confectioners' sugar
2 teaspoons cornflour	2 teaspoons cornstarch
3 egg whites	3 egg whites
1 teaspoon vinegar	1 teaspoon vinegar
1 teaspoon vanilla essence	1 teaspoon vanilla extract
175 g/6 oz castor sugar	¾ cup sugar
150 ml/¼ pint double cream	⅔ cup whipping cream
225 g/8 oz raspberries	2 cups raspberries

Lightly grease a 20–23-cm/8–9-inch sandwich tin, lightly coat with a little icing sugar and cornflour and tip out surplus.

Place the egg whites in a basin and whisk until stiff but not dry.

Blend the cornflour, vinegar and vanilla essence together and whisk into the egg whites with the sugar, 1 teaspoonful at a time, until well blended. The mixture will then be smooth and heavy.

Spread the mixture evenly in the tin and bake in a cool oven (140°C, 275°F, Gas Mark 1) for 1 hour. Remove and leave to cool in the tin before turning out.

Whisk the cream until thick and fold in three-quarters of the raspberries, pile into the centre of the pavlova and decorate with the remaining fruit. Leave to stand for about 1 hour before serving.

Note Pavlova cake may be made in advance and stored in an airtight tin for 3–4 days. The mixture may be baked on a piece of greased greaseproof paper on a baking tray, though it may spread a little.

Serves 8

Apricot mousse

Lemon soufflé

Lemon Soufflé

Metric/Imperial	American
3 lemons	3 lemons
3 large eggs	3 large eggs
150 g/5 oz castor sugar	⅔ cup sugar
4 teaspoons powdered gelatine	4 teaspoons powdered gelatin
50 ml/2 fl oz cold water	¼ cup cold water
150 ml/¼ pint double cream	⅔ cup whipping cream
Decoration	**Decoration**
whipped cream	whipped cream
chopped pistachio nuts (optional)	chopped pistachio nuts (optional)

Cut a piece of greaseproof paper long enough to go round the outside of a 750-ml/1¼-pint (US 1½-pint) soufflé dish and about 5 cm/2 inches deeper than the dish. Tie this round the outside to form a collar.

Finely grate the rind and squeeze the juice from the lemons. Separate the eggs. Put the lemon rind, juice, egg yolks and sugar in a basin over a pan of hot water. Whisk until just beginning to thicken.

Put the gelatine with the water in a small bowl and leave to soak for a few minutes, allowing the gelatine to swell. Place the bowl over a pan of simmering water and leave to dissolve, stirring occasionally. When it has dissolved stir into the lemon mixture. Leave in a cool place until just beginning to set.

Whisk the cream until it forms soft peaks. Fold into mixture. Whisk egg whites stiffly and fold into mixture. Turn soufflé into the prepared dish and leave in a cool place to set. Just before serving remove paper carefully. Pipe a little cream round the edge and, if liked, decorate with pistachio nuts.

Serves 5–6

Cold Gooseberry Soufflé

Metric/Imperial	American
2 teaspoons powdered gelatine	2 teaspoons powdered gelatin
150 ml/¼ pint water	⅔ cup water
0·5 kg/1 lb gooseberries	3 cups gooseberries
4 eggs, separated	4 eggs, separated
150 g/5 oz castor sugar	⅔ cup sugar
few drops green colouring (optional)	few drops green food coloring (optional)
300 ml/½ pint double cream	1¼ cups whipping cream

Prepare a 1·75-litre/3-pint (US 4-pint) soufflé dish with a collar of oiled greaseproof paper tied round, or a 2·25-litre/4-pint (US 5-pint) glass dish.

Place the gelatine in a small pan with half of the measured water and leave to soak. Stew the gooseberries in the remaining water until pulpy, then sieve to remove seeds.

Place the warm gooseberry purée in a bowl with the egg yolks, sugar and colouring. Whisk with a rotary or electric whisk until very thick and mousse-like, about 10 minutes.

Warm the gelatine to melt but do not boil. With a clean whisk stiffly whisk egg whites. Use same whisk to whip cream to a soft peak consistency. With a large metal spoon fold into the gooseberry soufflé mixture first gelatine, then one-third of cream (keep remainder for decoration) and lastly egg white. When just mixed turn into dish and chill.

When set whip remaining cream to firm peaks and pipe round top of soufflé to decorate. Remove paper collar just before serving. Keep at room temperature for 1 hour before serving.

To freeze   This will be easier to freeze in the glass dish than in a soufflé dish with paper collar round. Thaw in refrigerator for 8 hours. Keep at room temperature for 1 hour before serving. The soufflé will shrink slightly.

Note   Gelatine is not difficult to use so long as it is soaked well before melting. It should not boil but when crystals of gelatine are seen to be dissolved it should be poured over the soufflé mixture and folded in, making sure a puddle of gelatine is not at the bottom of the mixing bowl.

Serves 6

Cold Ginger Soufflé

Metric/Imperial	American
450 ml/¾ pint milk	2 cups milk
3 eggs, separated	3 eggs, separated
1 teaspoon ground ginger	1 teaspoon ground ginger
40 g/1½ oz castor sugar	3 tablespoons sugar
3 tablespoons ginger marmalade or chopped stem ginger	¼ cup ginger marmalade or chopped preserved ginger
2 teaspoons powdered gelatine	2 teaspoons powdered gelatin
50 ml/2 fl oz water	¼ cup water
200 ml/⅓ pint double cream	¾ cup whipping cream
few slices stem or crystallised ginger (optional)	few slices preserved or candied ginger (optional)

Prepare a 600–750-ml/1–1¼-pint (US 1¼–1½-pint) soufflé dish with a collar of oiled greaseproof paper round the outside or use a generous 1-litre/2-pint (US 2½-pint) glass dish.

Bring the milk to the boil. Beat the egg yolks, ground ginger and sugar in a bowl with a wooden spoon for 2 minutes. Pour on the boiling milk, stir and return to pan. Cook over a very gentle heat to thicken slightly. The mixture should not boil. Add the ginger marmalade or chopped ginger and leave to cool.

Place the gelatine in a small pan, add water and leave to soak. When the ginger mixture is cold melt the gelatine over a gentle heat, pour into the mixture and stir well. Whip the cream to a soft peak consistency; with a clean whisk whip egg whites to a firm snow. Stand the pan of ginger mixture in a bowl of ice and a little water. Stir with a large metal spoon and as mixture begins to thicken remove from ice and fold in first approximately 3 tablespoons (US ¼ cup) of cream (keep remainder for decoration) then egg white. Turn into dish and leave to set.

When set decorate with the remaining cream, whipped firmer. Pipe rosettes round edge and decorate these with slices of ginger if wished. Remove paper collar before serving.

Note   This type of soufflé does not freeze well and should be eaten on the day it is made. If milk and egg yolk mixture have boiled and curdled, turn quickly into a cold bowl and whisk. The mixture should not be chilled before gelatine is added.

Serves 4–5

Chestnut Cream Vacherin

Metric/Imperial	American
Meringue	**Meringue**
3 egg whites	3 egg whites
175 g/6 oz castor sugar	¾ cup sugar
Chestnut filling	**Chestnut filling**
250-g/8¾-oz can sweetened chestnut purée	8¾-oz can sweetened chestnut purée
150 ml/¼ pint double cream	⅔ cup whipping cream
1–2 tablespoons sherry (optional)	2–3 tablespoons sherry (optional)
marrons glacés (optional)	marrons glacés (optional)

Line a baking tray with silicone paper. Whisk the egg whites very stiffly. Add sugar 1 teaspoon at a time, whisking well after each addition.

Draw a 20-cm/8-inch circle on the silicone paper. Use half the meringue to fill circle and smooth it with a knife. Put spoonfuls of the remaining mixture on to the rest of the paper in seven heaps, drawing them up to a peak with the handle of a teaspoon. Bake in a very cool oven (110°C, 225°F, Gas Mark ¼) until crisp, about 2 hours. Remove and cool on a wire rack.

Put the chestnut purée in a bowl. In another bowl whip the cream until it forms soft peaks. Fold cream into the purée with sherry if used. Spread on to meringue base and arrange small meringues on top. Use the marrons glacés to decorate.

Note It is far better to cook meringues on the slow side, just gently drying them out. Use the coolest oven setting. Too hot an oven causes the sugar to weep out as a syrup and overcolours the meringues.

Serves 6

Chestnut cream vacherin

Strawberry Meringue

Metric/Imperial	American
Meringue case	**Meringue case**
4 egg whites	4 egg whites
225 g/8 oz castor sugar	1 cup sugar
15 g/½ oz flaked almonds	½ oz flaked almonds
Filling	**Filling**
300 ml/½ pint double cream	1¼ cups whipping cream
25 g/1 oz castor sugar	2 tablespoons sugar
2 teaspoons brandy or few drops vanilla essence	2 teaspoons brandy or few drops vanilla extract
0·75 kg/1½ lb strawberries, hulled and halved	6 cups strawberries, hulled and halved

Line two large baking trays with silicone paper, well greased greaseproof paper or foil. Mark out three circles: one 21 cm/8½ inches diameter, one 19 cm/7½ inches and one 14 cm/5½ inches.

Whisk egg whites until they form soft peaks. Add the sugar 1 teaspoon at a time, whisking well after each addition. Reserve 2 teaspoons of sugar. Divide the mixture between the circles. Smooth with a knife. Lift up meringue in peaks on smallest circle then sprinkle with remaining sugar and almonds, reserving a few for decoration. Bake on lower shelves in a very cool oven (110°C, 225°F, Gas Mark ¼) for 3–4 hours.

When meringue layers are crisp remove them from oven. Leave to cool. One hour before serving whip the cream, add the sugar and brandy or vanilla. Blend in a few of the halved strawberries. Spread half the mixture on the two largest meringues. Assemble cake in layers and press remaining strawberry halves round the edge. Pile the remaining cream on top layer and scatter with the remaining almonds.

Note Storing meringues: when meringues are cooked and thoroughly cooled, whether large or small, wrap in foil or arrange in an airtight tin, putting greaseproof paper between each layer. They will still be beautifully fresh in 2 months' time.

Serves 6

Coffee Meringues

Metric/Imperial	American
4 egg whites	4 egg whites
small pinch salt	small pinch salt
4 teaspoons instant coffee (powder or granules)	4 teaspoons instant coffee (powder or granules)
225 g/8 oz castor sugar	1 cup sugar
Filling	**Filling**
300 ml/½ pint double cream	1¼ cups whipping cream
2 tablespoons cold water	3 tablespoons cold water
225 g/8 oz raspberries	2 cups raspberries

Line two baking trays with silicone paper or with greaseproof paper which should be lightly oiled and dusted with flour.

Whisk egg whites and salt to a firm snow, whisk in the coffee until powder or granules dissolve. Add the sugar, 1 tablespoon at a time, whisking well between each addition. Using a star nozzle in a large piping bag, pipe the meringue into baskets: pipe a line of meringue 6 cm/2½ inches long on prepared tray. Pipe an oval round this to form the base. Pipe a further oval on top of the first to complete meringue basket. Meringue swells slightly in cooking so space at least 3·5 cm/1½ inches apart. Use up remaining mixture, making 12–16 meringue baskets. Dust with sugar and bake in a very cool oven (110°C, 225°F, Gas Mark ¼) for 2 hours.

Remove meringues from oven and leave for 1 minute. Lift on to wire rack to cool if really crisp on outside. If not easy to remove from trays, return to oven for a little longer then cool again slightly before removing from tray. When cold store meringues in airtight tins until 1–2 hours before serving.

To serve, whisk cream until beginning to thicken, add cold water and whisk until soft peaks form. Pipe cream into each meringue basket and top with a few raspberries.

Note For a crisp meringue fill less than 30 minutes before serving. For soft centred meringue fill 1–2 hours before serving. If frozen raspberries are used arrange at last minute so their juice does not seep into meringues. Very ripe, canned or cooked apricots also combine well with coffee meringues. Unfilled meringues will keep well in an airtight tin or bag.

Serves 6–8

Savarin

Metric/Imperial
Yeast liquid
1 tablespoon dried yeast
100 ml/4 fl oz warm milk
 (43°C, 110°F)
50 g/2 oz plain flour
15 g/½ oz sugar
Dough
½ teaspoon salt
175 g/6 oz plain flour
15 g/½ oz castor sugar
4 eggs, beaten
100 g/4 oz soft butter, not
 melted
Syrup and filling
6 tablespoons honey
100 ml/4 fl oz water
rum to taste
dessert apple and grapes

American
Yeast liquid
1 tablespoon active dry yeast
½ cup warm milk (110°F)

½ cup all-purpose flour
1 tablespoon sugar
Batter
½ teaspoon salt
1½ cups all-purpose flour
1 tablespoon sugar
4 eggs, beaten
½ cup soft butter, not melted

Syrup and filling
½ cup honey
½ cup water
rum to taste
dessert apple and grapes

Blend the yeast with the warm milk, flour and sugar. Leave until frothy, about 20–30 minutes.

Sift the salt with the remaining flour. Add with the sugar, eggs and butter to the yeast batter; beat well for 4 minutes.

Half fill a greased and floured 20-cm/8-inch fluted or plain ring mould and cover with a greased polythene bag. Leave to rise until the mould is two-thirds full. Bake in a moderately hot oven (200°C, 400°F, Gas Mark 6) for 20 minutes. Turn out on to a warm serving plate and prick with a skewer.

Prepare the syrup by warming the honey and water together; add the rum. Pour over two-thirds of the honey rum syrup while the savarin is still warm and leave to soak. Pour remainder of the syrup over the apple which has been peeled, sliced and cored, add the grapes and leave to soak. Fill the centre of the savarin and decorate the serving dish with the remaining fruit.

Savarin

Note To make rum babas use the savarin recipe and add 100 g/4 oz (US ⅔ cup) currants. Half fill greased dariole moulds and bake for about 15–20 minutes in a hot oven (220°C, 425°F, Gas Mark 7). To serve soak in syrup and sprinkle with rum.

Variation For a creamy version of the savarin, cut the savarin into two layers after soaking in the syrup. Fill with 100 ml/4 fl oz (US ½ cup) double cream and a 198-g/7-oz can of drained peach slices. Decorate with piped cream, glacé cherries and angelica leaves.

German Cheesecake

Metric/Imperial
Shortcrust pastry
175 g/6 oz plain flour
pinch salt
75 g/3 oz butter
25 g/1 oz castor sugar
approx. 2 tablespoons cold
 water
Cheesecake
225 g/8 oz cream cheese
4 egg yolks
100 g/4 oz castor sugar
25 g/1 oz ground almonds
finely grated rind of 1 lemon
142-g/5-oz carton soured
 cream
50 g/2 oz sultanas
50 g/2 oz chopped mixed peel
Meringue
1 egg white
50 g/2 oz castor sugar

American
Basic pie dough
1½ cups all-purpose flour
pinch salt
⅓ cup butter
2 tablespoons sugar
approx. 3 tablespoons cold
 water
Cheesecake
1 cup cream cheese
4 egg yolks
½ cup sugar
¼ cup ground almonds
finely grated rind of 1 lemon
5-oz carton dairy sour cream

⅓ cup seedless raisins
⅓ cup chopped candied peel
Meringue
1 egg white
¼ cup sugar

Make up the pastry in the usual way (see page 38), line a Swiss roll tin 18 × 28 cm/7 × 11 inches and crimp the edges. Cover with foil, then baking beans and bake in a moderately hot oven (200°C, 400°F, Gas Mark 6) for 15 minutes. Remove foil and continue baking for a further 5 minutes until pastry is completely cooked.

Blend the cream cheese with the egg yolks and sugar. Stir in the almonds, lemon rind, soured cream, sultanas and peel; mix well.

Remove pastry case from the oven and turn heat down to moderate (160°C, 325°F, Gas Mark 3). Pour the cheese mixture into the case and return to the oven for 45 minutes.

Whisk the egg white for the meringue until very stiff and whisk in the sugar a spoonful at a time. Remove the cheesecake from the oven and pipe the meringue over the top using a plain 5-mm/¼-inch tube.

Return the cheesecake to the oven and bake for a further 15 minutes. At the end of this time turn off the oven and leave the cheesecake for a further 30 minutes. Remove and chill.

Note This cheesecake improves with keeping for 2–3 days before eating, as it becomes more moist.

Serves 8

Chilled lemon cheesecake

Grapefruit Cheesecake

Metric/Imperial
4 teaspoons powdered
 gelatine
50 ml/2 fl oz cold water
0·5 kg/1 lb rich cream cheese
177-g/6¼-oz can frozen
 grapefruit juice
 concentrate, thawed
75 g/3 oz castor sugar
300 ml/½ pint double cream
75 g/3 oz butter
6 digestive biscuits,
 crushed
75 g/3 oz ginger biscuits,
 crushed
mimosa balls and angelica
 leaves to decorate

American
4 teaspoons powdered
 gelatin
¼ cup cold water
2 cups full fat cream cheese
6¼-oz can frozen grapefruit
 juice concentrate, thawed

6 tablespoons sugar
1¼ cups whipping cream
⅓ cup butter
¾ cup crushed graham
 crackers
¾ cup crushed gingersnaps

mimosa balls and angelica
 leaves to decorate

Place the gelatine in a small bowl with the cold water and leave
to stand for 5 minutes, then place in a pan of simmering water
and leave until the gelatine has dissolved and become clear;
remove and leave to cool.

Cream the cheese until soft and gradually beat in the grapefruit juice concentrate and sugar. Stir in the cooled gelatine.

Whisk the cream until thick but not stiff and fold into the
cheese mixture. Turn into a very lightly oiled 20-cm/8-inch
cake tin. Place in the refrigerator.

Melt the butter in a pan and stir in the crushed biscuit crumbs.
Press over the cheesecake and leave in the refrigerator for
several hours.

Turn out on to a serving dish and decorate with mimosa balls
and angelica leaves.

Serves 8

Chilled Lemon Cheesecake

Metric/Imperial
350 g/12 oz rich cream
 cheese
150 ml/¼ pint single cream
4 teaspoons powdered
 gelatine
4 tablespoons cold water
2 large lemons
3 eggs
100 g/4 oz castor sugar
150 ml/¼ pint double cream
8 digestive biscuits, crushed

25 g/1 oz demerara sugar

50 g/2 oz butter
chocolate curls to decorate

American
1½ cups full fat cream cheese

⅔ cup light cream
4 teaspoons powdered
 gelatin
⅓ cup cold water
2 large lemons
3 eggs
½ cup sugar
⅔ cup whipping cream
1 cup crushed graham
 crackers
2 tablespoons light brown
 sugar
¼ cup butter
chocolate curls to decorate

Butter a 20-cm/8-inch deep cake tin. Line first the sides, then the
base with greaseproof paper.

Mix the cheese with the single cream. Dissolve the gelatine
in the water in a small bowl placed over a pan of simmering
water. Grate the rind and squeeze the juice from the lemons, and
separate the eggs. Place the lemon juice and rind, egg yolks and
sugar in a large bowl over a pan of simmering water. Whisk
until thick and foamy, then remove from heat and whisk until
cool.

Blend together egg yolk mixture, gelatine and cheese mixture. Leave until thick but not set. Whisk egg whites until stiff,
lightly whip the double cream and fold into the cheese mixture.
Turn into the prepared tin and chill until set.

Mix the crushed biscuits with the sugar, melt the butter and
blend into the crushed biscuits, sprinkle over the cheesecake
and press down lightly. Chill until firm. Turn cheesecake out
on to a 25-cm/10-inch plate. Remove paper. Top with chocolate
curls.

Note Putting the crust on top of the set cheesecake then turning it out gives a very crisp crust.

Serves 6–8

Chocolate Rouladin

Metric/Imperial	American
3 eggs	3 eggs
75 g/3 oz icing sugar	¾ cup confectioners' sugar
40 g/1½ oz cocoa powder	6 tablespoons unsweetened cocoa
150 ml/¼ pint double cream	⅔ cup whipping cream
Chocolate sauce	**Chocolate sauce**
150 g/5 oz brown sugar	⅔ cup brown sugar
25 g/1 oz butter	2 tablespoons butter
1 tablespoon cocoa powder	1 tablespoon unsweetened cocoa
150 ml/¼ pint water	⅔ cup water

Grease and flour a Swiss roll tin 18 × 28 cm/7 × 11 inches.

Separate the eggs and beat the yolks until thick. Sieve the icing sugar and thoroughly beat in. Sieve the cocoa and stir in. Whisk the egg whites until stiff and fold in.

Turn into the tin and bake in a moderate oven (180°C, 350°F, Gas Mark 4) until mixture shrinks from edges of the tin, about 10–12 minutes. Turn out on to a floured cloth and cover with a damp cloth. Leave to become cold. Whisk the cream until thick, spread over the cake and roll up.

Make the chocolate sauce: place all the ingredients together in a small pan and heat gently until the sugar has dissolved. Boil rapidly for 3–4 minutes and serve hot or cold with the rouladin.

Note This is a very rich sweet and ideal for a dinner party.

Serves 6

Chocolate Rum Torte

Metric/Imperial	American
185 g/6½ oz plain flour	1½ cups plus 2 tablespoons all-purpose flour
2 tablespoons cocoa powder	3 tablespoons unsweetened cocoa
1 teaspoon bicarbonate of soda	1 teaspoon baking soda
1 rounded teaspoon baking powder	1 rounded teaspoon baking powder
150 g/5 oz castor sugar	⅔ cup sugar
2 tablespoons golden syrup	3 tablespoons corn syrup
2 eggs	2 eggs
150 ml/¼ pint salad or corn oil	⅔ cup salad or corn oil
150 ml/¼ pint milk	⅔ cup milk
Filling and topping	**Filling and topping**
150 ml/¼ pint double cream	⅔ cup whipping cream
50 ml/2 fl oz rum	¼ cup rum
75 g/3 oz plain chocolate	3 squares semi-sweet chocolate
chocolate curls	chocolate curls

Grease and line two 20-cm/8-inch sandwich tins.

Sift the flour, cocoa, bicarbonate of soda and baking powder into a large bowl. Make a well in the centre and add the sugar and syrup. Lightly beat the eggs and add with the oil and milk, beat well and pour into tins. Bake in a moderate oven (160°C, 325°F, Gas Mark 3) until well risen, about 30–35 minutes. Turn out and leave to cool on a wire rack.

Whisk the cream until thick and standing in peaks, fold in two-thirds of the rum. Sandwich the sponge together with flavoured cream. Melt the chocolate with the remaining rum and use to top cake; decorate with chocolate curls.

Serves 6–8

Pineapple Gâteau

Metric/Imperial	American
3 eggs	3 eggs
115 g/4½ oz castor sugar	generous ½ cup sugar
50 g/2 oz self-raising flour	½ cup all-purpose flour sifted with ½ teaspoon baking powder
25 g/1 oz cornflour	¼ cup cornstarch
Filling	**Filling**
150–200 ml/¼–⅓ pint double cream	⅔–¾ cup whipping cream
425-g/15-oz can pineapple rings and syrup	15-oz can pineapple rings and syrup
2 tablespoons apricot jam to glaze	3 tablespoons apricot jam to glaze

Line the base of a 23-cm/9-inch sandwich tin with a disc of greaseproof paper. Oil paper and sides of tin and dust with a little castor sugar.

Whisk the eggs and sugar in a basin until pale and very thick and mousse-like. If using a rotary whisk stand basin in sink in 5 cm/2 inches of very hot water. This is not necessary when an electric mixer is used. When whisk is lifted up the mixture should be thick enough to leave a trail which stays on the surface. Remove whisk, sift the flours over the surface and with a large metal spoon or plastic spatula just carefully fold in. Turn into prepared tin and bake for 15–20 minutes in a moderate oven (180°C, 350°F, Gas Mark 4) until spongy in the centre and just shrinking from the sides. Turn on to a wire rack to cool.

Whisk the cream and when thickening whisk in 1 tablespoon pineapple syrup. When soft and creamy but not yet forming peaks add two pineapple rings, chopped up. Using a bread knife, split the cake in two layers. Lift top half off by slipping a dinner plate between the layers. Fill with pineapple and cream and slip top back in place. Drain and cut remaining pineapple rings in half and arrange over top of cake.

Sieve apricot jam and heat with 2 teaspoons pineapple syrup. Brush over top of pineapple gâteau to glaze.

To freeze Make and fill the cake, decorate but do not glaze until thawed.

Note Take great care folding in sifted flours, as the more you stir the less light your sponge. Do not glaze cake more than 2 hours before serving as the glaze tends to soak into the sponge cake.

Serves 6

Chocolate rum torte

Coffee Cream Cake

Metric/Imperial	American
175 g/6 oz butter	¾ cup butter
175 g/6 oz castor sugar	¾ cup sugar
3 eggs	3 eggs
175 g/6 oz self-raising flour	1½ cups all-purpose flour sifted with 1½ teaspoons baking powder
Coffee syrup	**Coffee syrup**
225 g/8 oz castor sugar	1 cup sugar
450 ml/¾ pint water	2 cups water
1–2 tablespoons brandy or rum (optional)	2–3 tablespoons brandy or rum (optional)
50 ml/2 fl oz coffee essence	¼ cup strong black coffee
Decoration	**Decoration**
300 ml/½ pint double cream	1¼ cups whipping cream
few drops vanilla essence	few drops vanilla extract
walnut halves	walnut halves

Grease a 20-cm/8-inch cake tin and line base with a circle of greased greaseproof paper.

Cream the butter and sugar together until light and creamy. Lightly beat the eggs and gradually beat into the mixture adding 1 tablespoon of flour with the last addition of egg. Fold in the remaining flour. Turn into the prepared tin and bake in a moderately hot oven (190°C, 375°F, Gas Mark 5) for 45–50 minutes.

Make the coffee syrup by dissolving the sugar in the water over a low heat. Remove, add the brandy or rum and coffee essence. Turn the cake out of the tin and remove greaseproof paper, place on a deep serving plate, pierce all over with a skewer and pour over the coffee mixture. It is essential to pour the hot syrup over while the cake is still hot, otherwise the syrup will not be easily absorbed. Leave to soak for at least 12 hours.

Whip the cream and add a few drops of vanilla essence. When the cream is just forming peaks cover the top and sides of the cake and decorate with walnut halves.

Serves 10

Praline Ice Cream

Metric/Imperial	American
40 g/1½ oz whole unblanched almonds	⅓ cup whole unblanched almonds
40 g/1½ oz castor sugar	3 tablespoons sugar
4 eggs	4 eggs
100 g/4 oz icing sugar	scant cup confectioners' sugar
300 ml/½ pint double cream	1¼ cups whipping cream

Put the almonds and sugar in a heavy pan and place over a low heat, stirring occasionally until the sugar has melted and is beginning to caramelise (this may take about 15 minutes). Continue to cook until the mixture is an even golden brown and the nuts are glazed. Remove from the heat and pour on to an oiled enamel plate or baking tray. Leave until quite firm and cold. Turn into a grinder and grind coarsely.

Separate the eggs, place the yolks in a small bowl and whisk until well blended. In another larger bowl whisk the egg whites until stiff then whisk in the sifted icing sugar 1 teaspoon at a time. Whisk the cream until it forms soft peaks then fold into the meringue mixture with the egg yolks and praline. Turn into a 1·5-litre/2½-pint (US 3-pint) rigid container and freeze.

Serve in scoopfuls with sponge finger biscuits or wafers, or use to fill a meringue basket and serve sprinkled with flaked brown nuts on top.

Note If a grinder is not available the praline may be crushed with a rolling pin between sheets of greaseproof paper.

Serves 6–8

Coffee Ice Cream

Metric/Imperial	American
2 eggs	2 eggs
50 g/2 oz castor sugar	¼ cup sugar
2 tablespoons coffee essence	3 tablespoons strong black coffee
150 ml/¼ pint double cream	⅔ cup whipping cream

Separate the eggs. Whisk the egg whites until very stiff then gradually whisk in the sugar. Whisk the egg yolks and coffee essence together and whisk gradually into the egg whites. Lightly whip the cream and fold into the coffee mixture.

Pour into a 900-ml/1½-pint (US 2-pint) ice cube tray or shallow tin and freeze. This ice cream does not need any further beating.

Note If you do not have a freezer it is best to turn the refrigerator to its coldest setting 1 hour before freezing the ice cream. Turn back to normal setting once ice cream has been frozen.

Variation Fold in with the cream 50 g/2 oz (US ½ cup) finely chopped walnuts, lightly crushed meringue, or lightly crushed macaroons.

Serves 6

Hazelnut Shortcake with Peaches and Cream

Metric/Imperial	American
175 g/6 oz shelled hazelnuts	¾ cup shelled hazelnuts
175 g/6 oz butter	¾ cup butter
100 g/4 oz castor sugar	½ cup sugar
225 g/8 oz plain flour	2 cups all-purpose flour
300 ml/½ pint double cream	1¼ cups whipping cream
2 large peaches or 425-g/ 15-oz can white peaches	2 large peaches or 15-oz can white peaches

Place the nuts in a meat tin in a moderate oven for 10 minutes or until golden when the skins are rubbed off. Remove from oven and cool. Rub in a tea towel to loosen skins so they flake off. Grind nuts in a mill, mouli-grater, coffee grinder or mincer.

Cream the butter in a bowl and work in first the sugar then the nuts and flour. Knead with the hands to a smooth biscuit dough. Divide in three. Pat each portion out on a greased baking tray to a 20-cm/8-inch circle. (A flan ring is useful as each circle can be patted to fit this.) Bake for 8–12 minutes in a moderate oven (180°C, 350°F, Gas Mark 4) until just beginning to colour. Remove from oven and mark one circle into eight portions like a cake. Loosen shortcakes underneath with a palette knife but leave to harden on baking tray before moving to wire rack to cool. Keep in a dry atmosphere, or put in a biscuit tin for up to 2–3 days.

To finish, 1–2 hours before serving whip the cream and slice the peaches. Use one-third of the cream and half the peaches to sandwich the biscuit circles. Top with one-third of cream and the remaining peaches. Lay biscuit portions on top. Use the remaining cream to pipe a rosette of cream on each wedge.

To freeze Freeze biscuit dough, wrapped in polythene. Thaw, then pat out and bake. The shortcake is fragile and crisp when cooked and would lose its crispness if frozen.

Note If biscuit rounds have become soft, dry carefully in a warm oven and leave to harden and crisp again first on baking tray, then wire rack.

Serves 6–8

Grapefruit sorbet

Orange Sorbet

Metric/Imperial
75 g/3 oz castor sugar
300 ml/½ pint water
177-g/6¼-oz can frozen
   orange juice concentrate
1 egg white

American
6 tablespoons sugar
1¼ cups water
6¼-oz can frozen orange juice
   concentrate
1 egg white

Put the sugar and water into a pan and heat slowly until the sugar has dissolved. Allow this syrup to cool.

Add the undiluted orange juice concentrate to the sugar syrup. Blend them together, then pour the liquid into a 600-ml/ 1-pint (US 2½-cup) shallow plastic lidded container. Put the sorbet in the freezer or freezing compartment of the refrigerator for 30 minutes or until barely firm.

Turn into a bowl and mash down until there are no large pieces. Whisk the egg white until stiff and fold into the orange mixture, return to the container, cover and place in the freezer or freezing compartment until required.

Variation
Grapefruit Sorbet Substitute grapefruit juice concentrate for orange and serve in scooped out orange or grapefruit shells cut in a zig-zag pattern. Decorate with grated orange rind.

Serves 4

148

Melon Sorbet

Metric/Imperial
1 medium melon
juice of ½ lemon
4 egg whites
100 g/4 oz castor sugar
3–4 tablespoons maraschino
   cherries

American
1 medium melon
juice of ½ lemon
4 egg whites
½ cup sugar
4–5 tablespoons maraschino
   cherries

Cut the melon in half in a zig-zag pattern, remove the seeds and scoop out the flesh. Place in a liquidiser with the lemon juice and blend until smooth. Turn into a rigid 1·75-litre/3-pint (US 4-pint) container and freeze until beginning to set.

Whisk the egg whites until stiff and whisk in the sugar 1 tea-spoonful at a time.

Lightly whisk the melon until broken up and light; fold in the egg whites. Return to the freezer and freeze until set.

Remove from the freezer 5 minutes before serving and spoon into the bottom half of the melon shell. Top with cherries and replace top half of melon shell.

Note Use a type of melon that is in season in your area. For a special dish in the summer mix the spoonfuls of melon sorbet with a few fresh hulled strawberries.

Serves 6–8

Melon sorbet

Ginger Biscuit Roll

Metric/Imperial
300–450 ml/½–¾ pint double cream
225 g/8 oz ginger biscuits
crystallised or stem ginger to decorate

American
1¼–2 cups whipping cream
½ lb gingersnaps
candied or preserved ginger to decorate

Put half the cream in a bowl and whisk until it forms fairly stiff peaks. Use it to sandwich the ginger biscuits together in a long roll.

Arrange the roll on a serving dish and leave in a cool place or in the refrigerator overnight.

Next day whip the remaining cream and use it to cover the ginger biscuit roll completely. Decorate the roll with small pieces or slices of crystallised or stem ginger. To serve, cut diagonal pieces from the loaf shape or cut into slices.

Note Another simple yet special recipe on the same lines: soak Marie biscuits in rum and coffee essence then sandwich together with cream. Leave overnight then cover with cream. Decorate with halved walnuts.

Serves 4

Chilled Lemon Flan

Metric/Imperial
Flan case
8 digestive biscuits
50 g/2 oz butter
1 tablespoon castor sugar
Filling
2 large lemons
150 ml/¼ pint double cream
170-g/6-oz can condensed milk
Topping
lightly whipped double cream
fresh or crystallised lemon slices

American
Flan case
¼ lb graham crackers
¼ cup butter
1 tablespoon sugar
Filling
2 large lemons
⅔ cup whipping cream
6-oz can condensed milk
Topping
lightly whipped cream
fresh or candied lemon slices

Crush the digestive biscuits with a rolling pin. Melt the butter in a pan, add the sugar then blend in the biscuits. Mix well. Turn the mixture into an 18-cm/7-inch pie plate or flan dish and press into shape round base and sides of plate with the back of a spoon. Bake in a cool oven (150°C, 300°F, Gas Mark 2) for 8 minutes then remove and leave to cool. Do not turn the flan case out or it will crumble.

Grate the rind and squeeze the juice from the lemons. Mix together the cream, condensed milk and finely grated lemon rind. Slowly beat in the lemon juice. Pour into the flan case and chill for several hours until firm.

Just before serving decorate the flan with a whirl of lightly whipped cream and the lemon slices.

Serves 4–6

Syllabub

Metric/Imperial
1 large lemon
4 tablespoons sherry
2 tablespoons brandy
50 g/2 oz castor sugar
300 ml/½ pint double cream
lemon slices to decorate

American
1 large lemon
⅓ cup sherry
3 tablespoons brandy
¼ cup sugar
1¼ cups whipping cream
lemon slices to decorate

Finely grate the rind from the lemon and squeeze out the juice. Put the rind and juice in a bowl with the sherry, brandy and sugar. Stir until the sugar has dissolved. Pour in the cream and whisk until the mixture will form soft peaks when the whisk is lifted out. Spoon into individual glasses and leave in a cool place until required.

Top each glass with a slice of fresh lemon.

Note This syllabub can be made 1 day in advance as it keeps very well.

Serves 4

Chilled lemon flan

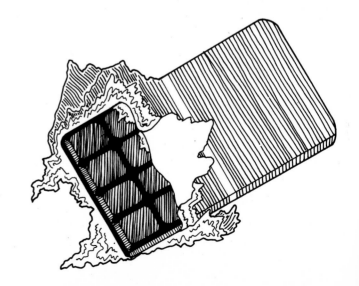

Chocolate dessert cups

Chocolate Dessert Cups

Metric/Imperial	American
175 g/6 oz plain chocolate	6 squares semi-sweet chocolate
15 g/½ oz butter	1 tablespoon butter
3 eggs	3 eggs
1 tablespoon rum (optional)	1 tablespoon rum (optional)
1 tablespoon coffee essence	1 tablespoon strong black coffee
grated chocolate to decorate	grated chocolate to decorate

Put the chocolate and butter in a bowl placed over a pan of hot (not boiling) water. Leave to dissolve, stirring constantly.

Separate the eggs. When the chocolate is completely melted remove it from the heat and beat in the egg yolks, rum if used, and coffee essence. Whisk the egg whites stiffly then fold them into the mixture.

Pour into four small cups or glasses and leave in a cool place until set. Just before serving top each with grated chocolate.

Note Serve mousses or creams in coffee cups, and choose small demi-tasse size cups for serving chocolate, coffee or caramel flavours. They look smart and are indeed different. Biscuits to go with these (or marshmallows for the children) are ideally served alongside in the saucer.

Serves 4

Traditional English Trifle

Metric/Imperial	American
6 small sponge cakes	6 small sponge cakes
strawberry jam	strawberry jam
50 g/2 oz ratafias, crushed	2 oz ratafia biscuits, crushed
5 tablespoons sherry or mixed sherry and fruit juice	6 tablespoons sherry or mixed sherry and fruit juice
8 maraschino cherries, chopped	8 maraschino cherries, chopped
1 tablespoon juice from cherries	1 tablespoon juice from cherries
Custard	**Custard**
2 eggs, separated	2 eggs, separated
2 teaspoons cornflour	2 teaspoons cornstarch
25 g/1 oz castor sugar	2 tablespoons sugar
300 ml/½ pint milk	1¼ cups milk
Topping	**Topping**
300 ml/½ pint double cream	1¼ cups whipping cream
15 g/½ oz split almonds	½ oz slivered almonds
5 maraschino cherries	5 maraschino cherries
angelica leaves	angelica leaves

Split the sponge cakes in half and sandwich them together with jam. Arrange in the base of a generous 1-litre/2-pint (US 2½-pint) serving dish and sprinkle the ratafias in between. Sprinkle the sherry, chopped cherries and maraschino juice over the sponge cakes.

Blend together the egg yolks, cornflour and sugar in a bowl. Warm the milk then pour it on to the egg mixture. Stir well, return the custard to the pan and cook over a low heat. Do not allow it to simmer or it will curdle. When it is thick enough to coat the back of a wooden spoon remove from heat. Strain custard over the sponge cakes and leave to cool and set.

Just before serving whip the cream with the egg whites until it forms soft peaks, then spread over the trifle. Lightly toast the almonds under the grill. Decorate with almonds, cherries and angelica.

Note If you are particularly fond of custard, double the quantity and use a larger serving dish. Crushed almond macaroons can be substituted for ratafia biscuits (see page 127).

Serves 6

Montelimar Pudding

Metric/Imperial	American
170-g/6-oz can evaporated milk	6-oz can evaporated milk
25 g/1 oz glacé cherries	2 tablespoons candied cherries
50 g/2 oz marshmallows	2 oz marshmallows
½ packet lemon jelly	½ package lemon-flavored gelatin
4 tablespoons boiling water	⅓ cup boiling water
juice of ½ lemon	juice of ½ lemon
25 g/1 oz castor sugar	2 tablespoons sugar
canned or maraschino cherries	canned or maraschino cherries

Chill the evaporated milk in the refrigerator. Chop the glacé cherries and cut the marshmallows into pieces using wet scissors.

Dissolve the jelly in the boiled water. Cool until it is thick but not set. Whip the evaporated milk until it is light and foamy. Add the cooled jelly, blending well.

Stir in the lemon juice, glacé cherries, marshmallows and sugar. Turn into a serving dish or mould and chill until set. Just before serving, turn out and decorate with canned or maraschino cherries.

Serves 4

Hot Banana Pudding

Metric/Imperial	American
6 ripe bananas	6 ripe bananas
50 g/2 oz butter	¼ cup butter
100 g/4 oz castor sugar	½ cup sugar
100 g/4 oz self-raising flour	1 cup all-purpose flour sifted with 1 teaspoon baking powder
1 egg, beaten	1 egg, beaten
generous pinch mixed spice	generous pinch mixed spice

Place the bananas in a large bowl and mash to a pulp.

Melt the butter and stir into the bananas. Add the sugar, flour, beaten egg and spice and mix well. Turn the mixture into a well greased 1-litre/1¾-pint (US 2¼-pint) ovenproof dish and bake in a moderate oven (180°C, 350°F, Gas Mark 4) for 40–50 minutes until golden brown and the pudding has shrunk slightly from the sides of the dish.

Serve hot with cream.

Note   This recipe is one of the best ways I know of using up ripe bananas and makes a delicious pudding.

Serves 6

Bread and Butter Pudding

Metric/Imperial	American
6–8 thin slices bread, buttered	6–8 thin slices bread, buttered
50 g/2 oz dried fruit	⅓ cup dried fruit
grated rind of 1 lemon	grated rind of 1 lemon
50 g/2 oz brown sugar	¼ cup brown sugar
1 egg	1 egg
300 ml/½ pint milk	1¼ cups milk

Well butter a shallow 900-ml/1½-pint (US 2-pint) ovenproof dish. Remove the crusts from the buttered bread and layer with the fruit, lemon rind and sugar. Pour over the egg blended with the milk and leave to soak for 30 minutes, then bake in a moderate oven (180°C, 350°F, Gas Mark 4) for about 30 minutes or until puffy and a pale golden brown.

Serves 4

Scandinavian Apple Charlotte

Metric/Imperial	American
75 g/3 oz butter	⅓ cup butter
175 g/6 oz fresh white breadcrumbs	3 cups fresh white bread crumbs
50 g/2 oz demerara sugar	¼ cup light brown sugar
1 kg/2 lb cooking apples	2 lb baking apples
juice of 1 lemon	juice of 1 lemon
2 tablespoons water	3 tablespoons water
50 g/2 oz castor sugar	¼ cup sugar
Topping	**Topping**
150 ml/¼ pint double cream	⅔ cup whipping cream
coarsely grated chocolate	coarsely grated chocolate

Melt the butter in a frying pan and fry the breadcrumbs slowly until crisp and golden, stirring frequently. When they are ready remove from heat and blend in the demerara sugar.

In another pan put peeled, cored and sliced apples, lemon juice, water and sugar. Cover and cook until the apples are soft, then mash to a smooth purée. Leave to cool.

Put half the cooled apple purée into a 1-litre/1¾-pint (US 2¼-pint) glass dish. Spread half the breadcrumbs on top. Repeat with a layer of apple and breadcrumbs. Leave to chill before serving.

Just before serving spread or pipe lightly whipped cream on top of the pudding and sprinkle with coarsely grated chocolate.

Serves 4–6

Apple Suet Pudding

Metric/Imperial	American
Pastry	**Pastry**
225 g/8 oz self-raising flour	2 cups all-purpose flour sifted with 2 teaspoons baking powder
100 g/4 oz suet, shredded	scant cup chopped suet
½ teaspoon salt	½ teaspoon salt
approx. 150 ml/¼ pint water	approx. ⅔ cup water
Filling	**Filling**
0·75 kg/1½ lb cooking apples	1½ lb baking apples
50 g/2 oz castor sugar	¼ cup sugar
50 ml/2 fl oz water	¼ cup water

Well oil a generous 1-litre/2-pint (US 2½-pint) pudding basin and piece of foil to cover.

Stir the flour, suet and salt together. Pour in three-quarters of the measured water. Using a table knife stir and cut the water in, adding remaining water as required to make a soft but not sticky dough. Take two-thirds of the dough and pat or roll out on a floured surface to a 20-cm/8-inch circle. Drop into the bottom of the oiled basin and with fingertips press dough up sides of basin until level with top. Pat or roll the remaining dough to the size of the top of the basin, about 18 cm/7 inches.

Peel, core and thinly slice the apples, layering in lined basin with the sugar. Add the water. Wet top edges of dough and cover with remaining dough, pressing edges together well to seal. Make a pleat in foil to allow room for expansion. Cover basin and press foil firmly under rim.

Place pudding either in a large saucepan with 3·5 cm/1½ inches of boiling water and boil for 2¼ hours, or in a steamer and steam 2½–3 hours. When cooked lift out and remove foil. Place a shallow serving dish on top and turn over, removing basin just before serving. Serve with cream or custard.

Note   Once water is added to pastry dough, pudding must be quickly completed to ensure a light suet crust. Keep cooking pan topped up with boiling water as necessary.

Serves 5–6

Praline Pancakes with Peaches

Metric/Imperial
Batter
100 g/4 oz plain flour
1 large egg
300 ml/½ pint milk
1½ tablespoons salad oil
Praline
150 g/5 oz granulated sugar
65 g/2½ oz unblanched almonds
Decoration
75 g/3 oz butter
425-g/15-oz can white peach halves
100 ml/4 fl oz brandy

American
Batter
1 cup all-purpose flour
1 large egg
1¼ cups milk
2 tablespoons salad oil
Praline
⅔ cup sugar
½ cup unblanched almonds
Decoration
⅓ cup butter
15-oz can white peach halves
½ cup brandy

Prepare batter and fry pancakes (see page 83). Oil a baking tray. Place the sugar and almonds in a small pan and heat gently without stirring – just shake – until sugar turns reddish brown. Turn on to oiled tray. Leave to set and harden undisturbed. When cold and set place in a thick polythene bag. Beat with a rolling pin or hammer until praline is nearly as fine as granulated sugar. Store in an airtight bag or container until used.

To finish, melt the butter and brush pancakes well. Sprinkle on 2 teaspoons of praline and roll up like a cigar. Lay in a shallow ovenproof dish. Complete remaining pancakes and stack in dish. Brush on remaining butter and sprinkle over remaining praline. Bake just before serving, in a moderate oven (160°C, 325°F, Gas Mark 3), for 15 minutes.

Drain and slice peaches, put in a pan with brandy and heat. Pour hot over pancakes and take immediately to table, set brandy alight with a match and serve.

To freeze Pancakes freeze well so can be made in advance. Praline may partly dissolve so do not fill and roll pancakes until the day of serving.
Note Praline keeps quite well in a screw-top jar so can be made in advance, but it becomes sticky in a damp atmosphere. To clean pan after making praline, cover and protect the hand holding the handle and while the pan is still hot pour in hot water. Return to heat to dissolve caramel.

Serves 4

Preston Whip

Metric/Imperial
½ packet lemon jelly

boiling water
150 ml/¼ pint double cream
2 (142-g/5-oz) cartons natural yogurt

American
½ package lemon-flavored gelatin
boiling water
⅔ cup whipping cream
2 (5-oz) cartons unflavored yogurt

Place the jelly in a measure and make up to 150 ml/¼ pint (US ⅔ cup) with boiling water, stir until dissolved and leave to become cold but not set.

Whisk the cream until it forms soft peaks. Stir the yogurt into the jelly and fold in the cream.

Turn into five individual ramekins or glasses and leave to set.

Serves 5

Lemon Pudding

Metric/Imperial
50 g/2 oz butter
100 g/4 oz castor sugar
rind and juice of 1 large lemon
2 eggs, separated
65 g/2½ oz self-raising flour

300 ml/½ pint milk

American
¼ cup butter
½ cup sugar
rind and juice of 1 large lemon
2 eggs, separated
½ cup plus 2 tablespoons all-purpose flour sifted with ½ teaspoon baking powder
1¼ cups milk

Cream the butter with one-third of the sugar, the lemon rind and egg yolks in a bowl, then add the flour, lemon juice and milk. Do not worry if the mixture is slightly lumpy at this stage.

Whisk the egg whites until stiff then add the remaining sugar a spoonful at a time, whisking well between each addition; fold into the lemon mixture. Pour into an ovenproof dish and stand in a meat tin containing 2·5 cm/1 inch of water. Place in a moderate oven (180°C, 350°F, Gas Mark 4) and bake for 45–50 minutes until golden and firm when gently shaken.

Note This pudding is delicious eaten hot or cold but will shrink slightly on cooling.

Serves 4

Pear and Chocolate Upside Down Pudding

Metric/Imperial
Topping
50 g/2 oz butter
25 g/1 oz demerara sugar

425-g/15-oz can pears

100 g/4 oz butter
100 g/4 oz castor sugar
2 eggs
100 g/4 oz self-raising flour

pinch salt
2 tablespoons cocoa powder

2 tablespoons pear syrup (from the can)

American
Topping
¼ cup butter
2 tablespoons light brown sugar
15-oz can pears

½ cup butter
½ cup sugar
2 eggs
1 cup all-purpose flour sifted with 1 teaspoon baking powder
pinch salt
3 tablespoons unsweetened cocoa
3 tablespoons pear syrup (from the can)

Grease a 20-cm/8-inch round cake tin or deep sandwich tin.

Melt the butter for topping and pour into tin and sprinkle demerara sugar over base. Drain the pears, reserving juice, and arrange these cut side down on butter and sugar mixture.

Cream the butter gradually adding first the sugar and then the whisked eggs a spoonful at a time. Sieve the flour, salt and cocoa together then fold into the mixture with the measured pear syrup, carefully, using a metal spoon.

Spoon the mixture over pears in tin. Bake for 35 minutes in a moderate oven (180°C, 350°F, Gas Mark 4) until firm and springy in centre of cake. Turn out so that sticky pears are on top to serve.

To freeze Bake and turn out of tin. Open freeze then wrap. To reheat, unwrap and thaw in original tin. Cover with foil and reheat.
Note The sandwich tin should be at least 4 cm/1¾ inches deep. Tie a collar of paper round or use a deep cake tin if no deep sandwich tins are available. For double quantity for ten people use a small meat tin 20 × 30 cm/8 × 12 inches.

Serves 4–6

Pear and chocolate upside down pudding

Entertaining
with a difference

Having friends in for a fondue party is a fun idea; not only does it make sure that you, the hostess, enjoy yourself but it keeps your friends busy cooking their own supper. Once they get the hang of it they will enjoy dabbling in the various sauces as they do in Switzerland and Austria.

For fondue bourguignonne you fry cubes of tender steak in oil on skewers and serve with a selection of sauces and salads. No need for potatoes, just serve crisp French bread with plenty of butter and a green salad. For cheese fondue, dip chunks of French bread into the hot cheese sauce and serve with crisp salad and dry white wine.

If you haven't a smart fondue set and can't beg or borrow one, use a little calor gas stove or, failing this, a picnic spirit heater. It is best to heat the pan containing the oil (you will need about 5 cm/2 inches of oil in the pan) on the hob of the cooker in the kitchen until a faint haze is rising, then transfer it to the fondue stove. If you have more than six guests you will, ideally, need two pans heated by a shuttle system from the kitchen. Remember that the oil will heat up more quickly with a lid on the pan, but keep an eye on it because it should not become too hot.

Mark the skewers with coloured tape or wools so that the guests will know which is theirs. If using metal skewers or forks be sure to let them cool before anyone pops one into his mouth.

Keep the oil hot by returning it to the cooker at intervals and not cooking more than eight portions of meat at the same time. Your guests can time their own steak cubes as some will like them rarer than others.

The sauces can all be made in advance. If you haven't time to make them all, use a bottled chunky tomato chutney instead of making the Provençal sauce.

A warming hot punch – Glühwein as this is called in the mountains – is the perfect accompaniment (see page 158). Lace it with cheap brandy if your drinks cupboard will stand it.

Fondue Supper

Fondue Bourguignonne

Metric/Imperial	American
175–225 g/6–8 oz rump steak, cut in cubes	$\frac{1}{3}$–$\frac{1}{2}$ lb rump steak, cut in cubes
600 ml–1 litre/1–2 pints salad or corn oil	$1\frac{1}{4}$–$2\frac{1}{2}$ pints salad or corn oil

Serves 6

Cold Spiced Mushroom Sauce

Metric/Imperial	American
100 ml/4 fl oz salad oil	$\frac{1}{2}$ cup salad oil
2 tablespoons wine vinegar	3 tablespoons wine vinegar
1 teaspoon chopped capers	1 teaspoon chopped capers
1 teaspoon chopped gherkin	1 teaspoon chopped sweet dill pickle
1 teaspoon chopped parsley	1 teaspoon chopped parsley
1 teaspoon snipped chives or very finely chopped onion	1 teaspoon snipped chives or very finely chopped onion
2 teaspoons tomato purée	2 teaspoons tomato paste
pinch tarragon or chervil	pinch tarragon or chervil
salt and pepper	salt and pepper
225 g/8 oz button mushrooms	2 cups button mushrooms

Put all the ingredients except the mushrooms into a screw-top jar and shake thoroughly until they are well mixed.

Wash, dry and finely slice the mushrooms. At least 1 hour before serving add the prepared mushrooms and leave them to marinate in the mixture. To serve, turn into a small bowl.

Serves 6

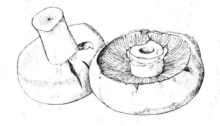

Horseradish Sauce

Metric/Imperial	American
150 ml/$\frac{1}{4}$ pint whipped cream	$\frac{2}{3}$ cup whipped cream
1 tablespoon grated horse-radish	1 tablespoon grated horse-radish
1 teaspoon cider or wine vinegar	1 teaspoon cider or wine vinegar
1 teaspoon sugar	1 teaspoon sugar

Blend all the ingredients together and serve in a small bowl.

Serves 6

Sweet 'n' Sour Mustard and Dill Sauce

Metric/Imperial	American
65 g/2½ oz castor sugar	⅓ cup sugar
2 tablespoons wine vinegar	3 tablespoons wine vinegar
2 tablespoons salad oil	3 tablespoons salad oil
2 tablespoons French mustard	3 tablespoons French mustard
½ teaspoon dried dill weed	½ teaspoon dried dill weed
salt and pepper	salt and pepper

Put the sugar and vinegar into a small pan and heat gently until the sugar has dissolved. If necessary brush the sides of the pan with cold water to dissolve any crystals of sugar. Bring the syrup to boiling point and simmer for about 15 minutes or until it has reduced by about one-third.

Remove the pan from the heat, allow to cool a little then blend in the salad oil, mustard, dill and plenty of salt and pepper. Pour the sauce into a small bowl and serve cold.

Serves 6

Curried Mayonnaise

Metric/Imperial	American
150 ml/¼ pint mayonnaise	⅔ cup mayonnaise
1 tablespoon lemon juice	1 tablespoon lemon juice
1 teaspoon curry powder	1 teaspoon curry powder
1 tablespoon chopped mango chutney	1 tablespoon chopped mango chutney
salt and freshly ground black pepper	salt and freshly ground black pepper

Mix all the ingredients together and turn into a small bowl to serve.

Serves 6

Hot Provençal Sauce

Metric/Imperial	American
0·5 kg/1 lb ripe tomatoes	1 lb ripe tomatoes
2 tablespoons salad oil	3 tablespoons salad oil
1 Spanish onion	1 Spanish onion
1 clove garlic	1 clove garlic
salt and pepper	salt and pepper
2 tablespoons vinegar	3 tablespoons vinegar
2 teaspoons sugar	2 teaspoons sugar
2 tablespoons soya sauce	3 tablespoons soy sauce
pinch basil	pinch basil
1 teaspoon chopped parsley	1 teaspoon chopped parsley

Put the tomatoes into boiling water for 10 seconds then remove them and put in a bowl of cold water. When they have cooled sufficiently peel and discard the skins. Cut the tomatoes in quarters, remove the seeds and chop the flesh. Heat the oil in a pan.

Peel and finely chop the onion, add to the pan with the peeled whole clove of garlic and fry until the onion is soft and transparent. Add the chopped tomatoes and continue to cook until the tomatoes have formed a purée, about 15 minutes. Remove the clove of garlic and stir in the seasoning, vinegar, sugar, soya sauce, basil and parsley. Turn into a small bowl and serve, preferably hot (but it may also be served cold).

Note   This sauce can also be sieved or liquidised, if preferred.

Serves 6

Hot provençal sauce

Cheese fondue

Cheese Fondue

Metric/Imperial	**American**
1 clove garlic	1 clove garlic
400 ml/scant $\frac{3}{4}$ pint dry white wine	1$\frac{1}{3}$ cups dry white wine
225 g/8 oz Swiss Emmenthal cheese, grated	2 cups grated Swiss Emmenthal cheese
225 g/8 oz Swiss Gruyère cheese, grated	2 cups grated Swiss Gruyère cheese
25 g/1 oz cornflour	$\frac{1}{4}$ cup cornstarch
salt and pepper	salt and pepper
1 tablespoon kirsch	1 tablespoon kirsch

Peel and crush the garlic very finely. Pour all but about 50 ml/ 2 fl oz (US $\frac{1}{4}$ cup) of the wine into a thick enamel or earthenware pan, add the garlic and grated cheeses and heat the mixture very slowly until all the cheese has dissolved. Do not allow it to boil.

Blend the cornflour with the remainder of the wine in a bowl to make a smooth paste. Add a little of the hot cheese mixture to the cornflour then add it to the pan. Carefully bring the fondue to the boil, stirring all the time until the mixture has thickened. Add salt and pepper to taste, stir in the kirsch and serve at once with lots of fresh French bread cut in pieces to dip into the hot fondue.

Serves 4

Glühwein

Metric/Imperial	**American**
2 lemons	2 lemons
1 bottle cheap red wine	1 bottle cheap red wine
600 ml/1 pint water	1$\frac{1}{4}$ pints water
8 cloves	8 cloves
1 stick cinnamon	1 stick cinnamon
50–100 g/2–4 oz castor sugar	$\frac{1}{4}$–$\frac{1}{2}$ cup sugar
50 ml/2 fl oz cheap brandy (optional)	$\frac{1}{4}$ cup cheap brandy (optional)

Peel the zest thinly from the lemons, cut a few slices of lemon for garnish, then squeeze the remaining lemons to extract the juice. Put the lemon zest, juice, wine, water, cloves and cinnamon into a pan, put on the lid, bring the mixture to just below simmering point and leave it at this temperature for 1 hour or more. Remove the lemon rind, cloves and cinnamon and add sugar to taste.

Serve hot with lemon slices floating on top. Add the brandy just before serving for a more potent drink.

Serves 6

Spanish Tapas

To add a Spanish touch to your next party, try serving the varied finger foods known as tapas. Not only are they tasty and easy to eat at an informal get-together, but you could serve them as a starter with paella (see page 160).

Serves 8–10

Cream Cheese and Nut Bites

Metric/Imperial	**American**
100 g/4 oz rich cream cheese	½ cup full fat cream cheese
salt and pepper	salt and pepper
milk	milk
50 g/2 oz chopped mixed nuts	½ cup chopped mixed nuts

Blend the cream cheese with a little salt and pepper and mix well, adding a little milk if necessary to make a smooth stiff consistency. Form into 12–16 balls and coat each in chopped mixed nuts. Chill before serving.

Mild Curry and Olive Eggs

Metric/Imperial	**American**
10 hard-boiled eggs	10 hard-cooked eggs
salt and pepper	salt and pepper
single cream	light cream
approx. 1 teaspoon concentrated curry paste	approx. 1 teaspoon concentrated curry paste
5 Spanish stuffed green olives	5 Spanish stuffed green olives

Halve the hard-boiled eggs. Remove the yolks and sieve. Season and blend with single cream to a smooth piping consistency. Add a little concentrated curry paste to taste. Then pipe the mixture into the egg halves. Decorate each with half a Spanish stuffed olive.

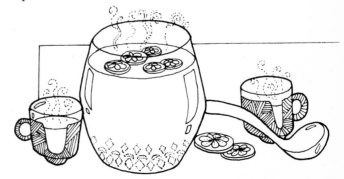

159

Cheese and Anchovy Puffs

Metric/Imperial	American
368-g/13-oz packet frozen puff pastry, thawed	13-oz package frozen puff paste, thawed
75 g/3 oz Gruyère cheese, diced	½ cup diced Gruyère cheese
4 anchovy fillets	4 canned anchovy fillets, drained
1 egg, beaten	1 egg, beaten

Make miniature pasties with puff pastry, filling each with a small piece of Gruyère cheese and a small piece of anchovy. Seal edges with egg and glaze. Bake until golden brown in a hot oven (220°C, 425°F, Gas Mark 7) for about 10 minutes. Serve hot.

Spanish Omelette Slices

Metric/Imperial	American
2 small tomatoes	2 small tomatoes
1 onion	1 onion
½ green pepper	½ green pepper
1 medium potato	1 medium potato
50 g/2 oz cooked ham, chopped	¼ cup chopped cooked ham
4 eggs	4 eggs
1 teaspoon salad oil	1 teaspoon salad oil
salt and pepper	salt and pepper
3–4 Spanish stuffed green olives	3–4 Spanish stuffed green olives

Peel and roughly chop the tomatoes, removing the seeds. Slice the onion thinly, chop the green pepper, discarding the seeds; peel and dice the potato. Mix with the chopped ham.

Beat the eggs lightly and add the ham and vegetable mixture. Heat the oil in an omelette pan, pour in the egg mixture and cook quickly for 3–5 minutes or until the eggs are set. Season to taste.

Scatter Spanish stuffed green olives over the omelette and leave to cool. Serve cold, cut in wedges.

For a buffet party serve tapas, with a bowl of stuffed green olives, attractively set out with wooden cocktail sticks to make the eating easier.

Paella

As the English know roast beef and Yorkshire pudding the Spaniards know paella. Each region has its own variation – near the sea more shellfish or seafood and less pork or poultry are used. Don't worry if you can't get all the ingredients: add more or less fish or meat to balance.

Metric/Imperial	American
350 g/12 oz chicken meat or 8 drumsticks	1½ cups chicken meat or 8 drumsticks
100 g/4 oz bacon	6 slices bacon
2 medium onions	2 medium onions
4 tablespoons salad oil	⅓ cup salad oil
1 clove garlic, crushed	1 clove garlic, crushed
sprig of fresh thyme	sprig of fresh thyme
generous litre/2 pints fresh mussels in shells	2½ pints fresh mussels in shells
100 ml/4 fl oz chicken stock	½ cup chicken stock
100–175 g/4–6 oz halibut or firm fish	¼–⅓ lb halibut or firm fish
100 g/4 oz garlic sausage, sliced	¼ lb garlic sausage, sliced
275 g/10 oz long-grain rice	1¼ cups long-grain rice
pinch saffron powder	pinch saffron powder
750 ml/1¼ pints liquid (mussel liquor with chicken stock or water)	1½ pints liquid (mussel liquor with chicken stock or water)
1 tablespoon salt	1 tablespoon salt
pinch freshly ground black pepper	pinch freshly ground black pepper
3 tomatoes	3 tomatoes
184-g/6½-oz can sweet red peppers	6½-oz can sweet red peppers
100 g/4 oz peeled prawns	⅔ cup peeled shrimp
225 g/8 oz cooked peas	1½ cups cooked peas
1 green pepper, sliced	1 green pepper, sliced
8 whole large Mediterranean prawns	8 whole jumbo shrimp

Cut the chicken into neat cubes and the bacon into 1-cm/½-inch squares. Peel and roughly chop the onions. Measure the oil into a paellera or large ovenproof open pan. Fry the chicken meat, bacon and onions until pale golden brown. Then add the garlic and thyme.

Rinse the mussels, using only tightly closed ones, clean and scrub well then put with the stock in a pan with a tight-fitting lid. Season and simmer until the mussels steam open (not more than 5 minutes).

Skin and bone the halibut and cut into 1·5-cm/¾-inch pieces. Cut the garlic sausage slices in half. Add to the paellera with the rice, saffron powder and the liquid. Mix well with a spoon, add the salt and pepper and bring to the boil. Cover with foil and bake in a moderate oven (180°C, 350°F, Gas Mark 4), stirring occasionally, for about 25 minutes, until the rice is barely soft. Remove from the oven.

Skin and pip the tomatoes, drain and slice the red peppers, and stir them into the rice with the peeled prawns, peas, mussels and green pepper slices. Arrange the large Mediterranean prawns on top, cover with foil and return to the oven for a further 10 minutes.

Serves 8

opposite Paella

Moussaka

Metric/Imperial

4 large aubergines, about
   1 kg/2 lb in weight
½ teaspoon salt
0·75 kg/1½ lb onions
2 cloves garlic
0·5 kg/1 lb tomatoes
salad oil
1 kg/2 lb shoulder lamb,
   coarsely minced
40 g/1½ oz flour
2 teaspoons salt
pinch pepper
½ teaspoon mixed dried herbs
150 ml/¼ pint stock
1 tablespoon tomato purée
2 tablespoons chopped
   parsley

Cheese sauce

40 g/1½ oz butter
40 g/1½ oz flour
450 ml /¾ pint milk
175 g/6 oz mature Cheddar
   cheese, grated
1 teaspoon made mustard
salt and pepper
watercress to garnish

American

4 large eggplant, about 2 lb in
   weight
½ teaspoon salt
1½ lb onions
2 cloves garlic
1 lb tomatoes
salad oil
4 cups coarsely minced
   lamb shoulder
⅓ cup all-purpose flour
2 teaspoons salt
pinch pepper
½ teaspoon mixed dried herbs
⅔ cup stock
1 tablespoon tomato paste
3 tablespoons chopped
   parsley

Cheese sauce

3 tablespoons butter
⅓ cup all-purpose flour
2 cups milk
1½ cups grated mature Cheddar
   cheese
1 teaspoon prepared mustard
salt and pepper
watercress to garnish

Slice the unpeeled aubergines in 1-cm/½-inch rounds, sprinkle with salt, leave for 30 minutes, then drain off liquid, rinse and pat dry. Peel and roughly chop the onions and crush the garlic.

Place the tomatoes in a bowl, cover with boiling water and leave to stand for 1 minute, drain, peel and slice. Fry the aubergines in oil, using as little as possible, and lift on to kitchen paper.

Heat 1 tablespoon oil in a large heavy pan, add the meat, stir and allow to brown, then add the onions and garlic and cook over the heat for 10 minutes. Stir in the flour and add the salt and pepper, herbs and stock with the tomato purée and parsley.

Make the cheese sauce: melt the butter in a pan, add the flour and cook over a medium heat without browning for about 2 minutes. Remove from the heat, mix the milk in stirring slowly, and return to the heat. Bring to the boil and add the cheese, mustard and seasoning. Allow the cheese to dissolve.

Butter a large shallow ovenproof dish, arrange in it layers of aubergines, meat mixture and tomato slices and finish with a layer of aubergine slices. Pour over the cheese sauce. Bake in a moderately hot oven (190°C, 375°F, Gas Mark 5) for about 45 minutes until golden brown, garnish with the watercress and grated cheese and serve with hot bread and butter.

Serves 8

Moussaka

Chicken Curry

Metric/Imperial	**American**
40 g/1½ oz lard	3 tablespoons shortening
4 chicken joints	4 chicken joints
2 onions, chopped	2 onions, chopped
25 g/1 oz flour	¼ cup all-purpose flour
1 tablespoon curry powder	1 tablespoon curry powder
300 ml/½ pint water	1¼ cups water
1 chicken stock cube	1 chicken bouillon cube
1 tablespoon mango chutney	1 tablespoon mango chutney
1 tablespoon blackcurrant jelly	1 tablespoon black currant jelly
salt and pepper	salt and pepper
1 dessert apple	1 dessert apple
25 g/1 oz sultanas	¼ cup seedless raisins

Melt two-thirds of the lard in a large pan and fry the chicken joints on both sides until golden brown. Remove from the pan and remove skin and bones carefully and cut into bite-size pieces.

Melt the remaining fat in the pan and fry the onions until soft. Blend in the flour and curry powder to taste and fry for 1 minute. Add the water and stock cube a little at a time, bring to the boil and simmer until the sauce has thickened. Stir in the chutney and blackcurrant jelly. Season with salt and pepper.

Replace the chicken pieces in the pan, cover and simmer for 30 minutes or until tender.

Meanwhile peel, core and chop the apple; stir into the sauce with the sultanas and cook for a further 5 minutes. Serve with boiled rice and side dishes.

Note Any of a selection of side dishes can be prepared in advance: two bananas sliced and sprinkled with lemon juice and coated in desiccated coconut, fried poppadums, sliced tomatoes and onions, peppers, mango chutney and peanuts.

Serves 4

Spaghetti Bolognese

Metric/Imperial	American
Bolognese sauce	**Bolognese sauce**
2 tablespoons salad oil	3 tablespoons salad oil
2 onions, chopped	2 onions, chopped
2–3 cloves garlic, crushed	2–3 cloves garlic, crushed
225 g/8 oz chicken livers	½ lb chicken livers
225 g/8 oz raw minced beef	1 cup raw ground beef
25 ml/1 fl oz sherry	2 tablespoons sherry
25 g/1 oz flour	¼ cup all-purpose flour
450 ml/¾ pint chicken stock	2 cups chicken stock
3 tablespoons tomato purée	¼ cup tomato paste
1 tablespoon marjoram	1 tablespoon marjoram
1 teaspoon basil or thyme	1 teaspoon basil or thyme
1 teaspoon salt	1 teaspoon salt
1 teaspoon sugar	1 teaspoon sugar
0·5 kg/1 lb spaghetti	1 lb spaghetti
50 g/2 oz grated Parmesan cheese	½ cup grated Parmesan cheese

Heat the oil in a large frying pan and add the chopped onions and crushed garlic. Cook gently for about 10 minutes until golden brown. Dice the chicken livers and add to the pan with the minced beef. Fry, stirring well, for 5 minutes. Pour on the sherry, cook for 2 minutes then blend in the flour and stock. Bring to the boil and add the remaining ingredients for the sauce. Simmer very gently for 35–40 minutes until thick and well reduced. Stir occasionally.

Place the spaghetti in a large pan of boiling salted water. Push it into the pan as it softens so that all is covered with water. Do not put a lid on the pan or it will easily boil over. Simmer gently for 12–15 minutes then test to see if it is tender by pinching between thumb and finger. It will crush and break if cooked. Simmer longer if not tender. Drain in a colander, rinse with a kettle of boiling water and if it needs to be kept hot for a short time return to the pan with 1 tablespoon of oil. Cover and shake well to coat with oil and prevent sticking.

Arrange the spaghetti on a hot serving dish, pour over the sauce and sprinkle with grated Parmesan cheese.

To freeze Bolognese sauce freezes well. Thaw and reheat to serve with freshly cooked pasta.
Note Extra minced meat can be used if your family do not like chicken livers or if they are unavailable. Freeze chicken livers whenever you cook chicken and keep them to make this sauce.

Serves 4

Classic Lasagne

Metric/Imperial	American
Meat sauce	**Meat sauce**
1 large onion	1 large onion
2 tablespoons salad oil	2 tablespoons salad oil
0·5 kg/1 lb raw minced beef	2 cups raw ground beef
1 clove garlic	1 clove garlic
pinch dried mixed herbs	pinch dried mixed herbs
2 teaspoons salt	2 teaspoons salt
½ teaspoon sugar	½ teaspoon sugar
pinch pepper	pinch pepper
5 tablespoons tomato purée	6 tablespoons tomato paste
250 ml/scant ½ pint water	1 cup water
White sauce	**White sauce**
25 g/1 oz butter	2 tablespoons butter
25 g/1 oz flour	¼ cup all-purpose flour
450 ml/¾ pint milk	2 cups milk
salt and pepper	salt and pepper
2 teaspoons salad oil	2 teaspoons salad oil
2 teaspoons salt	2 teaspoons salt
100 g/4 oz lasagne	¼ lb lasagne
150 g/5 oz Gruyère or Emmenthal cheese, grated	1¼ cups grated Gruyère or Emmenthal cheese
25 g/1 oz grated Parmesan cheese	¼ cup grated Parmesan cheese

First prepare the meat sauce: peel and chop the onion, heat the oil in a pan and fry the onion and minced beef until brown, stirring frequently. Crush the garlic and add with the other sauce ingredients, cover and simmer for 45 minutes.

Now prepare the white sauce: melt the butter in a saucepan, stir in the flour and cook for 2 minutes. Add the milk and bring to the boil, stirring. Simmer for 2–3 minutes and season to taste. Cover and keep hot.

Prepare the pasta: bring a large pan of water with oil and salt to the boil. Add the lasagne and boil for 8 minutes. Drain in a colander, refresh with cold water, then arrange on a clean, damp tea towel so that the pieces do not stick together.

Assemble the lasagne in three layers in a 1·75-litre/3-pint (US 4-pint) shallow ovenproof dish, starting with a layer of meat sauce, then a layer of pasta, then a layer of white sauce, sprinkled with Gruyère cheese. Continue in this way, ending with a layer of meat sauce. Sprinkle Parmesan cheese over the top.

Bake in a moderate oven (180°C, 350°F, Gas Mark 4) for 40 minutes or until the top is golden brown. Serve with a green salad.

To freeze This dish is a great standby to have in the freezer.
Note Well flavoured Cheddar cheese may be used but would not have the same consistency.

Serves 6

Classic lasagne

Spaghetti bolognese

Index